Table of Contents

A Message From John to Pastors and Leaders v

Instructions for Pastors and Leaders vii

Video Session 1: God's Pursuit - The Journey Begins! 1

Video Session 2: Protect Your Hunger 25

Video Session 3: Passion For His Presence 43

Video Session 4: The Friends of God 57

Video Session 5: What Hinders True Intimacy 81

Video Session 6: True Worship 99

Video Session 7: With Whom God Dwells 117

Video Session 8: Intimacy With the Holy Spirit 133

Video Session 9: The Promise of the Father 151

Video Session 10: The Language of Intimacy 171

Video Session 11: Full Assurance of Faith 187

Video Session 12: Drawing Near 201

Master Code Page 222

Appendix A: Our Need For A Savior 223

Appendix B: How To Be Filled With The Holy Spirit 226

A Message From John to Pastors and Leaders

I'd like to extend a warm welcome to you who have been called by God to lead His precious people through the Drawing Near journey. As leader of a church, Bible school, Bible study, family or cell group, you are valuable to God. You play a very important role in the lives of other believers!

One of the main reasons my wife, Lisa, and I founded Messenger International is to reach out and strengthen *local churches* through messages that are truly relevant, born from the heart of the Holy Spirit. The *Drawing Near* curriculum will be a transforming experience for you to bring unity, strength, vision, and intimacy with the Lord to believers.

The *Drawing Near Leader's Guide* is a vital tool to assist you as you are leading your group through this journey. Here are a few things to remember that will be of tremendous value to you.

- It's hard to want something when you don't even know it is missing. As leaders, we must remember that people come from many differing backgrounds and are at all different levels of relationship with the Lord. Many people haven't been truly intimate with Jesus for years, yet they seem satisfied with a bland religious life. Many others do not even realize they CAN have a passionate relationship with God, let alone that God Himself has invited them and promised them such a miraculous thing. Make your people aware this invitation (James 4:8) does exist, and it is for them, TODAY.

- Don't just talk to your people *about* drawing near to God. Help them do it. Help them *experience* the power of the Holy Spirit as they go with you through this treasure map.

- Remember to stress this is a journey—NOT just a ONE-TIME "adventure," but a LIFE of intimacy with God. The Lord offers us a *lifetime* of passionate love and closeness, which will strengthen us daily as we walk with Him in lifelong obedience. Remind your group that this is NOT a step-by-step formula, rather it is a passionate love affair.

- Finally, as you go through this curriculum, simply provide information and opportunities for people to grow closer to Christ through involvement in the local church. *Drawing Near* is an excellent opportunity to see believers come alive to God in a revival of intimacy and passion in their personal walk and through anointed service to the body of Christ!

Thank you so much for being a friend of this ministry. We so highly value you. I pray that we would yield to the greatest Lover in the universe; drawing closer to Him and helping others draw near as well.

EASY-TO-USE INSTRUCTIONS FOR PASTORS AND LEADERS

Welcome to *Drawing Near, A Life of Intimacy with God*. The goal here is not to give a seminary course, so you don't have to be a brilliant group leader or gifted teacher. We keep it simple, to the point, and stay focused on relationship, instead of rules. This is about living a life with God Himself; it's not about religious duties or regulations.

The objective is simply this:
- To prayerfully gather together
- To watch the video
- To learn the material
- To open things up in discussion and let God move!

Preparation

> *"Be diligent to present yourself approved to God, a worker who does not need to be ashamed, rightly dividing the word of truth."*
> 2 Timothy 2:15

Preparation time is never lost time. God will mightily bless you if you are a good steward and properly plan your sessions.

- Make sure you are working closely with the leadership in your church.

- Start your journey by reading the book *Drawing Near: A Life of Intimacy With God*. Use your Bible, and make notes as you read.

- There are twelve video sessions, each of which corresponds to a chapter in the workbook. Watch each video session and go over each chapter in the leader's guide workbook at least once BEFORE you meet with your group.

(It is not required, but it would prove very helpful if before you led your group, you went through the course one time on your own as a student using a Student Workbook.)

- Review your Leader's Guide, making sure you know the material and are ready for the discussion questions. See "Time" below.

- A complete transcript of each video session is included in your Leader's Guide and the Student Workbook.

- We've provided the answers for you.

Time

Tips Concerning Time...

Some sessions lend themselves to longer periods of time than others. Reviewing each session ahead of time will help you greatly in this regard. For instance, session four is heavy on doctrine and session nine deals with praying for the infilling of the Holy Spirit. These may take more time than others, so plan well and stick to your timetable in *all* sessions.

We give suggested times to move things along, *but these are subject to your discretion and the leading of the Holy Spirit.* In your pre-planning, you may see some items you want to spend time and focus on. On the other hand, there may be some things your group are well taught in, so you can quickly move forward.

You can complete a session in 60 to 90 minutes if you move along and are well prepared by going over the material in your Leader's Guide as you plan each session. Each group will probably differ in what time is spent where, depending on the background and diversity of people. Be flexible and mindful of schedules, and don't always try to cram everything in if things are flowing in a direction that God is obviously moving in. Trust God, pray, and get wisdom from the Lord for each session. Rely on Him as you and your group draw near.

Enhanced DVD Content

 We've included many bonus features on the DVDs.
When this icon appears on the screen during your sessions you may pause to watch the enhanced content (see Master Code page 222). Make sure you have previewed all videos and planned ahead what you will do. John's prayers in particular may prove to be a useful aid to your own prayer for your group, especially in the areas of salvation and infilling of the Holy Spirit.

How To Lead Your Group

How to Start a Session...

1. Open up by warmly greeting your group.
2. Pray a brief prayer for them and the session.
3. Thank them for participating, and tell them they are in for a great journey. This is going to change their lives as God draws them to Himself and they learn of and experience Him.
4. Let people know you are aware that some of them may not have completed their workbooks, or perhaps they've only done partial work. That's OK; they can still participate and it will be fine, <u>but</u> encourage them to find the time and go through their workbooks for each new session. As they sow, they will reap. They will get more out of this if they dedicate some time daily or weekly for it. (Note: See Student Workbook Instructions so you know what they should be doing.)

How to Go Through Each Session (it's easy)...

1. Start each session with a greeting and a brief prayer.
2. Watch the video.
3. After the video, go through the simple "academic" type questions (True/False, Fill in the blanks, etc.) in the workbooks, using your leader's notes and answers. Relax, enjoy leading, and go through the questions one by one. When indicated, give participants an opportunity to respond, *but*

make sure you provide the correct answers to your group. Don't spend too much time; move right along with these. They are simple, to the point, and are directly from John's teaching on the video (and the transcripts), so if people missed something, they can watch the video or read the transcript at home. The goal is to have them learn the material John is teaching.

4. Go through the personal, interactive-type discussion questions. Here is where you want to spend some time. These are the questions with this icon next to them. Though these may be very individual and personal we've provided sample answers for you to prompt discussion and help prepare you for leading your group. Be prayerful—*this is where you can really see God move.*

5. Finish each session as indicated in your Leader's Guide.

Important Helpful Hints…

- **You don't have to have all the answers.** Knowing everything is certainly not the point here. Let John's teaching speak for itself. For anything that comes up that you don't have answers for, simply say you don't know and encourage people to look it up in the Bible, to go back over John's teaching, or to ask their pastor. You can also respond at another time. Remember to always point people to the Word, and to pray for the answers they are seeking. Provide them with any resources that will assist them.
- **Keep things moving.** Never let any one person dominate a discussion, leaving the rest of the group as an audience. God has anointed you and appointed you as leader. When necessary, do not hesitate to gently but firmly interrupt and thank the person for their contribution. Just say, "Excuse me, but time is running short and we need to hear from some other folks, too." (Or, "We have more to cover tonight.")
- **Don't let things disintegrate into wars over doctrine.** The minute this begins to happen, tell people you "respect their positions, but this is not the time for a doctrinal debate." Then get back to the session.
- **Get to know your group.** Learn the group's personality; learn people's names, and prayerfully watch for cues from group members. You never know who may be in turmoil or trouble. Be prepared through the Word and through prayer to comfort, exhort, confront spiritual strongholds, and meet needs as they arise.

- Always keep your pastor (or whomever you report to) informed as you progress.

You want to remove the barriers that are hindering people's intimacy with God. These sessions will do that as you follow your leader's notes and walk your people through their journey to intimacy with God.

Ministry and Prayer in the Sessions

During this journey, always be sensitive for the opportunity the Lord may minister to people through you.

- **Prayer is essential!** Make sure you and your church are regularly praying for these sessions and believing God that lives will be deeply impacted.

- Pray that strongholds and barriers to God's presence in people's lives will be pulled down permanently.

- These sessions are the perfect opportunity to pray for people or to lead people in prayer, or to have them pray for one another at the end of the session.

- If your church offers qualified counseling, you may want to mention it is available for those who want it.

- Continually point people to the local church. Have materials available that provide information on how they can receive assistance and how they can be involved.

- Take joy in this, and let it show! Be excited for the sessions and ready to minister.

- *Remember, it's not about being perfect; it's about being His!*

"Legend"

As with any good map, we've included a legend. This will help you navigate on your journey.

- **Key Statement.** These statements are a handy way to summarize each topic.

- **Personal/discussion questions.** These are designed to go beyond "head" knowledge and instead help you to really grasp the truths being brought forth. Intimacy isn't necessarily only to be taught but rather lived and experienced. Take your time and wrap your heart around the questions that dig deep through the power of the Holy Spirit. Engage your group to use these opportunities.

- **Samaritan's Road.** This is based on Luke 10:33–34. The Good Samaritan had compassion as he journeyed along the road and saw someone in need. When you see this icon, it's your opportunity to do the same. Watch and see how God uses you as you step out in prayer and faith. Encourage your group to be bold about ministering to others.

- **Feet to Your Faith.** This journey isn't about academics or doctrinal debates. To be sure, you'll learn a lot of great biblical truth. But when you see this icon, you move from theory to practice, from religion to intimacy. Help your group to follow through with these.

- **Theology 101.** Don't be afraid of the word *theology*. It's simply about knowing God, and it doesn't get any better than that. We put these in to shed more light where needed.

When, Where, and Equipment

- Have the room set up and your sound/video checked well ahead of time.
- Use the best place and equipment you can get, and make sure you know how to use the DVD, TV, speakers, microphone, etc. The bigger the room or group, the bigger the video monitor you'll need.
- Be sure the sound is adequate as well. You don't want low volume or distorted sound to disrupt the meeting. You may need an audio/video person to assist you.

Besides taking care of those details, also have some extra student workbooks, *Drawing Near* books, pens, Bibles, and paper handy. Finally, you will need to be prepared to break into small groups when that time comes.

Video Session 1

God's Pursuit—
The Journey Begins!

"Draw near to God and He will draw near to you"
James 4:8

Welcome to *Drawing Near* with John Bevere! We pray this will begin a journey you will never forget, a life of intimacy with the living God.

In this first session, John boldly shares his hunger and longing, "I have never been so hungry for the presence of God and, even more so, to be intimate with Him as I have been in the last two years of my life. I have never wept as much as I have wept in the last two years in airplanes, airports, my hotel rooms, my bedroom, my office, and my car because of the presence of God and how real and how intimate He has become. I believe this is God's passion for every single one of us."

Do you hear this passion? Do you want this type of longing in your life?

Key Statement:
Intimacy with God is available to each one of us. This is God's passion.

This key statement starts you on your way. God's presence is for *you*. God's passion is for *you*. The very purpose of this Drawing Near Journey is to sweep *you* nearer to God and His presence, to personally engage *your* spirit, soul, and body in this most intimate endeavor. Keep in mind that this is not a mechanical process, but a wooing to a destination. Think of it as a trail guide or treasure map.

Leader's Notes

(2-3 minutes)

John starts the video sharing some very personal things about how God has become so real to him. Engage your group from the very start to help them understand that:

• THIS TIME TOGETHER, THIS MESSAGE *is for them* PERSONALLY.

• *It is God's will to deeply impact each of them in this very session and throughout this journey.*

We are led by the Spirit (Rom. 8:14) not told every little detail of what to do, with the Bible as our guide to daily living.

LESSON ONE

LEADER'S NOTES

(5 minutes)

In many things we do, how we start can determine how we finish.

• *It is important to make sure you tell your group from the very beginning that we are NOT creating a mechanical process. Rather it is more of a trail guide or treasure map. This is something you will want to repeatedly keep in your mind and remind your group of, as it is central to the book and the videos.*

• *You may want to share some example(s) of how God has brought (or wooed) you or someone you know through life in unexpected ways that fit with the idea of a guide or treasure map; a relationship as opposed to a life of step-by-step cold, impersonal processes.*

• *The goal is to gain further clarity of relationship versus formula.*

(10-15 minutes)

• **Encourage your group to NOT view intimacy with God by how they themselves think, but by biblical examples.**

As an exercise, consider having members of your group give other biblical examples of what true intimacy with God looks like.

Following a good map doesn't mean there will be no effort required, but it does keep you from unnecessary trouble and wasted time and energy.

As you seek this treasure (which is God Himself), you will come face to face with many heart-searching issues.

1. Ask yourself: Do I agree with John's declaration? Do I really believe it is God's passion to be intimate with me? [ ] Yes, I agree [ ] No way [ ] Not sure
Why?_____
_____

 2. Whatever your answer, can you picture in your mind how God might be intimate with you (or with anyone)? Describe it briefly here. What does it look like to be intimate with God?

There are many examples that may work here such as: praying often, attending church, having God speak to you and obeying His words, living a holy lifestyle, etc. But again, the point is not that intimacy looks like a set of rules or a nice, church-going person.

 3. Biblical Intimacy with God will bear the fruit of the biblical lifestyle. What are some biblical examples of what true intimacy with God looks like?

• *Jesus' life was anything but "normal." His intimate life with God was daily filled with prayer, adventure, fellowship, and risk.*

• *For Moses, intimacy with God meant that he would leave a lavish lifestyle, spend forty years as a shepherd, and then become a miracle-working deliverer.*

• *Esther, an orphan, became queen of a nation and was confronted with choices that would lead to her being used by God as an instrument to deliver her people.*

GOD'S PURSUIT

The Word of God proclaims in James 4:8, *"Draw near to God and He will draw near to you."*

Who draws near first? You do.

Key Statement:
There is something YOU can do that can literally cause God, who placed the stars in the universe with His fingers, to come to you!

This seems too good to be true. Even better is this: "You are the one who determines the level of your relationship with God, not God. In fact, God is more passionate about drawing near to you than you are to Him."

Wouldn't it be wonderful…

If those statements are true, then life takes on a whole new dynamic. Everything is changed—everything takes on new meaning and new purpose. Life would be far from drudgery or monotony or desperation—**life would be forever altered as you embark on the adventurous, exhilarating life of relationship with the God of the universe!**

4. Think about it. *Don't let this slip by.* Take a few moments to write below about how your life would change if you lived that intimately with God Himself right now:

_____
_____
_____
_____
_____

LEADER'S NOTES

(10 minutes)

Engage your group to show what a life of intimacy with God can look like.

• *Have fun with this. Many may think too religiously about this. Encourage them instead to let their imagination run wild as they consider living a life that resembles the life of a Bible character.*

• *This life would be very counterculture to today's prevalent lifestyles of sex, money, selfishness, greed, and divorce.*

• *Though we may never part the Red Sea or hold the fate of a nation in our hands, God does have a great adventure and many blessings for those who are willing to take this journey of intimacy with Him.*

• *Ask volunteers to share their answers.*

3

LESSON ONE

LEADER'S NOTES

Setting the stage...

The Bible communicates major themes. One of those themes is God's desire to actually commune with you—to be your friend, to be intimate with you, to have you walk and talk with Him as you live together in His kingdom NOW in this life on earth! In the video session, John puts it this way: "God's thoughts are toward you, you personally. Not the person beside you—we're talking about you."

This isn't something imaginary; it's the Word of God Himself. That is why you hear the excitement in John's voice and why he wants you to share in this. Let's look at some verses of Scripture to help us really get a hold on this as we begin:

Moses said, *"For he is a God who is passionate about his relationship with you"* (**Exod. 34:14, NLT**).

David said, *"Your thoughts toward us cannot be recounted to You in order...they are more than can be numbered"* (**Ps. 40:5**).

David also said, *"How precious also are Your thoughts to me, O God! How great is the sum of them! If I should count them, they would be more in number than the sand"* (**Ps. 139:17–18**).

Every grain of sand on this planet—on every beach, every desert, and every golf course—adds up to a lot of sand. Impossible to number, too much to comprehend, this is how God chose to reveal how numerous His thoughts are to each of us!

GOD'S PURSUIT

Jeremiah 29:11 states, *"For I know the thoughts that I think toward you, says the LORD, thoughts of peace and not of evil, to give you a future and a hope."* God actually made this statement to people who were disobedient, which further illustrates how much God longs for intimacy with each of us.

Using an example we can all relate to, John speaks of the many precious thoughts he has had for Lisa, his wife of twenty-one years. Yet all these would hardly fill a sandbox compared to God's precious thoughts toward each of us.

LEADER'S NOTES

Quickly ask for a few volunteers to offer their answers to 5 and 6, and then move on. If you need them, we've provided some answers that you can use as examples.

(5 minutes)

5. We all have people we care about. We understand what it means to not only think about those we love, but also to take action to show our love toward them. Can you think of some specific ways God has thought of you and provided for you throughout your life?

- *God gave me godly parents.*
- *I was in a car accident, unsaved and drunk, but I lived to tell about it and later became saved.*
- *I needed help with my college exams, so I prayed and found a great tutor.*

Read James 1:22. These are opportunities for you to encourage people to not just talk about drawing near to God, but to bear fruit as they are intimate with Him and led by Him in real life situations.

- *Simply ask your group if they had trouble with this.*

- *Spend a few minutes going over the sample answers we've provided if necessary, so people know what direction to be heading with this.*

This journey is for real, so let's take it a step further. You have listed some ways God has thought of you and has taken action to help you and to bless you. Now it's your turn to be like your master, Jesus.

6. What are some practical ways you could think of in which you could demonstrate God's love to someone in need?

- *Ask them to share testimonies in later sessions. Let them know they will find that not only will others get blessed, but they will too as they serve and see God move. (Remember to make a note of this and ask about it before your sessions are all finished).*

5

Lesson One

Leader's Notes

Sample answers:
- *A friend at work lost his wife to cancer and needs prayer and some meals made.*
- *The neighbor next door had an emergency and needed a baby sitter.*
- *The pastor said the church needs help with vacation Bible school.*

7. Consider writing down the name of a person(s) you will actually meet the need of:_____
*Sample: Bill Jones*_____.

Now let's put feet to our faith as we walk out this journey with God. Write down the date you will take action: _____. Make sure you follow through with it. Perhaps you can come back to the group and share the testimony about it as well.

Hot Pursuit and "Pull Over"...

The Bible contains countless examples of God reaching out to His people, desiring their response.

God provided the "burning bush" for Moses. Moses said, *"I will now turn aside and see this great sight"* (Exod. 3:3). Only after Moses turned aside did God speak.

8. "Turn aside" means to ___*depart*___ your course of ___*action*___. Moses would not have had that interaction with the Lord had he not ___*turned aside*___.

Young Samuel heard a voice four times, and then responded, *"Speak, for Your servant hears"* (1 Sam. 3:10). Then The Lord showed him things never known before.

It is interesting to note that to Samuel the voice sounded just like Eli, who was essentially Samuel's pastor.

God called to Samuel repeatedly. Yet God didn't reveal to Samuel who it was that was calling to him. *Only after Samuel properly responded to God's call did God speak with him.*

GOD'S PURSUIT

9. Why didn't God just go ahead and tell Samuel His message? Because God wants __us__ to know how to __recognize__ Him.

In Mark 6:48, we see Jesus walking on the sea, and He would have passed right by His disciples. But instead, they cried out, and Jesus turned and joined them in the boat, and they reached their destination together.

10. The New American Standard version reads, "And He __intended__ to pass by them." If they had not __cried out__ for Him, He would have __walked right by__.

Key Statement:
Our relationship with God is not one-sided.

We have a part to play. **The way we respond to God does make a difference in our relationship with Him.** If Jesus is Lord of our lives, we will respond in the ways He requires and not according to our own thinking.

Besides being Lord, Jesus is also the lover of our souls. In a healthy, loving relationship it is expected that we recognize one another's voices and respond appropriately to one another. The Bible is full of examples of people who came in contact with God, and their response to Him determined the outcome of their encounter.

11. Can you think of some other biblical examples?

LEADER'S NOTES

Lesson One

Leader's Notes

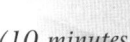

(10 minutes)

This is an important section and one you can have fun with as people get creative and look for examples. Ask your group for some examples, and you decide what the best ones are to focus on for discussion.

A. *(Blind Bartimaeus, Mark 10:46–52)* When blind Bartimaeus cried out to God, even though the crowd tried to stop him, Jesus healed him.

B. *(Woman with the issue of blood, Mark 5:25–34)* Although unclean, she believed in Jesus' mercy, virtue, and power; she risked shame just to touch even the hem of Jesus' garment and was healed.

C. *(Uzza, 1 Chronicles 13:9–10)* God is always to be held in reverence and fear. Like King Saul's disobedience to the words of the prophet Samuel in 1 Samuel 15:14–29, although Uzza's intentions were good, the result of presumption can be deadly. God desires obedience, not sacrifice or good intentions.

D. *(Job, Job 42:1–10)* When Job was confronted with the majesty of God, he repented and prayed for his friends, and then God turned his captivity.

Many times when God desires to speak to us, it is not at our convenience. He is the Lord of our lives, and we must know His voice and heed it.

John relates a story of how he was driving along the highway and the Holy Spirit told him to pull over because God had some things He wanted to say to him.

God then spoke to John, reminding him of 1 Thessalonians 5:17, which says, *"Pray without ceasing."*

12. Prayer is not simply a monologue, but rather a *dialogue*.

13. **God isn't saying He wants to talk to you without ceasing, but rather He is willing to** _communicate_ **without ceasing.** As a loving Father, God desires a continuing, two-way relationship of intimacy with His children.

A husband may be in a room with his wife and receive a single look, and he could write pages from what she has communicated with that simple gesture. Yet someone who didn't know her well could be in that same room and would have no idea of what she was "saying." But because that husband and his wife have become very intimate throughout their years of marriage, their levels of communication go far beyond mere words. *And so it is with God. There are other ways to communicate besides words, and the more we get to know Him, the easier it will be to recognize what and how He is communicating to us.*

Our God talks!

> "You will remember that before you became Christians you went around from one idol to another, not one of which could speak a single word"
> 1 Cor. 12:2, TLB

The apostle Paul shows one of the major differences between our God and all false gods. What is that difference? Our God talks. He is a talking, communicating God.

Where Are You?

Even after Adam and Eve sinned and fell from the profound relationship they had with Him, God did not first pronounce judgment on them. He said, "Where are you? Why have you left me?" God pursued them, spoke to them, and cared for them. This is a remarkable example of God's compassion and desire to stay in relationship with His people.

LEADER'S NOTES

LESSON ONE

LEADER'S NOTES

Point out the distinction that Enoch was a great prophet BECAUSE he walked with God, not the other way around. God does not favor us with His presence because we are someone great. Anything great that we might do would be a result of drawing near to Him.

(10–20 minutes)

The focus here is to get people to think about how God has pursued them, reached out to them in their own lives. Ask for volunteers to offer examples from their own lives. We've provided some samples to get things going for you if necessary.

The sample answers may provide an opportunity for you to use a bit of humor with this difficult subject of disobedience.

14. This is what God has been crying to His people ever since: "Why have you learned to be _____satisfied_____ without My presence?"_____.

15. Enoch walked with God, and God took him because he: [ ] was a great prophet [X] pursued God's heart.

God has made it known to us throughout the Scriptures that He is actually in pursuit of intimacy with us.

The question is how we will respond to Him.

Let's think about this...

16. What are some ways you may sometimes "fall from grace" and hinder your fellowship with God?
Like Adam and Eve in the garden, we may choose to disobey God in some way such as dishonesty, unforgiveness, etc.

17. What are some ways He reaches out to you and pursues to restore you?
- *People praying for us, sometimes even when we don't want them to.*
- *Pastor calls on us or maybe gives a sermon that "reads our mail."*
- *The Holy Spirit makes a verse alive to us and brings repentance to us.*
- *Something bad happens as a result of our disobedience, so we learn the hard way that it is better to obey.*

18. Knowing that God cares so deeply for you, what are some practical ways you can respond to Him as He reaches out to you?

GOD'S PURSUIT

- *Pray and ask God's forgiveness.*
- *Don't just pray, but follow through and change our behavior or make restitution.*
- *When we know that God is repeatedly reaching out to us or leading us to do something, obey immediately instead of continuing to ignore Him.*
- *Note to leader: You can suggest other examples that fit the personality of your group.*

The Promise or the Promiser...

19. Israel's destination when Moses led them out of Egypt was:

[ ] the Promised Land
[X] to worship in the desert.

Key Statement:
Seek God for who He is, not for what He can do for you.

Earlier we noted that the Bible communicates through major themes. The first we observed was that God has reached out to you, offering an intimate relationship. Another important theme of your journey is based on a question that John asks in this session:

"Why in the world would you want to take them out of Egypt and bring them into the Promised Land before you first bring them to the Promiser Himself? If you bring them out of Egypt straight to the Promised Land without first bringing them to the Promiser, they will make the Promised Land a place of idolatry. Then they'll start seeking God more for what He can do for them rather than for who He is."

LEADER'S NOTES

Lesson One

Leader's Notes

Read John's question again to your group and let them offer their observations. The point is to make sure this theme is driven home. Politely keep people on track and move the discussion along to the next exercise.

This is not just more information to ingest. It is TRUTH. Let's wrap our hearts around this so you can see a real impact on your life.

20. Why do you think so many people within the church automatically respond that the Israelite's destination was the Promised Land? Could it be:

- [ ] They are taught that way
- [ ] Our culture influences their thinking
- [X] Both
- [ ] Other

Below are some phrases that are both biblical and easy to remember. They convey this very important principle that John emphasizes throughout our Drawing Near journey.

This biblical theme is simply that we must seek:
- The Promiser, not the promise
- The Giver, not the gift

(5 minutes).

Again, this is a great opportunity to get creative with your group and have fun on this journey as you find these treasures together! Have people shout out their answers, but in an orderly manner.

21. Put some thought into this. Write below two or three more of your own phrases like those above. We must seek:

- *The One who blesses, not the blessing*
- *The Healer, not just the healing*
- *The Deliver, not just the deliverance*
- *The Creator, not just His creation*

Changing our mind-set, our attitude, and our very lifestyle to this biblical viewpoint is central to our success in this journey.

GOD'S PURSUIT

22. What are some ways that you may have fallen into the trap of serving God for what He can do for you instead of who He is?

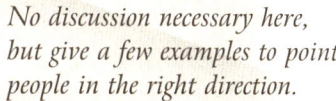

No discussion necessary here, but give a few examples to point people in the right direction.

- *Running around being very busy in the church trying to gain attention or a position or favor with God*
- *Judging yours/others' relationship with God by how many prayers got answered or how many tangible blessings you received (Note: Just because someone is walking in prosperity or always talking about their prayers being answered does not necessarily mean they are near to God. It could indicate the opposite—a shallow relationship that cares more about what they get from God then God Himself.)*
- *Falling away from God or being discouraged or angry every time things don't go your way. (Note: God chastises those whom He loves. Difficult times come to even the most spiritual among us and should not necessarily be viewed as a sign of not walking with God. Even Jesus suffered in His obedience to God. Remember Job; oftentimes it is in the valley of the shadow of death that we experience our most intimate times with God.*

23. Now what are some ways you can be just like Moses, Samuel, and the disciples, whom we looked at earlier? How can you turn aside, changing your course of action (the way you live, work, think, act and/or speak) to immediately respond to this call to seek the Creator instead of seeking the things He has created?

(5–10 minutes)

Ask for volunteers to share their answers to this very important question. Look for practical answers to focus on, and give some of your own as well.

Lesson One

Leader's Notes

- *Immediately change your prayer life so it is more balanced with an emphasis on worship and fellowship with your Creator, not just a list of things you want or even need.*
- *Instead of being busy doing what you think will "get you ahead," seek God's heart for your involvement in your church and in other areas of your life. God desires obedience, not sacrifice.*
- *Try giving more and accumulating less. Let God use you to bless others as opposed to always seeking more blessings for yourself.*
- *Leaders, give some other highly practical examples that stimulate thinking along this line.*

Finding More Treasure...

We pursue what we value, and everything has some value attached to it. A wise shopper will never pay more for an item than it is worth. If a home was worth $100,000, we wouldn't pay $200,000 for it. If a television wasn't worth more than $500, we wouldn't pay $2000 for it.

When major league baseball star Mark McGwire hit his 70th homerun, someone paid $2.7 million for the ball he hit. However, that ball has much less value only a short time later, because Barry Bonds has broken that homerun record. **The eye of the purchaser determines the value of something.**

What is our value as individual human beings? If we leave this question to mankind, our history paints a sad story of brutal wars, millions of abortions, divorce, slavery, prostitution, and more. **God must establish true value.**

Jesus makes this statement in Matthew 16:26, "*For what profit is it to a man if he gains the whole world, and loses his own soul? Or what will a man give in exchange for his soul?*"

GOD'S PURSUIT

Recent studies show the gross world product for one year was $35.8 trillion. That's beyond what we can imagine, and it doesn't include real estate. Jesus said if you give your soul even for all of that, you've made a bad deal.

God gave Jesus for us, and God does not make bad purchases.

This simple beginning of our journey has been filled with startling biblical facts, which can transform your very life. Let's finish this first portion with some more mind-boggling, humbling, and empowering truths.

24. In the video session John declares, "If you would've been worth one cent, one penny less to the Father than _____Jesus Himself_____, then the Father would have never given _____Jesus_____ in exchange for you."

25. This can be so difficult to believe. What are some reasons why we doubt that God values us as much as He values Jesus? Write your responses here.

Let your group know that answers could be anything, including responses such as:
- *I had an abortion.*
- *I was abused and feel dirty.*
- *I know I am a sinner.*
- *I am a good person, but I don't think Jesus would really love me.*
- *Jesus was perfect, holy, and just, and we feel completely unworthy in comparison.*
- *God may have created the world, but that doesn't mean He necessarily cares about me.*

LEADER'S NOTES

(10-15 minutes)

This is a very personal question (#25) and a great chance to reach hurting people. Understand that this is a very personal issue.

- *Spend the time to tell people that God's love toward them is an already established fact regardless of who they are or what they have done. We address this with scriptures a little bit further into this lesson.*

- *Then go over these sample answers, which act as a way to let people know of God's love.*

LESSON ONE

LEADER'S NOTES

The remedy for doubt can be found in Romans 10:17: "Faith comes by hearing, and hearing by the word of God."

• Why should God care about me?
• I want to believe it, and I try to be a good Christian, but I never seem to be able to be consistent, so I feel God doesn't love me as much as He loves Jesus.

Here are several more Bible verses that will bolster your faith and destroy the lie that you have no value to God:

• **John 3:16:** "God so loved the world that He gave His only begotten Son."
• **Psalm 49:8 (NIV):** "The ransom for a life is costly, no payment is ever enough."
• **1 Corinthians 6:20 (NLT):** "God bought you with a high price"
• **Ephesians 1:7 (NLT):** "He is so rich in kindness that he purchased our freedom through the blood of his Son."

In the Gospel of John, chapter 17, verses 22–24 (NLT), Jesus is praying to His Father God. Jesus makes a radical statement that has the power to further increase our faith and convince even the skeptics among us that God pursued us because He highly valued us. In verse 23, Jesus Himself says, *"Then the world will know that you sent me and will understand that you love them as much as you love me."*

Key Statement:
God loves you just as much as God loves Jesus!

26. What it means to me:

Take a moment to reflect. Write your feelings about what this incredible statement (made by Jesus Himself) actually means to you and how it will permanently change your life:

If your group seems to be stuck with this question, you may want to offer the following examples:

GOD'S PURSUIT

- *God actually will forgive me of the awful things I have done.*
- *There is hope for my future.*

27. How it changes my daily life:
Examples:
- *Now that I am forgiven, I can quit running from God. Now I can fellowship with God, worship Him, and be involved with my church.*
- *Because there is hope for my future, I can quit falling back into my addictions and through a close relationship with the Lord see my life and family restored.*

LEADER'S NOTES

28. Drawing near to God will naturally result in your sharing His love with others. Going through this curriculum is a perfect opportunity for you to open conversations with family, friends, and co-workers. Simply share what you are doing in your life right now. List here the names of at least one or two people you will share this amazing verse in John 17:22–24 with. Or you can tell them about the treasure you are finding on this journey. If you prayerfully look for the opportunity, God will arrange the details.

1 Peter 2:24 says, *"Who Himself bore our sins in His own body on the tree… by whose stripes you were healed."* Jesus lived a sinless life. It should have been us who were judged and condemned. Jesus willingly bore our judgment because He esteemed us better than Himself.

The Father loves us as much as He loves Jesus. Can you imagine Him staying with us and not leaving us even the way we have behaved in our lives? Yet still He draws us

• *Samaritan Road sections offer people the chance to be the Good Samaritan—to help others in need. Make sure you encourage people to DO this exercise; assure them that God will "show up" on their behalf as He has promised (James 4:8).*

• *Ask them to share testimonies in later sessions. Let them know they will find that not only will others get blessed, but also they will too as they serve and see God move. (Remember to make a note of this, and ask about it before your sessions are all finished.)*

Lesson One

Leader's Notes

(10 minutes)

Ask for volunteers to share their story, but let them know up front that they must keep it to 2–3 minutes so others can have an opportunity as well. Look for things to focus on as people share, things that you can use to minister with, of extraordinary ways God pursued people. Also share your own story if appropriate.

Here is your opportunity to leave the session on a high note. Go over the final two bullet points and finish this session by repeating James 4:8 as a promise.

Remind your group:
1. They should preview the next session and complete the personal discussion portions. If they like, they may complete the whole thing.
2. Pray for the group before they leave, or divide up in groups and have them pray for each other. Be led by the Spirit, but keep the focus on things that God may have brought to light from today's teaching.

to Jesus. Do you understand how God has pursued you? All of us have a story, a testimony of how God rescued us or touched us in some ways to bring us to Himself. Some are dramatic and exciting; some seem more plain and "vanilla." Either way, whether it looks wild on the outside or not, whether it is Hollywood, "average," or in between, God views your life as a major event. Whatever they were, list below some ways in which God has pursued you:

29. Before you knew Him as a Christian:
- *My sister prayed for me.*
- *A friend at work witnessed to me.*
- *My parents gave me a Bible.*

30. After you became a Christian:
- *Someone took me to a church picnic so I could meet Christian friends.*
- *At a Bible conference the minister prayed for me, and I received the gift of tongues.*
- *I read my Bible, and God showed me how to use my talents in the children's ministry.*

Today many in the church don't realize how valued they are by God.

- Don't let anyone tell you that you are not valuable, because when God paid such a high price for you, He demonstrated not only that you are valuable, but also that He is in hot pursuit of you.

- God has already made the move, but now He's saying, "I'm waiting. You're the one who's going to determine the level of your relationship with me."

You draw near to God, and He will draw near to you!

Video Script for Lesson 1
GOD'S PURSUIT

Good Morning.

We are beginning our first lesson of twelve on "Drawing Near" a life of intimacy with God. And our flagship scripture is going to be James Chapter 4, verse 8. And I want you to turn there with me this morning, James the 4th Chapter. And let me say this while you're turning there this morning. I have been in the ministry now twenty-one years. I have to say I have never been so hungry for the presence of God and even more so to be intimate with Him as I have been in the last two years of my life. I have never wept as much as I have wept in the last two years– in airplanes, airports, showers, my hotel rooms, my bedroom, my office, in my car– because of the presence of God and how real He has become and how intimate He has become. And I believe this is God's passion for every single one of us. And in James the 4th Chapter the 8th verse we read this: "Draw near to God and He will draw near to you".

Now I want you to say this with me. Draw near to God, and He will draw near to you. Who draws first? We do. There's something we can do, we can initiate, that will literally cause the One who put the stars in the universe with His fingers to come near me. Now I don't know about you but that really excites me.

What James is saying here by the Spirit of God is basically this. You're the one that determines the level of your relationship with God, not God. Did you get that? You're the one that determines the level of your relationship with God, not God. In fact, let me say this. God is more passionate about drawing near to you than you are to Him. Now let me just set the stage here. The Lord God says this to us in Exodus 34, Verse 14 in the New Living Translation. Listen to the scripture. Moses said, "for he is a God who is passionate about his relationship with you."

Did you hear that? I mean when I think about God being passionate for me I think about what David says in Psalms Chapter 40, verse 5. David says, "and your thoughts toward us cannot be recounted to You in order... they are more than can be numbered." Your thoughts Lord, toward us are more than can be numbered. Well how many are they if those thoughts are that many? Well if you go to Psalms 139 David says this, "Lord when I think about the thoughts that you have towards me and how precious they are. If I was able to number them they would outnumber every grain of sand that's on this planet." Now I want you to think about every single grain of sand that's on this planet–every beach, every dessert, every golf course. Now think about this: every grain. When I think about the thoughts that I've had towards Lisa in the last twenty-one years of our marriage, and you know I've had a lot of thoughts about her, okay. When I think a lot of precious thoughts– when I think about those thoughts– if I was able to number those thoughts up in twenty-one years, I don't think I'd get a sand box full and I'm doing better than most. Are you getting what I'm saying? God says, "The thoughts that I think towards you– you personally, not the person beside you, we're talking about you– outnumber every grain of sand that's on this planet. Are you getting how much He longs for you? And you know what He says in Jeremiah 29, Verse 11? He said, " For I know the thoughts that I think toward you... thoughts of peace and not of evil, to give you a future and a hope." And He said that to disobedient children. "Wow." So this is how much He yearns and longs for your intimacy.

Now if you think about this the Bible communicates major themes. You know one of the major themes is God's desire for you, for your intimacy, for communing with you. Now let me take a moment here and talk about this. Recently I was driving and I remember the Holy Spirit spoke to me and He said, "Son I want you to pull off." Now, how many of you know when God wants to initiate conversation it's usually at sometimes your most inconvenient times? Here I am driving down the highway and the Lord says, "Pull off I want to talk

Lesson One

to you." And you know this is true if you look at the Bible. Moses is in the backside of the desert and he is tending his father-in-law's sheep, right? And all of a sudden God wants to get his attention, so what does he do? He gets this bush to burn, right? And Moses checks this bush out and goes, "Wow, what do I do? Because here if I let go of these sheep they're going to scatter all over the wilderness, but you know what Moses said, I will turn aside and see this great sight." Now you know what that word turn aside means? It means depart your course of action. So Moses said, "I will depart the course of action." In other words, I am going to leave these sheep and they may scatter all over; it may take me a whole day to gather them back, but I'm going to check this out. And you know what the Bible says? When God saw that Moses turned aside, then God spoke. Now Moses would not have had that interaction with the Lord had he not turned aside.

Now somebody said, well God would have gotten his attention in another way. Well I don't know about that. I don't know if that's in line with the way scripture teaches. Because if you look at Samuel when he was a young boy–how many of you remember Samuel? God comes to him when he is a young man and God wants to initiate conversation and the Lord says, "Samuel". And you know Samuel hears the Lord's voice and who did it sound like? It sounded like his pastor, so he went running to Eli and said "Eli, Eli did you call me?" Eli said, "No I didn't call you; go back to bed." So Samuel goes back to bed and God comes in and goes, "Samuel". And Samuel goes running to Eli and goes "Eli did you call me?" "No I didn't call you, go back to bed". So God comes back again and says "Samuel." Samuel goes running to Eli, "Eli, Eli you called me. I know you called me." And Eli now, finally, this dense priest gets it through his head that maybe the Lord is calling this boy. So he looks at Samuel and says, "When you go back and He calls again, this time say your servant hears." So Samuel goes back to bed and the Lord goes "Samuel". And Samuel goes "Your servant hears, Lord." And God begins to show Samuel something that nobody had ever known before. Now if God would have been like sometimes people think He is, when He saw Samuel wasn't getting it the second time, he would have went "Samuel, no, no don't run to Eli; it is I the Lord your God who is speaking to you." But he doesn't do that. Why? Because He wants us to know how to recognize Him. He is our Lover. Do you understand that? And He wants us to know how to recognize Him.

If you notice, God the Lord is like that. In the book of Mark, there's the most amazing story. Jesus was walking across the water and you know what the book of Mark says? This is amazing. In Mark 6:48 Jesus was walking on the sea and this is what it says, "…and would have passed them by." Now the new American Standard reads, "…and he intended to pass them by." But you know what happens? When they cry out for Him, He turned and went into the boat and they were immediately on the other side. If they had not cried out for Him, He would have walked right by. So when I'm driving down the highway and the Lord says, " Pull off I want to talk to you." And I remember it, there's a rest stop a half a mile down the road and I immediately turned the car off. And as soon as I pulled the car off, the Holy Spirit said, " Son, did I not say to you pray with out ceasing?" And I said, "Yes Lord. Your word says that we are to pray without ceasing." He said, "Son, is prayer a monologue or is it a dialogue?" I said, "Well it's a dialogue." He said, "Yeah that's right; it is a dialogue; it's a two way conversation." He said, "So if I said to you– pray without ceasing– He said then that means that I am willing to communicate with you without ceasing." And I don't know about you, but I had a revival in my car right there, okay?

Now how many of you know it's not always with words? Now how many of you know there are other ways to communicate than words? He didn't say I am willing to talk to you without ceasing; He said I'm willing to communicate without ceasing. How many of you know my wife can give me one look and I can write three pages about what she just said? Now listen. If you're in the same room and she gave that same look, you couldn't write a thing, but I can write three full pages of what she just said. Now, I couldn't have done that twenty years ago because why? We've become really intimate in the last twenty-one years– I know that girl and she knows me. And sometimes it's frustrating because she knows me better than I know me sometimes. You understand what I'm saying? But we've become intimate in twenty-one years. And so this

is what the Lord was saying, "Son, I want to communicate with you."

If you remember Paul said this about the Lord. He said, you will remember now this is out of The Living Bible, 1 Corinthians the 12th chapter the 2nd and 3rd verse. Paul said, "you will remember that before you became a Christian, you went around from one idol to another not one of them could speak a single word." So Paul says the major differentiating thing between our living God, the real Lord and all false gods is– our God talks. He is a talking communicating God. Now when you think about somebody that much and you want to communicate with somebody that much, that means you're in hot pursuit of them. And this is what the Bible shows all throughout scriptures is God's hot pursuit of man. A lot of people when they read the scriptures do not read it accurately because you know what, they see things through the wrong eyes. How many of you know you've always got to read the scriptures through the character of God, interpreted through His character?

See, for example when Adam and Eve fell, the first thing He did was not proclaim judgement. What did he do? He said, "Where are you?" It was a cry of Adam and Eve "why have you left me." See can I say this, this is what God has been crying to His people ever since: "Why have you been satisfied without my presence?" I really believe the heart cry of God is this, "Why have you learned to be satisfied without My presence? Why do you not have intimacy with Me when I've made it available?" And so that's exactly what God is saying to Adam and Eve. "Where are you? Why have you left me?"

If you look at Enoch, Enoch was Adam's great, great, great, great, great grandson okay? You know what the Bible says about Enoch? The Bible says that Enoch walked with God. And it says, "He was not for God took him." Now this is what I really believe happened. Enoch, when he, listen, one day Enoch went up to his great, great, great, great, great, great grandfather Adam. You say how in the world can you go talk to your great, great, great, great, great, great grandfather. It's very simple. When you live to be 930-years-old, you're going to see your great, great, great, great, great, great grandchildren, okay? What a lot of people do not understand is that Adam was only, I think, 622 years old when Enoch was born. And Enoch went to Adam one day and he said, "Adam what was it like in the garden, tell me". And Adam began to weep and it wasn't tears of joy, it was tears of depression. Why? Because it's one thing to never know walking with God, it's another thing to walk with Him in His glory and lose it.

See I have ancient Hebrew writings that show the depression that Adam and Eve went through is unspeakable. They would sit in caves for days in depression because of what they had done. I mean Adam would even try to kill himself and God wouldn't let him. And so I believe that many of the descendants said you don't talk about the garden. But Enoch was hungry. Enoch said to Adam "Tell me what it was like; you walked with the Creator." And Adam went "Enoch I walked with Him. I mean Enoch He showed me how He set up the universe and put the earth in perfect equilibrium. How He set up the electromagnetic field and the seeds bring forth the fruit after their kind and the gravitational force and the universes perfect balance. And He began to speak about this and then He said, "You know Enoch, we named five billion species of animals together. God brought them to me, we discussed it, but the final choice He left to me." And Enoch was drooling; he was going "I want it." And so the Bible says he began to walk with God and this is the testimony that pleased Him. And listen, God just said, I've had it, I like this guy so much, you're out of here. And he was just a kid 365-years-old.

Enoch had a phenomenal prophetic ministry. He prophesied the coming of the Lord, okay. Do you realize this? Way, way back then he was the first one to see Jesus coming with ten thousands and thousands of his saints. Jude wrote about it, right? So he was a tremendous prophet, but God did not take him because he was a tremendous prophet. He took him because he pursued God's heart. He walked with God. If you continue through the Bible you will see that there is another man named Noah, who the Bible said walked with God. I love that; I love that. Because what do you do when you walk with somebody? You commune and share your heart. Isn't that right? Noah walked with God and you know what? The secret that was kept from the world that the world was unaware of for hundreds of years, it was first a secret kept between

LESSON ONE

God and Noah. Think of it, because God shared His heart with Noah, because Noah walked with Him.

God said to Abraham, He said "Abraham walk before me." Isn't that true? And Abraham walked before the Lord. If you look at God, what is the whole reason that He delivered the children of Israel out of Egypt? You know I ask churches this a lot. Let me ask you this. Where was Israel's destination when they came out of Egypt? Where were they heading? You're all saying the Promised Land and you're wrong.

What did Moses say to Pharaoh? Thus saith the Lord let my people go that they might worship me in the desert. Why in the world do you want to take them out of Egypt and bring them into the Promised Land before you first bring them to the Promiser Himself? If you bring them out of Egypt and bring them straight to the Promised Land without first bringing them to the Promiser then they'll make the Promised Land into a place of idolatry. And then they'll start seeking God more for what He can do for them rather than who He is. So Moses said "I'm going to bring you right to the place where I met with God at Sinai." And when Moses brings them out there in Exodus 19, Verse 3 you know what you're going to find? God says, "Go down and tell those people that I delivered them out of Egypt for one reason– to bring them to Myself. The whole reason He delivered you out of the world (Egypt is a type of the world) is to bring you to Himself."

If you look at Jesus He is the greatest example of God pursuing men and women because what did Jesus say to us, "The son of man came to seek and to save that which is lost." Not only did He come to save us He came to seek us out. And listen– that was when we were still enemies. So do you see how God has longed, longed, longed for His people? He has been in hot pursuit. Why? The whole reason He created us is to have intimacy with Him. He did not put Adam in the garden to have a worldwide ministry; He did not put Adam in the garden to build bridges and skyscrapers. He put Adam in the garden to have intimacy with God. Now out of that intimacy will come tremendous ministry, will come bridges, skyscrapers or whatever you're called to do; but the reason God created us was for us to walk in intimacy and inside of you is that desire to have intimacy with Him. And until it's satisfied you will never, ever be satisfied. "

Now let me say this– you pursue what you value, isn't that true? Now we're going to talk some more about the Lord here because the greatest example of God's pursuit of us is Jesus. How many of you know you pursue what you value? Right? Isn't that right? Now let me make this statement: if we are wise shoppers, how many of you know everything has a value attached to it? Everything has a value attached to it and if we're wise shoppers we will always purchase items, which are worth as much or more to us than what we give for it. Isn't that true? Think about it. If a home's worth $100,000.00 you are not going to go pay $200,000.00 for it right? If a television is not worth more than $500.00 to you, you're not going to go pay $2000.00 for it. Right? So if you're a wise shopper you're always going to pay what something's worth, right? Or less. Isn't that true?

Now the same thing is true with human beings. Here's the best example that I can think of. How many of you remember Mark McGwire when he hit his 70th homer? What was it? His 70th home run, right? Do you know how much the guy paid for that ball? 2.7 million dollars. Now I wouldn't have paid that much for it. It wasn't worth it. If I had the money I wouldn't of paid that. I didn't have that at that time but still don't have it. But anyway, I wouldn't have paid that much for that ball. But that guy paid 2.7 and you know what I read in the article then? There were people that would have paid more because that was the value of that ball then. Today I'm sure that nobody would pay 2.7 million because Barry Bond's has broken that record. Isn't that right? So you see the value of something is determined by the eye of the purchaser.

The value of an item is determined by the eye of the purchaser. So what is our value? You cannot look at what our value is based on what man says because how many of you know what is highly esteemed among men is an abomination before God. If you look at the way human beings value human beings it would be a sad thing because if you look there are people that abort their babies every single day because those babies are going to be inconvenient to them. There are husbands that

22

leave their families because they think their relationships are not worth working for anymore. Right? So they place little value on their families. You look at prostitutes. Everyday they give their bodies to be sold; they place a value upon their own bodies sometimes as small as $100.00. So what human beings see is the value of a person is not the true value. All true value has to be established by God. Isn't that right?

Now listen to this. Jesus makes this statement. Listen carefully. In Matthew 16:26, He says, "For what profit is it to a man if he gains the whole world, and loses his own soul? Or what will a man give in exchange for his soul?" Now look up at me. What Jesus is saying here is this. He's saying–if you give your soul for all the wealth that's in the world you have made an unprofitable deal. Now you know what, I have found recent studies show, you know what the gross world product was recently for one year? 35.8 trillion dollars. Trillion. I mean that's beyond what you can even imagine; you understand that's not even counting the real estate. 35.8 trillion dollars. Jesus said if you give your soul in exchange for that you've made an unprofitable deal. In other words you've given something of more value for something of less value. Okay? So what's the value? What is our worth? You know what the Bible says? For God so loved the world that He gave His only begotten son. Now listen, listen to this. God gave Jesus for us. Now listen. How many of you know God does not make bad purchases? Because let me read this to you. The Bible says in Psalm 49, Verse 8 the ransom for a life is costly. No payment is ever enough. And the Bible also says in 1 Corinthians 6, Verse 20 God bought you at a high price.

And again He says the Father is so rich in kindness that He purchased our freedom through the blood of His son. So God gave Jesus for us and how many of you know that God doesn't make a bad deal? You know what that tells me? If you had been worth one cent, one penny less to the Father than Jesus Himself then the Father would never have given Jesus in exchange for you. Jesus is the Father's most prized possession and yet Jesus was given for you, and if you had been the only one He would have still done it. Listen to what Jesus says because this will confirm what I just said. John 17, Verses 22 through 24 in the New Living Translation. Listen to these words. "Then the world will know that you sent me and will understand that you will love them as much as you love me." Now how many of you know that the Father really loves Jesus? Jesus said, "Father then the world is going to know you love them as much as you love me." If you had been worth one cent less to the Father than Jesus Himself, He never would have given Him for you. Do you understand how much He has been pursuing us?

I will never forget this. I was first born again and I would have been filled with the Holy Spirit just for a few months and I was driving in my car and the Lord spoke to my heart something that riveted me. He said, "Son, do you know that I esteem you better than myself?" Now when I heard that do you know what my first impression was? This is not God; this is not Jesus. I almost said get thee behind me Satan. I'm driving. I'm going wait a minute– wait. You esteem me better than yourself? You're Jesus. You're the one that created the universe; you esteem me little peon John Bevere, more than yourself? I said, I am sorry I will not believe this is you unless you give me three scriptures out of the New Testament. I won't believe you. You know the Lord never has a problem with that. Do you realize that? He actually likes it and so immediately I heard the Lord say this to me, "What does Philippians, Chapter 2, Verse 3 say?" Now that was a scripture I had memorized. Now listen, I'm going to quote it to you. Paul said. "Let nothing be done through selfish ambition or conceit, but in lowliness of mind let each esteem others better than himself." I said no, no, no, no, no. I'm in my car. Just this is the way I am in my car. I said, No, no, no, no, no. I said that is Paul talking to the Philippian Christians, and he is telling the Philippian Christians that they are to esteem each other better than themselves. That is not talking about you esteeming me better than Yourself. He said, "Son I never tell my children to do anything that I don't do Myself. Wow! I kind of backed off. He said, "Son that's the problem with parents. They tell their kids not to do something they do and then they wonder why their kids do it. They tell their kids don't you speak evil about your teacher, yet they talk about their pastor around the dinner table. Then they wonder why their kids have a problem with rebellion. You see what I'm saying? That was just a little extra added there in case you didn't know.

Lesson One

So I said, "Well, that's one you need to give me two more." I mean I wasn't convinced. And then the Lord said to me (I'll never forget this), "Son who hung on the cross? Me or you?" And all of a sudden it hit me– I should have been the one who went to hell– I should have been the one who should have been judged. He didn't do one thing wrong. Yet He hung on that cross bearing my shame, my sickness, my disease, my punishment, and my judgment all because He esteemed me better than Himself. And that broke me; I started weeping in the car. And then the scriptures just came springing up from my heart; 1 Peter 2:24, "who Himself bore our sins in His own body on the tree…by whose stripes you were healed."

I was completely broken and you know what's amazing? Even though now I was completely broken and convinced He said, "Are you ready for your third scripture?" I said yeah because I already knew. He said, "What is Romans Chapter 12, Verse 10 say"? Let me read it to you, Romans Chapter 12, verse 10, listen to this. Romans Chapter 12, verse 10 says this, "Be kindly affectionate to one another with brotherly love, (now listen) in honor giving preference to one another." He said, "Son I said you are to give preference to one another or esteem each other better, right? He said am I not the first born of many brethren." He said, " I prefer my brother over Myself." So here's the Father who loves us as much as He loves Jesus and He never would have sent Him if we would have been worth one cent less than Jesus. Here's Jesus who says I esteem you actually better than myself.

When you think about the Holy Spirit can you imagine Him staying with us and not leaving us, even the way we behaved and still drawing us to Jesus when we were still enemies? Do you understand how God has pursued? And you know what is really sad– so many in the church have misunderstood His hot love and pursuit of us just like Israel did because you know what God said to Israel? He said in the book of Malachi, now you have to understand, this is after over 1,000 years of pursuing them. He said, I have loved you with an eternal love and yet you say how have you loved us. In other words they missed the fact that He had been in hot pursuit of them and loved them so much. And their response was– yet how have you loved us? And yet today I find people in the church that don't realize how valued they are by God. When God spoke that to me He wasn't just speaking that to me; He was speaking that to every one of his children. That's how valuable you are. Don't you let anybody ever tell you, you aren't valuable because when God pays that kind of a high price for you, not only are you valuable, but He is in hot pursuit of you. So James says, "draw near to God and he will draw near to you." He has already made the move but now He is saying, " I'm waiting. You're the one that's going to determine the level of your relationship with Me."

PROTECT YOUR HUNGER

Video Session 2

PROTECT YOUR HUNGER

Key Statement:
Walking closely with God is for all who hunger.

1. [ ] True or [X] False: World-renowned ministers such as Billy Graham and Oral Roberts have a greater opportunity to walk closely with God than you do.

2. [ ] True or [X] False: Ministers are to have a closer relationship with God than congregation members.

3. [X] True or [ ] False: You're the one, not God, who determines your level of relationship with God.

 4. Why is it that we tend to think that those "in full-time ministry" can be closer to God than the rest of us?

[X] They have to read and pray; we don't.
[X] It is their job.
[X] They're called and we're not.
[X] It is easier for them.

5. When it comes to living intimately with God, why is there no real difference between those who are full-time ministers and those who are not?
(5 minute discussion)

Here are some possible answers you might see:
• We are all human and face the same daily challenges.

LEADER'S NOTES

(3–5 minutes)

Much like the first session, you will want to make sure you stress that the truths in the sessions are for everyone in your group.

1. Intimacy with God is available to each one of us. This is God's passion.

2. This intimacy is not reserved for specially gifted personalities, rather it is available for all who hunger and thirst for more of God.

(5 minutes)

This is an excellent opportunity to answer a question that is in the back of the minds of many people.

• **If you are an ordained or full-time minister,** *you can help your group understand that you have no special "direct*

25

Lesson Two

Leader's Notes

line" to God and that you have many of the same challenges that all of them have. You may also want to point out something that many will find surprising—at times it seems more difficult for you to be close to God because of the realities and difficult challenges of ministry.

- **If you are not an ordained or full-time minister,** this is an excellent opportunity for you to share how God has blessed you with the opportunity to lead and have an intimate walk with Him even though you are not a "minister."

- Whether or not you are a minister, briefly share and/or open for discussion:

A. Your journey of becoming close with God and how you are still growing.

B. How many of the challenges we all face are similar regardless of title, career, or vocation. This is a good topic for open discussion among a group.

- *God has called us all to a life of intimacy with Him.*
- *We all have jobs, careers, etc. that God requires us to be faithful in.*
- *Whatever career or vocation we have must be carried out with faith, prayer, holiness, and servanthood.*
- *Ministers are no "better" than anyone else.*
- *We all face the same temptations.*

NOTE: Some may contend that there is indeed a difference. Open debate can be a good way to learn and bring interest to the session. But be a strong leader; keep it short and friendly, and steer the debate to the truth.
(5 minutes optional):

- *Remind the group that the issue is personal relationship with God, NOT daily duties or work schedule. Remember Mary and Martha (Luke 10:41–42).*
- *Of course a minister's work schedule is different from a plumber's or an executive's.*
- *Point out that though a minister "gets paid" to read the Bible and pray, there is no such thing as buying your way to intimacy with God.*
- *A religious title such as "Reverend" or simply reading and praying a lot "because it's your job" does not make anyone close to God.*
- *Remember the Pharisees—they had a great religious position and title—studied and prayed all the time, but according to Jesus they were often furthest from God.*
- *Most importantly is the fact that the Bible is clear that God offers intimacy to us all equally.*

PROTECT YOUR HUNGER

6. Can you support your answer with scriptures?

Acts 10:34–35: "God shows no partiality. But...whoever fears Him...is accepted by Him."

1 Timothy 2:4: "[God] desires all men to be saved and to come to the knowledge of the truth."

Romans 2:11 (KJV): "There is no respect of persons with God."

Ephesians 5:17–18 (paraphrased): God desires us all to be filled with the Spirit.

Colossians 3:23–25 (paraphrased): Whatever you do, do it with all your might, for there is no partiality with God.

1 Thessalonians 4:1–5 shows that we should abound more and more in the Word and holiness in a lifestyle with God.

- There are many other "more popular" scriptures you can add to this list, including many we will go through as we continue our journey.
- Feel free to add your favorite scriptures about this.

God desires interaction. God has given us a timeless invitation to draw near to Him, and He is waiting for us to respond.

You are the one who determines the level of your relationship with God, not God.

Some of the most spiritual people we know will never be seen standing behind a pulpit. God desires that every born-again child know Him deeply and intimately!

LEADER'S NOTES

(5 minutes)

Ask volunteers for their answers, and give some of your own.

LESSON TWO

LEADER'S NOTES

7. How would you rate your level of relationship with God? *(Circle those that apply)*

Shallow	Consistent	Distant
Complacent	Discouraged	Confused
"On fire," hungry	Deep, intimate	Backslidden

8. From the answer(s) circled above, why do you place yourself into this category?

No discussion is necessary here. This and the next question are obviously very personal subject matter.

- *Your group may be widely diverse, so most likely they will have given many types of answers.*
- *Instead of discussion, simply encourage people—whether they are hungry and on fire for God or they are discouraged or not walking with the Lord—to keep coming to these sessions, growing in God.*
- *Seek to get people involved in church. This is one of the best ways they can grow in the Lord.*

9. What is holding you back from a deeper and consistent relationship?

No discussion is necessary here.

- *The answers to many of the things that hinder people's intimacy with God will be found within these continuing sessions, and you may simply want to let your group know that and encourage them to keep drawing near.*

PROTECT YOUR HUNGER

10. What could ignite you to grow deeper in God? List ways and things you can do to change your level of relationship in order to be able to continually be drawing near to God:

Below are samples of some answers you may get or you could offer as examples for discussion:

- Continuing to come to these sessions.
- Walking in the fear of God, identifying and repenting of sin.
- Reading the Word of God regularly, praying regularly.
- Not hanging around the wrong people.
- Being more involved in church.
- Be faithful in a daily time of devotions.
- Get counseling to overcome _____
- Stop gossiping.
- Read good Christian books.
- Be part of a prayer group.
- Don't hang around _____ sin.

[handwritten note: Who? Knows by experience ✓]

An Invitation...

11. If God has given us this amazing invitation to draw near, why aren't more people walking in intimacy with God? *There is a lack of hunger in the body of Christ.*

"As the deer pants for the water brooks, so pants my soul for You, O God. My soul thirsts for God, for the living God. When shall I come and appear before God? My tears have been my food day and night, while they continually say to me, 'Where is your God?' When I remember these things, I pour out my soul within me. For I used to go with the multitude; I went with them to the house of God, with the voice of joy and praise, with a multitude that kept a pilgrim feast"
Ps. 42:1–4

LEADER'S NOTES
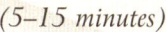

(5–15 minutes)

This is where you can spend some time to encourage people to press on with God. The point here is that there are practical ways in which we live our lives that can cause us to walk more closely with God—NOT formulas, but good biblical habits and attitudes that nurture our relationship with God.

- Ask for a few volunteers to share their answers.

- Remind the people in your group that the "ball is in their court," and there are practical things they can do to grow in the Lord. If they draw near to God, He will draw near to them!

Lesson Two

Leader's Notes

12. What is the key to David's hunger and thirst? *"When I remember these things, I pour out my soul within me" (v. 4).*

13. The Hebrew word for *remember* is *zakar*. It means more than just remember or recall. *Zakar* means to ____retain____ in ____thought____.

14. It is important for us to ____protect____ as well as to ____increase____ our hunger for Him, and we do it by ____retaining____ Him in our soulish ____thoughts____.

Hungry or Content?

15. [ ] True or [x] False: "Lord, increase my hunger for You" is a biblical prayer in order to increase your hunger for God?

16. True or [ ] False: The degree that you fill your ... the things of this world is going to determine ...se to His call to draw near?

(3–5 minut...

Tell your grou... something you an... very seriously. Make s... take it seriously and have answered these questions with care. Do not ask for people to share their answers, but you as the leader may prayerfully consider setting the example and sharing some of your life story answers here.

17. Take some time to step back and honestly examine your life:

• What is your soul satisfied with?

• What is your everyday motive for getting up in the morning and going to work?

• What does your life revolve around?

PROTECT YOUR HUNGER

- Is it consumed with worldly cares and desires (cars, houses, money, food, entertainment, career goals, etc)?

Key Statement:
God wants all of His people to love hearing His voice more than they love the things of the world.

In Revelation 3:14–20 God speaks to the Laodeceian church, saying, *"And to the angel of the church of the Laodiceans write, 'These things says the Amen, the Faithful and True Witness, the Beginning of the creation of God: "I know your works, that you are neither cold nor hot. I could wish you were cold or hot. So then, because you are lukewarm, and neither cold nor hot, I will vomit you out of My mouth. Because you say, 'I am rich, have become wealthy, and have need of nothing'— and do not know that you are wretched, miserable, poor, blind, and naked—I counsel you to buy from Me gold refined in the fire, that you may be rich; and white garments, that you may be clothed, that the shame of your nakedness may not be revealed; and anoint your eyes with eye salve, that you may see. As many as I love, I rebuke and chasten. Therefore be zealous and repent. Behold, I stand at the door and knock. If anyone hears My voice and opens the door, I will come in to him and dine with him, and he with Me."*

"Bow down Your ear, O LORD, hear me; for I am poor and needy"
Ps. 86:1.

18. What is the difference between the Laodicean church and David?
- *The Laodicean church had some wealth and saw themselves as in need of nothing.*
- *David, who had much more wealth, saw himself as one who was poor and needing more of the presence of God.*

LEADER'S NOTES

read

Lesson Two

Leader's Notes

19. How do these scriptures relate to the stories John tells of the two different churches he preached at?

- *Like the Laodicean church, the Cree Indian youth were satisfied with the relatively little wealth they had. They were indifferent because they were filling their souls with television.*
- *Like David in Psalm 86, the youth of the northwestern church, although they had more wealth, had chosen to satisfy their soul with the right things—they were still hungry for the things of God.*

Key Statement:
You are in control of your spiritual appetite, not God. You will hunger for what you feed on.

We have all heard of the "junk food junkie," the person who seems to crave, even need, lots of sugary sweets and salty snacks or fast food. Our bodies quickly develop poor habits if we don't control them. When we don't eat at all, our bodies scream out for nourishment.

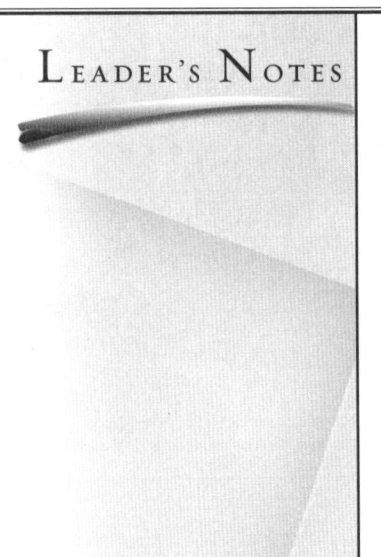

us God Speaks 2

The g____ you____ hunger for God you can create one!

20. What happens when you don't feed yourself spiritually? The __*opposite*__ occurs. Your spirit gets __*quieter*__. When we lose our hunger for God, it is because we __*have not*__ been feeding ourselves with __*His presence*__ and __*His word*__.

If you feed on a steady diet of the Word of God, it will be easy to set aside time for prayer, study, and communing with your heavenly Father. It will flow naturally, and you will crave the awesome presence and a life of intimacy with the living God.

PROTECT YOUR HUNGER

Key Statement:
The more of God you get, the more of God you crave.

21. Hunger is your spiritual thermometer. The first sign of backsliding is *your loss of hunger for His presence and His Word*. We don't wake up one day and suddenly, accidentally find ourselves in sin; the road to sin begins when *we lose our hunger*.

That is why Proverbs 4:23 tells us to guard our heart. We must watch over it and protect it. God tells us that the most valuable possession is our heart, yet we constantly give ourselves over to things that are of no profit to us and that even harm us.

LEADER'S NOTES

"THEOLOGY 101"

REACHING GOD'S SUMMIT

In 1953 Sir Edmund Hillary and a Sherpa tribesman, Tenzing Norgay, succeeded in becoming the first two men to reach the top of the world's highest peak, Mount Everest in Nepal. The queen of England knighted Hillary for the achievement. The majestic mountain in the Himalayan range rises in a snow-covered peak at over 29,000 feet high. Few men actually survive a climb to the top as they face avalanches, strong winds, crevasses, and nearly vertical surfaces. In addition to these daunting challenges, the thin air makes the climb next to impossible.

(OPTIONAL) (10 minutes)

Talk about this classic and inspiring true story:

• *Involve your group in an exciting discussion on the parallels they see.*

• *Don't be afraid to be passionate as you encourage people to see how their own life is a real-life drama with God!*

Lesson Two

Leader's Notes

Remind your group:

1. They should preview the next session and complete the personal/discussion portions. If they like, they may complete the whole thing.

2. Pray for the group before they leave, or divide up in groups and have them pray for each other. Be led by the Spirit, but keep the focus on things that God may have brought to light from today's teaching.

There are many similarities that can be drawn between a successful journey to the top of this majestic summit and our life with God. An expedition up a mountain requires preparation, teamwork, physical stamina, mental endurance, the ability to take risk in venturing forth into the unknown, and more.

22. What other parallels can you see?
_____
_____
_____

23. How can you encourage and challenge yourself on your own life's spiritual expedition using this inspiring example?
_____
_____
_____
_____

Finish on a high note. Go over the two points on the right.

- God is waiting to satisfy us with His goodness.

- Let's keep our hearts hungry and not take His call to us lightly, for when we draw near to Him, He has promised to draw near to us!

Video Script for Lesson 2
PROTECT YOUR HUNGER

Now we are going to begin this morning in James Chapter 4 and we're going to read one verse, and that's verse 8. And James says, " *Draw near to God and he will draw near to you."* So now who draws first? We do. There's something we do, we initiate that will literally cause the One who placed the stars in the universe to come near me. Now that turns me on. You understand what I'm talking about? I mean that excites me. You understand?

Now what James is saying by the Spirit of God here is this: you are the one that determines the level of your relationship with God not God. Do I need to say that again? You're the one that determines the level of your relationship with God, not God. Now there are a lot of people in the church in the back of their minds they think there were just certain individuals that were born with a star over there crib. You know what I'm talking about. People like Oral Roberts, Benny Hinn and you know Billy Graham. No, these people walk close with the Lord because they drew near. In fact some of the people that I know personally that walk closest to the Lord are people you're never going to see behind pulpits because they choose to draw near. It has nothing to do with ministry. It has to do with walking intimately with God. And that is what we were created for and you will never be satisfied until you live it. Can you say "Amen". And so that's what this is all about.

Now the question, the first question we must ask is if God is giving us this amazing invitation to draw near why aren't more people walking in intimacy with God? The first and foremost reason is this it is the lack of hunger in the people in the body of Christ.

Go to Psalms 42 and let's begin there, Psalms 42. This is an amazing scripture written by David. Psalms 42, Verse 1 we read, *"As the deer pants for the water brooks, so pants my soul for you, O God.* (Now listen to these words) *My soul thirsts for God, for the living God. When shall I come and appear before God? My tears have been my food day and night, while they continually say to me, 'Where is your God'?"* Look at the next verse: *"When I remember these things, I pour out my soul within me."* Now do you see how passionate David is? Do you see how hungry and thirsty he is? Now notice he says the whole key to his hunger and thirst is found in verse four. He says when I remember these things I pour out my soul within me.

Now the Hebrew word for remember there the Hebrew word is Z-A-K-AR. W.E. Vines is an expert in Hebrew words says this, "Just as its English part, so this Hebrew word means this, it means more than to just recall." How many of you know what I mean by that? That means to recall something right? It means more than to just recall, this is what it really means, it means to retain in thought. This certainly applies to the scripture so what David's literally saying here is this: when I retain desire for God in my thoughts it causes me to pour out my soul within me.

So what we are saying is it is important for us to protect as well as to increase our hunger for Him and we do it by retaining Him in our soulish thoughts.

Now many people in the body of Christ pray this incorrectly. They pray: Lord, increase my hunger for you, all right? Yet this is not accurate. I remember when my wife prayed for this in the shower. She was praying, she said, "Lord increase my hunger, John's hunger, my children's hunger for You." And the Lord spoke back to Lisa and said, "Lisa that is incorrect. It's not My responsibility to increase your hunger." He said it's your responsibility. Now there is a scripture that says this, Proverbs, write it down and you can look it up later. Proverb 27, Verse 7 says this-- listen carefully. *"A satisfied soul loathes the honeycomb."* Did you hear what I just said? The satisfied soul loathes. What does loathe mean? Hates the honeycomb.

Now think of Thanksgiving Day all right. Many of us we wake up Thanksgiving morning and we fast breakfast, why? Because we have a feast coming our way, right? So we do without and we get our-

Lesson Two

selves really, really, really hungry, right? So when we get that, when that turkey comes out and here comes that stuffing, here comes the sweet potatoes, the whipped potatoes and the salad and all this stuff and the pumpkin pies and man we eat like a pig right? Then a couple hours later we leave and go to the in-laws house. Okay now, mother-in-law can be a better cook than mother– you understand what I'm saying– she could be even more gourmet. She brings out turkey, dressing and all the other stuff we had at the other house and what do we go– ugh. Why? We are already stuffed. So now the very thing we hungered for a few hours ago we are actually loathing now and saying I don't want it. This is exactly what the word of God means when it says the soul that is full with the things of this world when God brings the sweet honeycomb by we'll actually loathe it. Now to take this a step further it is proportional. We may not be stuffed with the world, but how many of you know we may be kind of loaded with it, filled with it? You understand?

Let me give you an example. Many, many times when I travel, cause I travel 200,000 miles a year, you know I'll be in one city and they'll feed me and then in a couple hours I'll be in another city and the first thing they'll say to me is do I want to go eat. And I'll go, "You know what I'm really not that hungry." And I may even go to the restaurant with him and watch them eat, but I don't want the food. I don't loathe it but I'm not interested because I just had a meal a few hours ago. So it's not that I'm loaded, I'm just satisfied. So I'm not loathing it, I'm just disinterested in it. Now, if you take a guy who hasn't eaten in two days and you put him in front of that meal he is not going to be indifferent towards it, he's going to chow it. Why? Because he's hungry, you see what I'm saying? Now, this is exactly what God is saying here. He's saying: to the degree that you fill your soul with the things of life is going to determine your response to His call to draw near.

Now go with me to Revelations 3 and I'm going to give you an example of this, Revelations the third chapter. To the degree that you fill yourself with the things of this world, is the degree you're going to respond to His call to draw near. In Revelations, Chapter three, now just let me say this, in chapter 2 and chapter 3 in the book of Revelations we have seven letters from Jesus to seven churches in Asia, okay. John was just secretary. If you'll notice, if you have the red-letter edition, your words are in red, right? So John is the secretary here. He's just taking dictation. These are Jesus' words to His seven churches in Asia. Now, how many of you know that if these seven letters to these churches from Jesus are in the Bible that means they have prophetic application? What does that mean? They apply to us today. They weren't just for these historical churches, right? And to take this even one step further, I believe these seven churches could also be because prophecy can always have several meanings. I think they are chronological; I think that if you looked at the first church is kind of descriptive of the early church and what happened. How she lost her first love and then you keep going and you'll find out that the last church could kind of be descriptive of the church today because right after the seventh church, you'll find in Chapter 4, Verse 1, I heard a voice in heaven saying come up hither with the sound of a trumpet. Well how is Jesus going to come for the church with the voice of an archangel and the sound of a trumpet? He's going to say come up; He's going to catch away the church, right? So that's why I could believe this seventh church could apply today.

Look what he says about this seventh church, Chapter 3, Verse 14. *"And to the angel of the church of the Laodiceans write, these things says the Amen, the Faithful and True Witness."* What does faithful mean? It means it will tell you the truth every time. What does true mean? He will tell you the truth whether you like it or not. How many of you know an unsaved used car salesman will tell you what you want in order to get what you got? Jesus will never flatter you. He will always tell you the truth because He loves you. The used car salesman wants to take what you got and he wants to take advantage of you. You got what I'm saying?

He said in verse 15, *"The beginning of the creation of God: I know your works, that you are neither cold nor hot. I could wish you were cold or hot. So then, because you are lukewarm, and neither cold nor hot I, will vomit you out of My mouth."* So He says to this church. He said it not to the city, you're not cold, and you're not hot. In other words you're indifferent, you're lukewarm, indifferent. Now what caused this church to be indifferent with the things of the

Lord? You'll see it right here, Verse 17. *"Because you say, 'I am rich, have become wealthy, and have need of nothing'– and do not know that you are wretched, miserable, poor, blind, and naked–."* So notice, He said that they are saying I am rich, become wealthy and in need of nothing. So obviously this church has filled itself with what it possessed.

Now look up at me please. A very shallow, legalistic assessment of this would be, okay this church had a lot of material things, that's why they were lukewarm. That is very shallow and not true. Because let me tell you about David. David left his son Solomon 4,000 tons of gold, 40,000 tons of silver and so much bronze you couldn't even count it. Now I'd like to leave my kids that much, I mean that's a pretty good inheritance. So in other words David has got so much money he's got stockpiles of gold and silver. But yet you want to hear about how David talks about himself? Are you ready for this? He says in Psalms 86,verse 1, *"Bow down your ear, O Lord, hear me; for I am poor and needy".* These guys got 4,000 tons of gold that he just leaves one son, we don't even know what he left the other sons and he says I'm poor and needy. So you can obviously see his poorness or neediness is in the fact that he is desperate for God. He says my tears have become my food day and night, saying where is my God? I want to be in His presence, in His throne room. So now let me say this. This church in Laodecia had far less material goods than David had but yet they said I am rich. They were satisfied; they were satisfied with the little they had.

Can I give you a classic example of this? Back in the early 1990's I was asked to preach to the Cree Indians up in Northern Canada. And I mean, man you had to fly to Montreal, and then you had to fly in a prop plane another hour and a half North, and then you had to drive another hour and a half North to get to this reservation. And every year they had this big camp meeting. They had about 1,000 people come underneath this tent. I remember these people were the last Indian Tribe to go on a reservation in North America. They had only gone on reservation 25 years, before that and I remember going into this camp and it was amazing the hunger in the twenty-five, twenty to twenty-five year-olds and older. I mean man they were gunning for the front seats. They were leaning in, they were taking notes, and they were like hungry listening.

Then I was noticing the twenty-five and unders are all sitting there like this. They're in the back outside the tent, just indifferent. So finally I just got fed up. One service I went running out after them. I left the tent and I started preaching to them out there and they were just sitting there like this: like this guy from another world. All of a sudden I couldn't believe the indifference in these kids, and all of a sudden I started noticing their shirts– they had L.A. Lakers shirts, they had Piston Caps, they had Bulls shirts, Chicago Bulls shirts– and I realized they had just gotten TV's in the last twenty years up on their reservations. The other ones had never had it and these kids choose to fill themselves with the TV and it caused them to be indifferent to the word of God, whereas the adults couldn't care less about the TV. I watched them live because I was in among them living with them. I watched. The adults couldn't care less; they still went on the moose trails for nine months out of the year. You understand? I mean my host father who had just turned 100 and he still walked the moose trails from September to May. So here is the older people–they chose themselves to fill with the word of God; here the younger people– they were indifferent cause they were filling their souls with all the stuff happening in the world from the television. You understand what I'm saying?

So now listen, a couple months later an interesting thing happened. I fly to the Northwest part of the United States and I do a Friday night service for this church. Now this Friday night service was open to the whole church, everybody in the area okay? But I come into this service and this interesting thing occurs. There are seven hundred people in the service. Five hundred of them are sixteen, seventeen, eighteen, and nineteen and twenty-year-olds; two hundred are all the other age groups. So I'm sitting there and I have to tell you it was fun preaching. I got done preaching that night and you know what I found in myself? All of a sudden I'm surrounded three to four rows deep circled by a bunch of sixteen, seventeen, eighteen, nineteen and twenty-year-olds and they were firing questions at me like crazy and they're just sucking the anointing out. I mean the words were just pouring out of me and we just keep talking. Finally I looked down at my watch and it's almost midnight. Midnight! And I looked around and I said this is amazing. Look at how hungry these young people are.

Lesson Two

Where are the rest of the people? So the young people looked at me and said, "Can we take you to lunch tomorrow? We want to talk some more." So we reserved an entire upstairs room in a restaurant and we all picked up at lunch the next day.

Now here's to open up to everybody, you know what's amazing? I met the pastor and then I met the youth pastor and then I understood immediately what was going on. The pastor was full of cares and worries and the things of the world. The youth pastor was on fire. So you know how the Bible says like priest like people? Say it like this: like pastor like people, that's why you guys are so hungry. You see what I'm saying? Your pastor is hungry for the word of God. That's why I always find it easy to preach here.

So here you've got young people that don't have a lot. Now how many of you know that the Northwest part of the United States is very, very rich? How many of you know those young kids were driving some pretty nice cars, all right? But here they are hungry and there are the Indians and all they have is a TV and yet they're not hungry. Why? Because they chose to fill their soul with the wrong thing. The young people even though they had nice cars they were hungry for God and they were sucking the anointing out of me. You understand what I'm saying? All right now, what is the remedy for this indifferent church? Jesus says that (I'm going to read out of the NIV) in verse 20, He says. *"Behold, I stand at the door and knock. If anyone hears My voice and opens the door, I will come in and eat with him and he with me."* So you know a lot of preachers use this verse for the unsaved. They say hey the Lord's standing at the door knocking. This is not about unsaved people; He's talking to the church. He's saying I'm at the door of your heart knocking and I want to come in and have intimacy. If anybody hears My voice they'll open. You know what keeps us from hearing His voice? Being full of the things of this world.

Why do you think God has to take Moses and send him from Egypt to the backside of the desert? To get Moses' soul quiet so that he can hear the word of God, so that even when God sends him back to Egypt he's not going to be distracted by Egypt. That is the thing that God wants to do with every single one of His people: get you to the point of where you love hearing His voice more than the things of the world. So even if you are in the world you are not distracted by it, you're sensitive to Him. And so the Lord says I'll come in and dine with him and he with Me. How many of you know now this was particularly true back then but it's still true today– the highest level of fellowship comes when what? We enjoy a meal with somebody. That is when there is a connection. I mean my wife, I love that she does this she makes sure that every night we eat a meal together as a family. All four of my boys sitting around the table and she and I, and I'm telling you I love that. Because there is a soulish tie an intimacy, a social intimacy that will be deeper in a meal than in any other setting. I mean between people, I'm not talking between a husband and wife, between people, all right? That's why the Bible says don't eat with a person who says they are Christian yet they are living in sexual immorality because if you are going to partake of what is now because there is an exchange. So Jesus says if you just hear My voice and open, I am going to serve you the bread of life Myself. I'm going to reveal Myself. I'm preaching myself happy. Goodness! Oh, so anyway, oh, my goodness let's go on.

Hunger– now let me say this to you: hunger is the key element to whether or not we will pursue intimacy with God. Therefore we need to keep in mind that we are in control of our appetite, not God. The question is what appetites and cravings are we going to develop. There is a spiritual principal folks that will always apply, are you ready? We will hunger for what we feed on. We will hunger for what we feed on. I remember when I first got saved; I got saved in my college fraternity in 1979. Now I was a junk food junky. You know what a junk food junky is right? Now I think that is a great term for that, okay? Because how many of you know a junky is someone who is addicted to something right? I was addicted to ho ho's, twinkies and ding-dongs, you understand? Man, my idea of a gourmet meal was a Big Mac and fries and a coke from McDonalds okay? I am a complete junk food junky and I remember I was in my fraternity. I was standing in the fraternity kitchen looking for something to munch on, cookies or something like that, and I heard the Holy Spirit speak this. He said, "Your body is my temple. Take care of it." Now, no health food guy said anything to me; the Holy

PROTECT YOUR HUNGER

Spirit did. And I remember right then that I realized you know what, if I had a Ferrari I would not put recycled oil and dirty gas in it and yet I can replace that Ferrari but I can't replace this body.

So God started changing the way I started eating. Sodas were the first things that went then bleached flour and all that stuff. I started learning and educating myself on how to eat right. Now that was good because it was going to keep me healthy, right? But there was an added benefit. You know what the added benefit was? I noticed my appetite started changing. See it used to be when you put a Big Mac and a fries in front of me, and then you put a piece of fish, fresh fish and a wild mix field green salad and whole grain bread, I'd go "ugh" to the fish and the whole grain salad I'd go "give me the Big Mac". After two years of eating healthy I noticed that if you put a Big Mac in front of me and you put a piece of fish in front of me I'd go to the fish because I actually had an appetite for it. Because why? You will hunger for what you feed on. That's why kids when all they eat is cake and candy, you put something healthy in front of them and they go yuck. But my kids my wife was feeding them avocados from birth and all this healthy food and they started enjoying healthy food. You see what I'm saying? Well the same thing happens to us spiritually. We're going to hunger for what we feed on.

Have you ever wondered why you like watching a movie for three hours but if somebody talks richly about the word of God you get bored after thirty minutes? Well maybe it's what you are feeding on. See people that hunger and watch a lot of sports they're going to hunger for ESPN. Now do you watch ESPN? Absolutely, I enjoy it but that's not what I'm feeding my spirit on. You understand what I'm saying? So you've got to look at what you're feeding yourself on and you've got to take an assessment of what you are dieting on. What you are feeding your soul on is what I'm talking about, not natural food. I mean if all you ever talk about is shopping then guess what? You're going to get real excited at the stores but you're going to get bored in the services because you're feeding yourself with that. There's nothing wrong with it but you see you can take it to an unhealthy extreme.

I remember when I was back in Bible School I was working forty hours a week, going to Bible School at night and really seeking God. And I remember one weekend my roommate said to me, "hey John, let's go play touch football" and I said, no, no, no I'm going to spend time in the Word. I remember he left and I opened up my Bible and I remember this, I couldn't get anything. I'm sitting there reading and it was like words on a page. It was like heavens were closed. And I screamed out in my apartment. I said "God how come you're not speaking to me, how come the Bible just seems so, so lifeless?" And the Holy Spirit spoke to me and said, "Go out and play touch football." I said, what? He said, "Go play touch football." And then He gave me a scripture, Ecclesiastes chapter 12. Listen to this, Ecclesiastes the twelfth chapter Verse 12. It says, *"Of making many books there is no end, and much study is wearisome to the flesh."* That is why Jesus looked at his disciples when they were so busy ministering that they didn't have time to eat and He said, come apart and rest awhile. In other words what He's saying is come apart and lest you come apart, right? In other words we live in a body, right? And part of our flesh is our brain and you need to give it recreation. Recreation means recreation.

Now what I find in the church today is that most people don't have a problem with that extreme. Where most people have a problem with is they're feeding themselves with too much of the other. See that's what we are talking about tonight. Let me just say this, why do we feed ourselves physically? Hopefully your answers should be this: to get nourishment. We're really getting excited over this today I can see this. The main reason you eat is number one, nourishment. I was looking at my staff yesterday and I shocked one of them. I said we better get that over with, we need to go and eat. I better get that over with so I can spend time with the Word tonight. My staff went "need to get that over with"? You've got to understand the way I look at food. Taste is a benefit but I only eat because of nourishment. Doug and I talked about this yesterday. We are weight lifting a lot, we're in the gym and we eat small meals, several to keep the protein intake, so we can keep the body healthy, right? Because it's the temple, right? And sometimes I wish I didn't have to eat. I wish I could eat some of that manna bars like Elijah and run forty days and forty nights. You understand what I'm saying? But a benefit is it tastes good. Okay. That's a benefit. But the main reason we eat is for nourishment.

Lesson Two

Now let me ask you a question: can you imagine yourself carrying on full speed the way you do? And I know you are busy people because most of you here are very successful people and the Bible says you don't work you don't eat. So you've learned that principle. Thank God your pastor has taught you that. But can you imagine carrying on full speed like you do and not eating any meals? Go three days and keep working just as hard as you always work and tell me what is going to happen. You're going to lose strength and keel over. I mean you're out there working construction, guess what? You are going to fall over if you keep on going and you don't eat a meal for three days. Right? So now what happens when you don't eat for a few days, what does your body do? It screams I'm hungry. No, nobody is familiar with that. Come on, what does it do? It screams at you, I'm hungry, feed me. Right?

Guess what happens when you don't eat spiritually? The opposite occurs. Your spirit gets quieter. That's why it is so easy to neglect your spiritual nourishment before your physical nourishment because your spirit doesn't scream it gets quieter. Now how many of you know that when you go without eating for three, four, five days (and it really happens about the fifth day) your appetite leaves physically? If you've ever gone on a fast for five or more days, you'll notice when you hit about the fifth day (some people it happens about the fourth or third, but with me it was five) you hit the fifth day and your appetite is gone. I mean eating a shoe looks as good as eating a piece of meat. Why, what happened? It is gone until hunger returns and that's usually about forty, fifty days later and that's when starvation sets in. That's what happened with Jesus. Afterward He hungered. After the forty days He hungered. Now what I've noticed when you go on a long fast like that your hunger totally leaves, all right? And you know the only way you can redeem your hunger is to eat small meals, several and that causes your appetite to return.

So what I've noticed is that when people lose that hunger to be with God alone it means you haven't been feeding yourself with His presence and His word for awhile and you're going to have to do it in short intervals. Get the scripture and open it up and just read half the scripture. Don't read it all don't try to force it in because how many of you know that if you go without food for four days, you eat a big meal you may die physically. Take short meals and start meditating on the scripture. Then thirty minutes later take another scripture meditate and just stop and let the Lord's presence start ministering to you. And what happens is once He speaks one thing to you, bam, your hunger is back. See because once you've tasted His presence you're like a junky, you're like an alcoholic you are never the same again. This is what Peter is talking about when he says don't be drunk with wine whereas in excess, but be continually filled with the Holy Spirit. In other words wine is a counterpart. That is why you have winos and alcoholics who have got to have another drink, right? That is a perversion of the way we are supposed to live in the spirit. When you taste of the heavenly gift, when you taste of His presence, man, you are like there's nothing like it.

Wait, let me tell you something, I preached to thousands, millions. Excuse me, I mean our books are in the millions, we've been all over the world. But I'm going to tell you something if I had to choose. If I had to choose between the presence of God and having intimacy, I'd take that. I'd say to someone else you can have it because there is nothing better. Moses tasted it, and that's why Moses never once said he wanted to go back to Egypt, but Israel was constantly saying we want to go back to Egypt because they never tasted it. I mean think of it, they lived in the slums. He lived in the wealthiest house in the world, the richest grandfather, the richest man in the world was his grandfather, and he never once said he wanted to go back to Egypt. It was better for me back in Egypt. But they were constantly saying "I want to go back to Egypt" and they lived in slums. It has to do with your hunger. What do you feed yourself with? Let me say this your hunger is your spiritual thermometer. How many do you know what is the first thing that leaves when a person gets the flu and they are sick? Their appetite. The first sign that you back slid is your loss of hunger for His presence and His word. See backsliding doesn't begin when a guy suddenly finds himself in bed with a girl; it started when he lost his hunger.

Let me end this session with Proverbs 4:23 says above all else guard your heart. You know what is amazing? It baffles me. The world will spend

thousands, tens of thousands of dollars when they bring the 112 carat diamond to the Smithsonian and they will have it in unbreakable glass and a pad that when weight changes of one-tenth of an ounce all the alarms go off. If the temperature changes inside the glass the alarm goes off. The electric eye beams for after hours, armed guards with guns, all to protect a rock– a rock– a stone. And yet we open up, we watch anything, we listen to anything and God said the most valuable thing you've got is your heart not a rock. And even us believers will protect our little rocks and but yet we will open our heart to anything and feed ourselves on anything and then we wonder why we're not taking this invitation to draw near so earnestly. Amen.

PASSION FOR HIS PRESENCE

Video Session 3

PASSION FOR HIS PRESENCE

Key Statement:
Are you seeking God for who He is or what He can do?

In this video session John talks about some people he has met in his worldwide travels. He divides them into two groups:

A. _Those who are seeking God for what He can do for them._

B. _Those who are seeking God for who He is._

These two groups can be likened to:

A. _The children of Israel._

B. _Moses._

The Israelites...

1. The Israelites had waited in miserable captivity for the promised deliverer for _400 years_.

2. What did the children of Israel do after they finally realized that God had sent them a deliverer? _Bowed their heads and worshiped._

LEADER'S NOTES

(3–5 minutes)

After greeting the people and opening in prayer, do a brief recap of sessions 1 and 2 by referring to these statements:

1. Intimacy with God is available to each one of us. This is God's passion.

2. This intimacy is not reserved for specially gifted personalities, but rather is available for all who hunger and thirst for more of God.

Set this session up with the Key Statement.

(5–10 minutes)

• *Simply go through these questions as usual with the group, providing the answers as necessary.*

• *Then open it up for discussion, asking for ways in which people see the behavior of the Israelites in themselves.*

• *This can be humorous and lighthearted as well as sobering. Look for examples of both in your group's responses, and focus on those.*

Lesson Three

Leader's Notes

3. Did the Israelites keep their worshipful attitude?
   No

4. What did they do at the first sign of opposition?
   Complained

5. What does this reveal about what was in their heart?
   As long as God was doing for them what they wanted when they wanted it, they were happy. Otherwise, they complained.

6. When we complain, what does it say to God? "I ____*don't like*____ what You are doing in my life. If I were ____*You*____, I would be doing it ____*differently*____." This is an ____*insult*____ to God's ____*character*____.

Moses...

"By faith Moses, when he became of age, refused to be called the son of Pharaoh's daughter, choosing rather to suffer affliction with the people of God than to enjoy the passing pleasures of sin, esteeming the reproach of Christ greater riches than the treasures in Egypt; for he looked to the reward."
Hebrews 11:24–26

Point out the contrast between Moses and the people of Israel.

7. What is the difference between Israel's and Moses' suffering?
   Israel was born into suffering; they had no choice. Moses was born to riches, yet he chose suffering for Christ as greater riches.

8. Moses chose God's presence over His _____
   promises

Israel's reward was a better lifestyle. Moses' reward was God's manifest presence.

44

PASSION FOR HIS PRESENCE

Let's check our own hearts. 2 Corinthians 13:5 says, *"Examine yourselves as to whether you are in the faith. Test yourselves. Do you not know yourselves, that Jesus Christ is in you?—unless indeed you are disqualified."*

How do you stack up to the attitude of the children of Israel? Spend some time in prayer and meditation, and answer these thought-provoking questions.

What does your thought life reveal?
Philippians 4:8 says, *"Finally, brethren, whatsoever things are true, whatsoever things are honest, whatsoever things are just, whatsoever things are pure, whatsoever things are lovely, whatsoever things are of good report; if there be any virtue, and if there be any praise, think on these things"* (KJV).

9. There are many things that can consume our thought life, such as money, finances, clothes, jewelry, vacations, or sexual and lustful thoughts. We can also be consumed with love, patience, kindness, gentleness, and Scripture. List what things consume your thought life below. What are the things your mind tends to dwell on?

_____
_____
_____
_____
_____

What do your words reveal?
James 1:26 says, *"If any man among you seem to be religious, and bridleth not his tongue, but deceiveth his own heart, this man's religion is vain"* (KJV).

Try this to really see where you stand. As you go through your day, examine what your response is to friends, family, co-workers, your boss, and others that you come into contact with.

LEADER'S NOTES

(15–20 minutes, for questions 9-15)

7. Read 2 Corinthians 13:5, and remind your group that they are on an adventure, a real-life journey. This is where God can really move for them.

• Go through each of the following questions. Make sure you have a volunteer read each scripture verse *before* you open it for discussion. Let the group know they are comparing themselves with the attitudes of the Israelites, not the people themselves.

• Open each of the questions by asking volunteers to share their answers, but lay the ground rule that you know this is personal and people should be thoughtful before they share.

• This is also an excellent opportunity to remind people that you as the leader reserve the right to facilitate the meeting as necessary to keep it moving along and focused on God.

Lesson Three

Leader's Notes

- Do you find that your actions and words are polite, sarcastic, helpful, egotistical, or grateful?
- When you come home after a long day, do you respond to others out of anger or hostility, or are you withdrawn because you are stressed from the pressures of daily life?

Being daily intimate with the Lord as David was will enable you to rise above circumstances and cause you to be filled to overflowing, speaking words of faith and encouragement to yourself and those around you.

10. After having done this, what did your words reveal about yourself?

_____
_____
_____
_____

11. Write below how you react under stressful circumstances:

_____
_____
_____
_____

12. What can you do to rise above these circumstances and be like David?

_____
_____
_____
_____

What do your deeds reveal?
Colossians 3:17 says, *"And whatsoever ye do in word or deed, do all in the name of the Lord Jesus, giving thanks to God and the Father by Him"* (KJV).

In the home, at the office, at church, or at school, actions generally speak louder than words. Think about how you act in your daily routines.

- When someone asks for help, do you say "yes" and then never follow through and then make up an excuse the next time you see them as to why you were unable to help?

- Do you assist your children out of a loving heart when they ask for help, or are you complaining the whole time because the "game" is on and you just missed a great play?

- At work do you do half a job or a good job? Or do you work as unto the Lord and always give your best?

13. No one will react perfectly in any situation all of the time, and that is not the goal. The goal is, however, to be mindful of what we are doing and why we are doing it. If we are living out of a deep relationship with the Holy Spirit, in everything we do our actions can bring glory to the Father God. Write what your deeds reveal below:

_____
_____
_____
_____
_____

14. We are in the third session of the Drawing Near journey. Write below how the first few sessions have impacted you so far:

_____
_____
_____

LEADER'S NOTES

LESSON THREE

Leader's Notes

15. Now here's the real question. In light of your thoughts, words, and deeds above, what would you like to see in your life as a result of going through these sessions? Don't be afraid to dream big and believe God, and don't hesitate to seek assistance from your group leader and your church:

_____
_____
_____
_____
_____
_____
_____

Key Statement:
It is God's presence that separates us from all the others on the face of the earth.

16. What is omnipresence? It is the presence of the Lord _*that is everywhere*_.

Psalms 139:7 says, *"Where can I go from Your Spirit? Or where can I flee from Your presence?"*

(3–5 minutes)

Ask your group to get creative and come up with some scriptures. They can shout them out as long as it is done decently and in order. You may want to read over "Theology 101" together before doing this.

17. What are some other verses you can think of that show God's omnipresence?
- *Jeremiah 23:23–24 (paraphrased):* "Can any hide himself in secret places that I shall not see him? Do not I fill the heaven and the earth, says the Lord?"
- *Matthew 28:20:* "Lo, I am with you always."
- *1 Kings 8:27:* "Behold, heaven and the heaven of heavens cannot contain You.

PASSION FOR HIS PRESENCE

LEADER'S NOTES

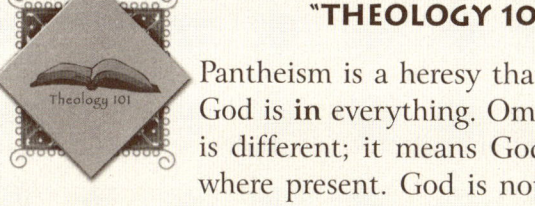

"THEOLOGY 101"

Pantheism is a heresy that says that God is **in** everything. Omnipresence is different; it means God is everywhere present. God is not in everything. He is in some specific places in manifestation as He chooses. For example, He is in His temple, yet it cannot hold Him. He is there when we pray and call upon His name, yet He is also in heaven. And He fills heaven and earth as well. God is truly the Great I Am!

18. What does the word *manifest* mean? It means to bring from the <u>unseen into the seen</u>, to bring from the <u>unheard into the heard</u>, and to bring from the <u>unknown to the known</u>.

19. God's manifest presence is when God reveals Himself to not only our <u>spirits</u>, but also when our <u>mind</u> and our <u>senses</u> become <u>aware of His nearness</u> as well. This is the presence every believer should be <u>passionately hungry</u> for.

Key Statement:
"Manna-festations" don't satisfy.

John offers a number of examples from his travels as well as the Bible on the difference between seeking God Himself and seeking manifestations.

Lesson Three

Leader's Notes

(3–5 minutes)

Ask your group to get creative and come up with other scriptures for question 22. They can shout them out as long as it is done decently and in order.

Finish the session on a high note:

- *Read the Key Statement and the scripture.*
- *Then boldly proclaim: "Let us draw near with a true heart in full assurance of faith…and God will draw near to us!"*

Remind your group:

1. They should preview the next session and complete the personal/discussion portions. If they would like, they may complete the whole thing.

2. Pray for the group before they leave or divide up in groups and have them pray for each other. Be led by the Spirit, but keep the focus on things that God may have brought to light from today's teaching.

20. Why don't manifestations satisfy?
Just as the manna never satisfied the children of Israel in the wilderness, so manifestations are never given to satisfy your deeper longings. Manifestations are not an end in themselves.

21. What are some of the results that occur when believers exalt manifestations above seeking the Lord Himself?
- *It turns others off from the true presence of God.*
- *It can result in a mental relationship with God that is mechanical and spiritless.*

22. Who are some people in the Bible who experienced God's manifest presence?
- *Adam and Eve, Genesis 3:8*
- *Abraham, Genesis 12:7*
- *Samuel, 1 Samuel 2:21*
- *Solomon, 2 Chronicles 1:7*

Key Statement:
Today we are all authorized to come into God's presence.

"Therefore, brethren, having boldness to enter the Holiest by the blood of Jesus, by a new and living way which He consecrated for us, through the veil, that is, His flesh, and having a High Priest over the house of God, let us draw near with a true heart in full assurance of faith, having our hearts sprinkled from a evil conscience and our bodies washed with pure water."
Hebrews 10:19–22

Let us draw near with a true heart in full assurance of faith…and God will draw near to us!

Video Script for Lesson 3
PASSION FOR HIS PRESENCE

Good Morning. Well, it's great to be here with lesson three of Drawing Near and are you enjoying this? All right. Well, listen to where we are going to begin this morning is first of all I want you to open your Bibles up with me to Exodus the fourth chapter, Exodus chapter four. Oh you are going to love this today. Isn't the word of God delicious? Exodus the fourth chapter. Now let me say this: I have been in the full time ministry for twenty-one years; for seven years I worked on two major church staffs, one had a staff of 450 and the other had a staff of 150. They were very large churches. And then for the last fifteen years I have been traveling all over the world and in working in churches and serving in churches I should say, and now traveling all over the world, I have been everywhere in the world except Antarctica. I have not preached to the penguins yet. But anyway, I'm working on that.

I have discovered something especially in the last fifteen years in all my travels and that is this: I find there are two major categories of people in the church. You can draw a line right down the middle and you can separate these two groups of people in church. Are you ready for who they are? Number one, those who are seeking God for what He can do for them. Number two category: those who are seeking God for who He is. First group of those seeking God for what He can do for them is like a woman marrying a man because he has a lot of money. She doesn't marry him because of who he is, she marries him because of what he can do for her. She loves him but for all the wrong reasons. These two groups of people can be classically seen in the children of Israel and Moses. They are perfect examples of what I've seen in the church.

First people I want to look at: the children of Israel. Turn with me to Exodus the fourth chapter. Now let me say this and I've got to set this up. Abraham's descendants, the children of Israel, have been in captivity now for over four hundred years in Egypt correct? They were promised that a deliverer would come and set them free, correct? Correct. And so for hundreds of years they are talking about a deliverer. Now I want you to stop and think about this. Your great, great grandfather talked about a deliverer but he was born and he died and he never saw Him. Your grandfather talked about the deliverer to you, but he was born and he died and he never saw the deliverer. Your father talked about the deliverer to you but he was born, he died and never saw the deliverer. You know what was running through your mind? Am I going to be the one or am I going to die and not see this deliverer. You understand what I'm saying? They are being cruelly treated by the taskmasters; they have stripes on their back. They live in the slums, life is rough. They live their life to build somebody else's inheritance. All right? And yet God sends a man named Moses and God gives him His signs and His word on the mountain and then Moses realizes that he is the deliverer, right? Because he was raised in Pharaohs' house as a prince but he knew he was a Hebrew and yet here God now appears to him and says go and tell Pharaoh to let my people go you are the deliverer. He throws down his staff and it becomes a snake, he picks it up and it becomes a pole and all these signs. So Moses comes and before he goes to Pharaoh he first of all goes to the leaders of Israel, which are thousands of them, all right?

Look at Exodus chapter 4, verse 29, *"Then Moses and Aaron went and gathered together all the elders of the children of Israel. And Aaron spoke all the words which the Lord had spoken to Moses. Then he did the signs in the sight of the people. So the people believed; and when they heard that the Lord had visited the children of Israel and that He looked on their affliction, then they bowed their heads and worshiped."* Can you imagine that atmosphere? Your great, great grandfather died, your father died, your grandfather died and now you are looking at the deliverer. Can you imagine the prayer service and the worshipping that was going on in that place? Some of them were weeping and some of them were rejoicing. Can you imagine? I mean God, He sent the deliverer and they believed. Everyone say, "they believed". *They believed.* Isn't it wonderful? But then Moses turns

Lesson Three

right around and goes right into Pharaoh, brings the same word and Pharaoh goes oh yeah, yeah right. So you guys want to go out and worship this God in the desert? I guess you guys aren't busy enough. Pharaoh increases their hardship.

Now I want you to think about it. They are working from sunrise to sundown building bricks and they have to meet their quota of bricks. Pharaoh says I guess you are just too lazy, huh? Why don't you go out and get your own straw, we won't provide for you anymore. I want you to think about it. You're working from sunrise to sundown. You go eat a meal and collapse. Now after Moses preaches the word of God you have to get up two hours before sunrise gather straw and maybe a few hours after sundown and gather straw. So their hardship increased, you getting this? As soon as Moses preached their hardship went up. Do you know what they said to Moses? They said stop preaching. Get out of here. We were much better off before you came along. But now how many of you know that in God's mercy He delivered them? So He delivers them out and leads them to the Red Sea, great leader, huh. And Pharaoh gets his finest chariot and says let's go butcher them.

So go to Exodus 14 and I want you to notice what happens. Now how many of you know when Pharaoh, after all those children were put to death in Egypt, the firstborn? How many do you know of those people left Egypt with rejoicing? I mean they left with their gold, they plundered them, isn't that right? There wasn't one sick or feeble among them, isn't that right? And they were rejoicing and dancing out of Egypt, right? But then Moses leads them to the Red Sea and Pharaoh is now marching on them, right? And I want you to see the attitude change. Are you ready for this? Moses 14 or excuse me Exodus 14, all right verse 10. *"And Pharaoh drew near, the children of Israel lifted their eyes, and behold, the Egyptians marched after them. So they were very afraid, and the children of Israel cried out to the Lord.* (How religious.) *Then they said to Moses, 'Because there were no graves in Egypt, have you taken us away to die in the wilderness? Why have you so dealt with us, to bring us up out of Egypt?'"* Look at verse 12. *"Is this not the word that we told you in Egypt, saying, 'Let us alone that we may serve the Egyptians'? For it would have been better for us to serve the Egyptians than that we should die in the wilderness.'"*

Right there that indicates what is in their heart: they are serving God and what He can do for them. It would have been better for us to stay in Egypt. Now what happens? God splits the Red Sea and walk across dry ground, correct? Correct. Then they turn around and look at the most powerful nation in the world's military buried under the sea. I mean they are oppressive for four hundred years, buried and do you know what the Bible says? Miriam and all the women take the tambourines and they go out and have them a prayer service like we've never seen in America. I mean can you imagine 800,000 women dancing and singing to the Lord? I mean, wow, what a praise service. I mean they are jubilant with joy right, right? Three days later– not enough food, not enough water– oh you brought us out here to die. Let's get a leader and go back to Egypt. So what are we saying? As long as God is doing for them what they want when they want it they are praising, we're happy. But when God is not doing for them what they wanted when they want it, they are complaining. Now, how many of you know God hates complaining? Want to know why God hates complaining? Can I give you a little secret? I used to wonder why, why is it one of the big ones that God hates. I'll tell you why-- because complaining says to God I don't like what You are doing to my life, but if I were You I would do it differently. There is an insult to His character. Sure got quiet on that one didn't it.

Now, lets take a look at Moses. Now go with me to Hebrews the 11th chapter, and we're going to take a look at Moses verse 24. We read, *"By faith Moses, when he became of age, refused to be called the son of Pharaoh's daughter,* (verse 25) *choosing rather to suffer affliction with the people of God than to enjoy the passing pleasures of sin, esteeming the reproach Christ greater riches than the treasures in Egypt; for he looked to the reward."* Do you realize how much is in there? First of all look up at me. He chose to suffer. Now how many of you know Israel did not choose to suffer? They were born in it. Moses chose it. He chose it. Why did he choose to suffer? Because of why? He esteemed the reproach of Christ's greater riches then the treasures in Egypt for he looked to the rewards.

What was the reward? Well let's go to Exodus 33 and you're going to see it. Exodus 33 and we'll look for what the reward was. Now watch this in Exodus

52

33 look at verse 1. God says, *"Then the Lord said to Moses, depart and go up from here, you and the people whom you have brought out of the land of Egypt, to the land of which I swore to Abraham, Isaac, and Jacob, saying, 'To your descendants I will give it.' And I will send My angel before you, and I will drive out the Canaanite and the Amorite and the Hittite and the Perizzite and the Hivite and the Jebusite. Go up to a land flowing with milk and honey; for I will not go up in your midst, lest I consume you on the way, for you are stiff-necked people."* Look up at me. God says all right Moses go on down, get the people and go to the Promised Land, the land which I promised Abraham, Isaac and Jacob and I am going to send a choice angel and I'm going to drive out all the "ites". Okay? But I'm not going Moses, I'm not going. Now, I am so glad He said this to Moses. I'm glad He didn't say this to the children of Israel because if He would have said this to the children of Israel they would have had a party and gone. If they would have taken Egypt without God I'm sure they would have taken the Promised Land with an angel because they were constantly saying let's go back to Egypt, right? But I want you to notice what Moses says. Look at Verse 15. *"Then he said to Him, 'If your Presence does not go with us, do not bring us up from here."* Would you look up at me? Moses said, God you can forget that Promised Land if Your presence isn't going because I would rather have Your presence than Your promises even in this desert. How many of you know the desert spoke of a place of suffering, a place of hardship, a place where there was not abundance? Moses said I would rather have Your presence without the promises if I have to choose than the promises without Your presence. Israel would have said we'd take the promises who cares about the Presence. That separates the difference between the two groups of people that I have seen in the church in the last fifteen years, those seeking God for what He can do and those who are seeking God for who He is.

Now I want to talk about the presence of the Lord. There are two presences' of the Lord that the Bible speaks of. First one is omnipresence. What is that presence? That is the presence of the Lord that is everywhere. David said in Psalm 139 Verse 7, *"Where can I go from your Spirit? Or where can I flee from Your presence?"* So omnipresence describes Him as being in all places, right? So David goes on to say in Verse 8, *"If I ascend into heaven, You are there; if I make my bed in hell, behold, You are there...I could ask the darkness to hide me and the light around me to become night. But even in darkness I cannot hide from you."* So in other words that is the presence of the Lord but the Lord says I will never leave you nor forsake you.

The second presence of the Lord in the scripture speaks of His manifest presence. Manifest presence is what Jesus spoke of in John Chapter 14 Verse 21 where He says, "He who has My commandments and keeps them, it is he who loves Me. And he who loves Me will be loved by My Father, and I will love him and manifest Myself to him." Now look up at me please. That word manifest in the Greek means this: to bring from the unseen into the seen, to bring from the unheard into the heard, and to bring from the unknown into the known. This is the way God reveals Himself to not only our spirits but is when our mind and our senses become aware of His nearness as well. Now that's the presence that every believer should be passionately hungry for, Amen. See let me say this. In my years and years of traveling I have met ministers, you know they long to have a large ministry and they'll never get it. And unfortunately what happens is they quit or they turn to other things because they are not passionate for His presence. I've met other ministers in traveling for years that had big ministries and realized that large ministries don't satisfy you and then they ran into trouble. But then I've met ministers who have very large ministries and yet they are like Moses. They are like John, you know I hold on to this loosely because I know God called me to lead this large church but I'm so passionate for Him. I've met other ministers that have very small ministries and yet they are very complete and satisfied because they walk in the presence of God. Some of you who walk closest to the Lord and really enjoy His manifest presence are some of the people you will never see behind pulpits, they are not in ministry.

I have to look at my own life and I will be very honest with you, you know we have what people would call success. We are now on in television in 214 nations in the world, books in the millions (they're in twenty-six languages), we have an office with four employees in Sydney, Australia, we have employees in America, employees and an office in the United Kingdom, amassed some of the largest churches and conferences. But you know what, I

Lesson Three

prayed this and I prayed this just recently, and I've been praying it a lot and I really mean it when I pray it. I said Lord if I have to choose between Your presence and anything You are having me do, I said I will take Your presence in a heartbeat and give it to somebody else because let me tell you something, there is nothing like His presence and when you've tasted His presence you know it– you'll never be the same again. And that's what happened to Moses, he tasted God's presence at the burning bush. Israel had a chance to turn Him down. God said I brought you to this mountain to reveal Myself to you and when He did they ran back because whenever you get in the presence of the Lord He exposes things and if you are heart is not clean then you want to back away. Remember what Adam and Eve did as they hid from the presence of the Lord in the garden? Do you remember that? The first thing they did in the garden was they hid from the presence of the Lord.

If you look at people all throughout scriptures you're going to find out that they were in hot pursuit of His presence. Now let me say this because I need to take a little side step here. I have met people that have been hungry for the presence of God and they've become so hungry for the manifestation of His presence that they have gotten easily sidetracked. I have been in meetings before where people start laughing hysterically, or they start weeping, or they start shaking or doing something and yet God is not in the building, His manifest presence. And what it is, is those people at one time were touched by the Lord and they did laugh, or maybe one time He really, really touched them and they wept or maybe one time He touched them and they shook. And so you know what they're doing? They are looking for God in the manifestation instead of looking for God and then experiencing the manifestation. See Elijah experienced great manifestations of the Lord's presence but he knew where God was. I mean the wind blew, the earth quaked, there was the fire and he says no God's not in that but then there was the still small voice. Elijah was not seeking the manifestations; he was seeking the One who caused them. See I've literally been in meetings, I remember one in Singapore. I was there and I remember the presence of God came in the building and people started laughing hysterically. And there had been an evangelist in that area just recently and he has a manifestation of that and it was a genuine manifestation of God. But I remember when they started laughing, as soon, just as quick as the Lord came He left them. His manifest presence just left and now there was laughter and no presence. I stopped them and I said, look you all are seeking a manifestation instead of seeking Him. And I said manna never satisfied the children of Israel. I said think about it. In Deuteronomy 8, verse 2 and 3, that God gave manna to the children of Israel for one reason: to let them know man should not live by bread alone but every word that proceeds out of the mouth of God.

Now what does the word proceed (not proceeded) mean, present tense? Where does the word proceed out of the mouth of God in His presence? So God was saying I didn't give you the manna to satisfy because man does not live by bread alone. He lives by every word that proceeds: in other words man lives in My presence and receives My word. That's what man really needs as well as the bread. So God was saying to Israel, manna was never given to satisfy you. Even so God says that in the New Testament manifestations were never given to satisfy. It's Him; He is the only one that can satisfy us. That's why Elijah wasn't looking for the manifestations he was looking for the One who was in it. He was looking for the still small voice. So I told the people in Singapore, I said, stop this, stop this right now. I said look we are not looking for a manifestation here we are looking for a person, His name is Jesus. And all of a sudden the presence of God came back in and it was amazing the healing and the deliverance's that occurred in that meeting.

All right now go back to Exodus. Are you in Exodus 33 still? All right look at this now. I want to look at the fifteenth verse again. Then Moses said to God, "*If your Presence does not go with us, do not bring us up from here.*" Remember "here" is the place in the desert, right? Look at verse 16. "*For how then will it be known that Your people and I have found grace in your sight, except You go with us? (Now look at this.) So we shall be separate, Your people and I, from all the people who are upon the face of the earth.*" What does that mean? What separates us from all the people on the face of the earth? The presence of God. Moses says that is what differentiates us from all the unbelievers, the presence of the Lord, yet how many believers have learned how to live satis-

fied without it. Why is it when Jesus walks in the temple the angels started screaming? Because it was the presence of the Spirit of God upon Jesus. Why is it men like Charles Finney walked into a factory and the whole factory shut down and within minutes he was preaching to 3,000 employees and many of them get saved? Because the presence of God that he walked in. Why is it that Smith Wigglesworth can walk down the train and the Catholic priest kneeled down and said, "My God you convict me of my sin?" Because of the presence he walked in. Why is it John G. Lake can have the bubonic plague placed right in his hand and the thing die? Because of the presence of the Lord. That's what separates us from all the people that are on the face of the world.

Now if you go through scriptures you'll find out that this is what all of the people are in hot pursuit of. If you look at Genesis 3:8, the first thing Adam and Eve hid from is the presence of the Lord when they sinned. If you look at Enoch and Noah, Enoch and Noah walked with God-- they walked in His presence. You look at Abraham, Abraham said in Genesis 24 verse 40, he says, for the Lord in whose presence I have walked will send an angel with you and make his mission successful, so Abraham said I have walked in the presence of the Lord.

Samuel, if you look at 1Samuel 3:19 through 21 it says, *"So Samuel grew, and the Lord was with him and let none of his words fall to the ground."* Why did God not allow any of His words to fall to the ground? And the Lord gave Hannah three sons and two daughters-- meanwhile Samuel grew up in presence of the Lord. Samuel's words carried such weight because he spoke what God had placed in him. Remember Jesus said the same thing: I only speak what I hear my Father speaking. See Jesus lived in the manifest presence of God.

Look at David. David said in 2 Samuel 7:26, may the dynasty of your servant David be established in your presence. The first thing that David said when he had sinned in the incident with Bathsheba, he said do not banish me from Your presence or take the Holy Spirit from me. I want you to look up at me and I want talk about the presence of the Lord on a person's life. Psychologists tell us, listen carefully, this is amazing. Psychologists tell us that the relationships that we've had for the last five years of our life directly influence our character and our personalities. Did you hear that? The relationships with friends over the last five years of our life directly influence our personality and our character. Now I agree with that. You want to know why? Because the Bible says whoever walks with the wise shall be wise. The Bible also says do you not know that evil company corrupt good morals, right? So I agree with you, there's a lot of things psychologist's say that I don't agree with. But this is one thing that I do agree– the relationships and personalities we've had in the last five years of our life shape our life and our personalities, right? Look at David. You know what the Bible says about David? Are you ready for this? 1 Samuel 22 verse 2 says this, *"And everyone who is in distress, everyone who was in debt, and everyone who was discontented gathered to him. So he became captain over them. And there were about four hundred men with them."* Now think about this. He's in the desert for fourteen years and whom does God bring around? Everybody that's in distress, everybody that is in debt and everybody that is grumpy. Now you think you hang around four hundred people like that and you're going to become grumpy and you're going to become distressed, right? You know what, that's not what happened. David spent so much time in the presence of the Lord that he influenced their lives and made them some of the greatest men of renown in the whole Old Testament, those grumpy distressed men. David spent so much time in the presence of the King, he made them kingly; he made them noble. See when you spend a lot of time in the presence of the Lord, guess who is going to influence you? The Lord Himself. That's why the people that walk closest to the Lord that I know are stately ambassador-like people. There's air about them when you get around. I'm telling you, when you get around him and you're just like, I remember I felt this about T.L. Osborn. Whenever I was with T.L. Osborn I felt like I was with an ambassador and that man let me tell you something you didn't mess around in that man's presence; you couldn't because there was such a presence on him.

So unfortunately we have people in the New Testament today who have a greater opportunity to spend time with the Lord than even David and are not taking advantage of it. Because David passed beyond what he was supposed to be able to do He

Lesson Three

walked with God and that's why David was prophetic– because he saw into the realm of God and he prophesied the Messiah and prophesied things to come because he walked so closely with the Lord– and yet he was an Old Testament saint. The greatest tragedy in the Old Testament is when Moses brought the people to meet with God and they ran back. God said I brought you out of Egypt to bring you to Myself. He comes down to reveal Himself and they all run away. They say Moses we can't handle it. Do you understand what I'm saying? How tragic. Israel could have had what Moses had. See Moses face shone like the sun. I mean they were always okay when Moses was around but let him go to the mountain and they started messing up. He's just like David. You see what I'm saying? Yet those people wouldn't be changed like David's four hundred men. Some people just won't be changed, amen.

Now today let me say this in the last couple minutes before we close. The children of Israel when they ran away from God, God said all right I'm going to have to set up a Tabernacle. I'm going to have to have a family of men, Aaron and his son's who will come to Me for the people. Now today in the New Testament every one of us are authorized to come into the presence of God. In the days of Moses and Aaron only six men could come in to the presence of the Lord– Moses, Aaron, Nadab, Abihu, Eleazar, Ithamar– Aaron's four sons. But today you know what the Bible says? Listen to this. Hebrews Chapter 10, verse 19 says, *"Therefore, brethren, having boldness* (or confidence) *to enter the Holiest by the blood of Jesus."* Now look up at me.

What is the holiest? If you remember the Tabernacle had the outer court, it had the holy place and had the what? It had the most holy place. The outer court is where the laver was and the brazen altar. The holy place was only where the priest could go, right? And that had what? The lamp stand, it had the table of showbread and it had the incense altar, correct? Which incense speaks of what: praise and worship; lamp stand speaks of illumination; table of showbread speaks of revelation. But as much as the priest had experienced in that place he still hadn't been in the presence of God. He had illumination and revelation but hadn't been in the presence of God. It is the most holy place.

Now today listen to what the Bible says, *"Therefore, brethren, having boldness to enter the Holiest* (the most holy place) *by the blood of Jesus, by a new and living way which He consecrated for us…let us draw near "With a True Heart."* (We're going to talk about that in the next session.) *"Let us draw near with a true heart in full assurance of faith, having our hearts sprinkled from an evil conscience and our bodies washed with pure water. Let us hold fast the confession of our hope without wavering, for He who promised is faithful."* And then in Hebrews 6:19 it says, this hope now remember he just said let us hold fast our hope, *"This hope we have as an anchor of the soul, both sure and steadfast, and which enters the Presence behind the veil."* Today we are authorized to come into the Presence behind the veil by a new and living way but He says we've got to draw near with a true heart.

Video Session 4

THE FRIENDS OF GOD

Key Statement:
You cannot talk about drawing near to God without addressing the issue of holy fear.

1. This is where the typical "seeker-friendly" or "seeker-sensitive" messengers part ways with the truth.
   - These teachers are numerous and may be in any __denomination__ or __nondenominational church__.
   - They speak or write of a God who desires men and longs to bless them, yet they __omit His holiness__.

2. Why do they do this?
   - Many do it out of __well-meaning__ intentions. They may have experienced or seen the tragedy of __legalism__, so they go to __the other extreme__.
   - Others just desire to see people __loved and nurtured__.
   - Some do it for the wrong reasons, such as __to develop a greater following__.

LEADER'S NOTES

(3–5 minutes)

After greeting the people and opening in prayer, do a brief recap of sessions 1–3 by referring to these statements:

1. Intimacy with God is available to each one of us. This is God's passion.

2. We are to seek God for who He is and not what He can do for us.

Set this session up with the Key Statement. Mention to the group that this session is a very in-depth, intense, and exciting study and will require a bit more time to complete.

Move quickly through these questions, providing answers for your group. If you are comfortable, you may see if there are any quick questions before moving along.

Lesson Four

Leader's Notes

- But those who have fled the grip of legalism and preach of only a loving, kind God who compensates for our lawlessness and worldliness are reactionary in their motive and tactics. These teachers preach an "easy Lord" at the expense of the very goal they are trying to accomplish. They desire people to come to know God, but by _leaving out_ the _fear of the Lord_, they in essence shut out the presence of the Lord to men.

A Real Life Drama...

> "God is greatly to be feared in the assembly of the saints, and to be held in reverence by all those around Him"
> Ps. 89:7

John relates the powerful and true story of a large national conference in Brazil for which he was asked to speak. It was well planned, with many ingredients for success, including a fine location, large auditorium, well-known personalities, and talented musicians with great praise and worship music happening. The auditorium was packed with thousands of believers, yet despite all the outward appearances of success, John says he sensed no real presence of the Holy Spirit. "All of a sudden God opened up my eyes and I started noticing what was happening," he says.

Move quickly through these questions, providing answers for your group.

3. What were some of the signs of complacency in the crowd?
- There were people standing with _their hands in their pockets_ looking _up at the ceiling_.
- There were other people with their arms _crossed_ during worship looking _down at the floor_.

THE FRIENDS OF GOD

- Some were ___whispering___ to one another.
- Others were ___walking in and out___ getting something like ___it was a show___.

John waits for this to change, but it doesn't; it goes on all through praise and worship. Then the leader goes up and starts reading from the Scriptures, and still there is no change in the crowd's attitude. They are simply not paying attention.

"I thought OK, this will change, but it doesn't; it goes on all through praise and worship. Now I'm getting angry.

– John Bevere

By the time John is introduced, it has been an hour or hour and a half. John then boldly confronts those in the crowd. Let's see what we can glean from what took place.

The following questions are very basic and relationship oriented:

A. You are sitting and talking to someone sitting across the table from you, and the whole time you are sitting and talking to them they are sitting there with their hands in their pockets looking around, or sitting there with their arms crossed looking down, or they are whispering to someone sitting next to them. Will you continue to speak to them?'

LEADER'S NOTES

59

Lesson Four

Leader's Notes

B. If you were to go over and knock on the door at someone's house to visit, and every time you go to visit, they just come to the door and say, "Oh, it's you again; come on in," would you continue to go?

4. Of course the answer to both questions is "no." But why? *They are not paying attention to you; they are disinterested. When you are not treated with love, respect, or even common courtesy, you don't want to speak or visit with someone.*

5. What do you think this has to do with God? *Everything. He is the One who created you and everything around you. He deserves respect, honor, and praise.*

6. These people assembled together to do something much more important than hanging out with friends or visiting family—they presumably came to worship Almighty God. Yet, if it is so simple and even obvious how to behave in a relationship with a friend or family member, why do you think this huge crowd of Christians behaved so poorly, so disrespectfully to God Himself?
Sample answers may be as follows:
- *They did not have an intimate relationship with Him.*
- *No one taught them about worship.*
- *They were used to a show and not worshiping God.*

7. What was the biblical reason that there was no tangible presence of God? (Ps. 89:7)
"God is greatly to be feared in the assembly of the saints, and to be held in reverence by all those around Him."

8. **Why is it** we find ourselves respecting, even worshiping famous personalities more than God Himself? This is a very prevalent problem in Western culture, so take some time to think about this and write down your answers:

60

THE FRIENDS OF GOD

A. You can't "see" God, but you can see and often directly experience these people.

B. The media make sure we easily and constantly see and "experience" famous personalities, but God waits patiently for us to draw near to experience Him.

C. We feel we know these famous people or dignitaries. We feel close with them and feel that they are worthy of respect and our attentions because of their fame, position, and/or attainments.

D. We want to be like them. We desire their minds, bodies, power, abilities, fortunes, and more.

E. The famous person is in a position of great power and influence, so we almost have to respect, revere, and pay attention.

LEADER'S NOTES

(15–20 minutes)
Make sure you have read these answers ahead of time and are well prepared. Ask for volunteers to provide their answers. Read the answers below to your group if their answers do not cover these.

(Discuss with answer "C")
• *This is a great learning topic for discussion, and it is one everyone can relate to. Read this answer to the group and open it for discussion by simply asking if anyone has ever thought of what you've read here. Do they have any comments on this very common cultural problem? Famous people want us to feel very close to them. Famous people want us to believe that they care about us, love us, and respect us and that they feel as close to us as we feel close to them. This is one of the ways they increase their fame and fortune. However, just try being intimate with Madonna, Michael Jordan, or the president of the United States—and you will quickly find they do NOT want your intimacy. What's more, you could find yourself imprisoned if you try to get too close to them! Yet God Almighty is immeasurably closer to us than any famous person, and*

Miraculous Drama in Real Life

"Now I have no way to adequately describe this, but I'll try. The only way I can think of is if you're standing on the end of a runway and a 777 jet is getting ready to take off on the runway right in front of you. That kind of a violent mighty wind came blowing into that auditorium. When it did, thousands of people started screaming, but the wind was much louder. I was standing frozen, and I got goose bumps on my goose bumps. I was petrified, but a good petrified. There was such an awesome presence in that building for about a minute and a half. It then just gradually died out, leaving people sobbing, collapsed in their chairs and weeping. So I thought to myself, 'You can't make one wrong move in this atmosphere, buddy.'"

—John Bevere

Lesson Four

Leader's Notes

He does desire our intimacy! Furthermore, of course, God will do much more in and for our lives than even the most revered public figure.

(Discuss with answer "D")
• *This is another engaging topic for learning about the fear of God. Read this answer to the group and open it for discussion. We emulate sports figures, movie and rock stars, politicians, and business persons. The list of people we want to be "just like" is endless. The sad irony is, of course, that we will never be just like a Donald Trump, a Nelson Mandela, a Tiger Woods, Nancy Reagan, or a Billy Graham. We can covet being like them all we want, but it's not going to happen, even if we get close to them. Yet Jesus is the one famous personality that WANTS us near Him. He desires us to want to be like Him! The beauty of this is that God is the most famed, most beautiful, most powerful, most influential, most able "person" there ever was! He is the one "ultra-famous personality" who actually invites you—gives you 24/7 (24 hours per day, 7 days per week) access—to His very inner chamber! He wants you to*

Real Life Drama in the Old Testament...

Leviticus 10:1: *"Nadab and Abihu, the sons of Aaron, each took his censer and put fire in it, put incense on it, and offered profane fire before the LORD, which He had not commanded them."* (Some translations say "unauthorized," "strange," or "unholy" fire.)

9. At this time only ___six people___ were authorized to come into the presence of God.

10. The word *profane* means:
[ ] Hot   [ ] A food offering
[ ] To treat poorly [x] To treat what is sacred as common

11. Another meaning for *profane* is "to ___treat___ what is ___holy___ as ___ordinary___."

12. Webster's dictionary gives profane a one-word definition: ___Irreverent___.

13. Even though Nadab and Abihu were authorized to come, what happened when these two men came into the presence of God with irreverence?
"So fire went out from the LORD and devoured them, and they died before the LORD" (Lev. 10:2).

Let's not gloss over this or view it too lightly. This is a serious biblical example, written and recorded for our admonition. These were two young men, leaders in their country. This was a remarkable occurrence that doubtless affected everyone. Moses himself was their uncle and Aaron their father.

14. What did Moses say to Aaron about this?
"This is what the Lord spoke, saying: 'By those who come near Me I must be regarded as holy; and before all the people I must be glorified'" (Lev. 10:3).

THE FRIENDS OF GOD

- This is called a "____universal and eternal____ decree."
- *Universal* means it applies to every ____created being in the universe____.
- *Eternal* means ____it has always been____ this way, and ____it will always be____ this way.

How many of you know Scripture has the "should be's" and "must be's"? You would be wise to know what the "must be's" are.

—John Bevere

Real Life Drama in the New Testament...

15. In Acts 5, we see a real-life story of two more people. In the midst of a celebration of thanksgiving, what happened when Ananias lied?
    ____God struck him dead.____

16. Three hours later, what happened to Ananias's wife, Sapphira, when she lied to Peter?
    ____God struck her dead too.____

17. What happened to the whole church when this took place? ____Great fear came upon the whole church.____

18. We are to be drawing near to God, guarding our hearts with all diligence. Go to your Bible in the Book of Acts, chapter 5, and verse 3. Something filled the heart of Ananias, so that he kept back part of the money and lied to God. It was:
[ ] Greed   [ ] Envy   [ ] Care for the church
[ ] Care for his family   [X] Satan

LEADER'S NOTES

draw near to Him so you may be transformed into His very image and become the person you should be!

(Discuss with answer "E")
- What better platform could you hope for from which to minister the majesty and fear of God. Use this as an opportunity to point out that:

- If we pay homage to men and women in power, heads of state, CEOs, and military leaders, how much more should we revere, respect, and fear the God of the universe, who holds all power, might, and dominion in the palm of His hand.

- God commands the waves of the sea. The heavens drop at His presence, and He is the One who has the power to cast our souls into hell.

- Jesus is the Person we should bow to, more than all men combined. In fact, one day every knee shall bow.

Lesson Four

Leader's Notes

19. Even though Ananias told the lie to Peter, whom does Peter say that Ananias lied to?
The Holy Spirit

20. In Acts 5:9, Peter says Ananias and Sapphira tested:
[ ] Satan   [ ] Peter
[x] The Holy Spirit [ ] The church

Key Statement:
God is not only a God of love, but He is also a holy God.

We need to be sober and vigilant, very cautious about what we allow into our lives. Satan is like a roaring lion, seeking whom he may devour (1 Pet. 5:8), and he seeks to enter our very hearts. Let's not give him any opportunities.

What are your eyes seeing? Consider this brief list of things that your eyes may let into your heart:

- The Word of God
- Television
- Pornography
- Books
- The beauty of nature, the beauty of your children
- The latest catalog of items that the world tells you will make you a success or that you need for your home or to keep up with society
- The Internet

21. "Gut check" time: Which, if any, of the above pertain to you? What other types of things?

_____
_____
_____

THE FRIENDS OF GOD

22. Which of the above are good, which seems "neutral," and which is plainly sinful?

LEADER'S NOTES

How about your ears? Consider this brief list of things that your ears may let into your heart:
- Music
- Preaching/teaching
- Prayer
- The radio
- Gossip, rumors
- Counseling
- Family, friends, or co-workers talking

23. "Gut check" time: Which, if any, of the above pertain to you? What other types of things?

24. Which of the above are good, which seems "neutral," and which is plainly sinful?

65

LESSON FOUR

Leader's Notes

What is your pride pushing you toward? (Not all forms of pride are necessarily evil.)

- Competition with your neighbor (better house, car, spouse, etc.)
- Desire for position or a title or name within your church
- A personal pride to be had that causes a desire to walk before God in sincerity
- Desire to be free from sin so you can feel clean and whole before God and man
- Athletics, music or career goals

25. "Gut check" time: Which, if any, of the above pertain to you? What other types of things?

_____
_____
_____

26. Which of the above are good, which seems "neutral," and which is plainly sinful?

_____
_____
_____

Take some personal prayer time. Pray about your answers to these questions. Ask God to reveal to you what needs to go and what is good to keep. Draw near to the Holy Spirit, asking for Him to empower you by the Word, prayer, and fellowship so you can do the things He shows you.

THE FRIENDS OF GOD

At the end of the group session, ask for prayer about anything you may want help with.

Key Statement:
It takes the fear of God *and* the love of God to keep us on the path of life.

27. How can we be intimate with someone we fear? So what then is the fear of the Lord?

- It is **not** ___*to be scared of God*___.
- It has nothing to do with the ___*spirit of fear*___.
- The fear of the Lord is when we venerate Him. We ___*respect*___ His presence. We ___*honor*___ Him. We ___*revere*___ Him and ___*tremble*___ at His Word. We ___*love*___ what He ___*loves*___. We ___*hate*___ what He ___*hates*___. What is ___*important*___ to Him is ___*important*___ to us.
- When we fear God, we will ___*obey*___ even when we don't ___*understand*___ or see the ___*benefit*___ of it.
- Psalms 25:14 says, "The secret of the LORD is with those who ___*fear*___ Him."
- Psalms 25:14 in the New Living Translation reads, "___*Friendship*___ with the LORD is reserved for those who ___*fear*___ him."

**Knowing God as our loving heavenly Father keeps us from the ditch of legalism.
The fear of God as Lord and King keeps us from the ditch of a fleshly lifestyle.**

LEADER'S NOTES

Lesson Four

Leader's Notes

Friendship with God?

Key Statement:
"Friendship with the LORD is reserved for those who fear him" (Ps. 25:14, NLT).

28. Not everyone is God's friend. More specifically, not everyone within the church is God's friend. Why?
Not everyone walks intimately with God. Friendship is reserved for those who fear Him.

Abraham, God, and Isaac...

29. God told Abraham to sacrifice his son Isaac. Abraham feared God. What are some of the actions that Abraham took that proved it?
Though God didn't give him a reason, Abraham rose early the next morning and began doing all things God had commanded him.

30. What can you learn from the fact that Abraham "rose early the next morning" after God told him to sacrifice Isaac?
Because he feared God he immediately obeyed even when he did not understand.

31. How does this contrast with so many of us who say, "God has been dealing with me for several weeks"?
By putting off God we reveal our lack of fear of God.

32. In the events that transpired regarding the sacrifice of Isaac, what wonderful facet of His personality did God reveal to Abraham for the first time?
Jehovah Jireh, the Lord Provides.

THE FRIENDS OF GOD

33. In your life, what are some times when you have walked with God through a difficult period, and He then revealed Himself to you in a way that was perfect for that situation?

_____
_____
_____

34. For Abraham and Isaac, God revealed Himself with a "new" name—The Lord Who Provides. With what "names" has God revealed Himself to you personally?

_____
_____
_____

LEADER'S NOTES

Two righteous men, one friend of God...

35. Although both Abraham and Lot were righteous, we see an exciting but sobering fact about what took place in Sodom and Gomorrah.

- We see a righteous man who knows __*what God is going to do even before He does it*__ and even __*helps God make up His mind*__ about doing it.

- We see another righteous man who is as __*clueless as the rest of the world*__.

36. Why? Because one man __*feared*__ God. The other man __*didn't*__.

69

Lesson Four

Leader's Notes

37. Here is a tough question, but one worth exploring. Be honest. In what ways (or maybe when) in your life do you see yourself:

- Like Abraham, a friend of God, in intimate dialogue with God.

- Like Lot, clueless about what God is doing.

- In what practical, really doable ways can you apply this lesson so the Holy Spirit transforms your life into friendship with God? This is a life-time journey, so think in terms of taking one step at a time and being faithful at it. When we are faithful in little things, God will make us ruler of bigger things (Matt. 25:21).

John relates the events of Moses and Israel and then of Jesus in the New Testament as he quotes Jesus' words in John 15:15, "No longer do I call you servants."

38. Why would God call us servants as opposed to friends?
To protect us. (He doesn't take delight in Ananias and Sapphira situations.) God doesn't share His intimate things with you until you are very firm in who you are and very firm in who He is—very firm in the fear of the Lord.

THE FRIENDS OF GOD

"No longer do I call you servants, for a servant does not know what his master is doing; but I have called you friends, for all things that I have heard from My Father I have made known to you"
John 15:15

LEADER'S NOTES

Search your heart...

"You are My friends if you do whatever I command you."
John 15:14:

39. What does the word *if* mean in that verse? It means you __have to satisfy this__ in order to have that.

40. What is Jesus saying here? He is saying *not everyone in the church is His friend, but only those who tremble at His Word and fear God.*

"THEOLOGY 101"

LEGALISM and LAWLESSNESS

Optional:
Any discussion about this would be optional. If you decide to skip this "Theology 101" then continue with question 41.

~More understanding~
" It takes the fear of God *and* the love of God to keep us on the path of life."

—John Bevere

A dictionary definition of *legalism* is "strict conformity to the letter of the law rather than its spirit." You can see the Pharisees as examples of this in the New Testament (Matthew 23; John 8). On the outside they looked like they were close to God by obeying many laws and rules, but Jesus at one point said that their hearts actually looked like dead men's graves.

LESSON FOUR

LEADER'S NOTES

Lawlessness can be described as rejecting any law or all law: living in lasciviousness, which is an excessively fleshly lifestyle as opposed to a Spirit-controlled life. Both legalism and lawlessness can rob us of the joy of God's grace and the truth and power, and they can actually keep people from the kingdom of God.

The legalist tends to be scared of God, trying to please Him through perfectly keeping the letter of the law, often focusing on externals (what to wear, when to work and worship, what to eat, etc.). On the other hand, those who practice lawlessness tend to take God for granted. They have no healthy fear of God, so they live according to their fleshly desires but call it freedom in Christ. But God is looking for those who will worship Him in spirit and in truth.

(John 4:24; 1 John 3:18; see also chapter 8 of the book *Drawing Near* for more about this).

There is danger in landing in a ditch on either side of this road. We can be too rigid and legalistic, not understanding that God desires an intimate relationship with us. Or we can go too far with our so-called freedom in Christ and live a life of sin and lawlessness—a life that only seeks the blessings of God, not God Himself. Consider these sobering words from Jesus about Judgment Day:

Matthew 7:21–27: "Not every one that saith unto me, Lord, Lord, shall enter into the kingdom of heaven; *but he that doeth the will of my Father which is in heaven.* Many will say to me in that day, Lord, Lord, have we not prophesied in thy name? and in thy name have cast out devils? and in thy name done many wonderful works? And then will I profess unto them, I never knew you: depart from me, ye that work iniquity. *Therefore whosoever*

The Friends of God

heareth these sayings of mine, and doeth them, I will liken him unto a wise man, which built his house upon a rock: And the rain descended, and the floods came, and the winds blew, and beat upon that house; and it fell not: for it was founded upon a rock. *And every one that heareth these sayings of mine, and doeth them not, shall be likened unto a foolish man,* which built his house upon the sand: And the rain descended, and the floods came, and the winds blew, and beat upon that house; and it fell: and great was the fall of it" (KJV, emphasis added).

Our motivation for obeying God should be love.

"And this is love, that we walk after his commandments"
2 John 6, KJV

"For this is the love of God, that we keep his commandments"
1 John 5:3, KJV

"You have become estranged from Christ, you who attempt to be justified by law; you have fallen from grace"
Gal. 5:4

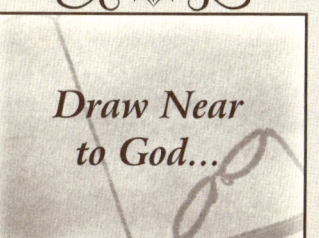

We are to live balanced, holy lives, obeying the Word of God by the power of the Holy Spirit in the fear of the Lord.

Here again we see the beauty of our flagship verse, James 4:8. If we draw near to God, He will draw near to us and lead us and empower us to live the way He desires us to live!

Leader's Notes

LESSON FOUR

LEADER'S NOTES

To finish this session, think about John's message and what happened with the church in Brazil.

• *Tell your group as you refer to question 41 that right now you are going to check your hearts and believe God together for this session and all the rest of the sessions.*

• *Pray together for people to come with fear and reverence, joy and expectation that God will move in each service as you are all drawing near to Him. Pray for a real move of God, asking the Holy Spirit to knit your group together for great things as you proceed.* **Be expectant for God to move in this very session.**

This also might be a good time for people to share short testimonies of what the Lord has done through the series so far.

41. Now really search your heart. What is YOUR attitude when you attend these sessions?

Is it:
- Indifferent? Complacent?
- Irreverent like the crowd in Brazil?
- Expectant? Filled with the Spirit?

Do you come:
- To learn some things?
- To spend time with church friends?
- Because everyone else is coming?

Or Do You Come to Meet God!?

If you have been like the crowd in Brazil was, ask for God's forgiveness right now and expect the Holy Spirit to move!

Attend the sessions with reverence toward God. Be prayed up, prepared for the lessons, and expectant to experience God Himself!

Everyone in the church can be God's friend; that's the invitation in James 4:8:

Draw near to God and He will draw near to you.

Video Script for Lesson 4
THE FRIENDS OF GOD

It's great to be back here again with you this morning as we continue in our fourth lesson of drawing near a life of intimacy with God. Our flagship scripture for this book has been "draw near to God and he will draw near to you." We are the ones that determine the level of our relationship with God, not God. Let me say this, with all the other lessons that we've done an insatiable hunger has been placed in my heart to pursue Him. Now, you cannot talk about drawing near to God without addressing the issue of Holy fear. This is the point where seeker friendly, seeker sensitive messengers and truth will part ways. These teachers, which are numerous and can be in any denomination or non-denomination, speak or write of a God who desires men and longs to bless them, yet they omit his holiness. Many do this out of well meaning intentions. Why? They have experienced or seen the tragedy of legalism, so they go to the extreme other side. Others just desire to see people loved and nurtured. These are good intentions.

Lastly, there are some who do it for wrong reasons, such as to develop a greater following. But those from the first two categories, who have fled the grip of legalism and preach of only a loving kind God who compensates for our lawlessness and worldliness, are reactionary in their motives and tactics. These teachers preach an easy Lord at the expense of the very goal they are trying to accomplish. They desire people to come to know God, yet by leaving out the fear of the Lord they in essence shut out the presence of the Lord to men.

Psalm 89:7 says *"God is to be greatly feared in the assembly of the saints, and to be held in reverence by all those around Him."* You will never find the Lord in an atmosphere where He is not held in the utmost respect and reverence. I'll never forget when I first learned this. Back in 1996 or 7 I was asked to do a national conference in the nation of Brazil. It was a huge conference and they did a very smart thing. They had the speakers travel to the three largest cities instead of the people all having to travel to one city. The three cities were Brasilia, San Paulo, and Rio De Janeiro. The three speakers were Benson Idahosa from Africa, another person and then myself. My first city was Brasilia, the capital. I remember flying down all Thursday night, spending Friday afternoon in prayer in my room and I was ready for service. Now, I remember when they picked me up and drove me to the service, we were many blocks away from the auditorium and there were cars everywhere. We drove up through a sea of cars to a huge parking lot to the reserved spot and I get out of the car and I can hear the singing that's coming from the inside of this massive auditorium. This is because the building has a gap between the ceiling and the upper wall so you can get an airflow coming through the building in this sub-tropical climate. I can hear them singing from the inside. They escort me into the auditorium and they take me right up to the platform. And you know these Latinos can play. They were singing in Portuguese and I couldn't understand a lick of what they were saying but I could tell they were good musicians and singers. And as good as they are there isn't a drop of the presence of God in this place. I am talking about His manifest presence. Remember His omnipresence speaks of Him being everywhere; His manifest presence speaks of when we can sense Him with our senses, when He comes out of the unknown into the known. There wasn't a drop of the manifested presence of God and I'm sitting there thinking, whoa, wait a minute, this is a believer's conference. This huge auditorium is packed; there isn't an open seat anywhere that I can see. The singing is good, so what's going on? So I said Lord where is your presence? All of a sudden God opened up my eyes and I started noticing. There were people standing with their hands in their pockets looking up at the ceiling, there are other people with their arms crossed during worship looking down at the floor, some were fumbling with their purse, some whispering to one another, and others walking in and out getting something like it's a show. I thought okay, this will change but it doesn't– it goes on all through praise and worship.

Lesson Four

Then the leader comes up and starts reading from the scriptures and I still see people with their arms crossed, hands in their pockets, looking down at the floor whispering, even muttering from people talking etc., not paying attention. Now I'm getting angry. I'm talking Texas-spitting mad-angry! And by the time they introduce me it's been an hour or hour and a half, and I walked up to the pulpit and put my elbow on it and leaned there and just looked at them– stared at them– didn't say a word. Now how many of you know, after about 45 seconds of just staring and no activity on the platform, everybody stops what they are doing and they look up thinking "what happened, the show has stopped". So I didn't say to them, "it is great to be in Brazil, I'm so happy to be here for the first time." I just looked at them and realized I had every eye in that place on me and this is exactly what I said: "I've got two questions. Question number one: you're sitting and talking to someone sitting across the table from you and the whole time you are sitting and talking to them they are sitting there with their hands in their pockets looking around, or sitting there with their arms crossed looking down, or they are whispering to someone sitting next to them. Will you continue to speak to them?" They all said no. I said, "if you were to go over and knock on the door at someone's house to visit and every time you go to visit they just come to the door and say 'oh it's you again come on in'. Would you continue to go?" They said no. I said I've been in this building for an hour and a half. I haven't felt a drop of the presence of God and the reason is because Psalm 89 says that God is to be held in reverence by all those around Him. If the prime minister of your nation had walked onto this platform tonight he would've gotten ten times more respect than the presence of the Holy Spirit. If Pele` your greatest soccer player came here tonight you would've been on the edge of your seats anticipating every word because he's such a national hero. He would've gotten much more respect than the Holy Spirit did tonight.

God will never come into a place where he is not held with the utmost respect because He is a great King. And I began preaching to them about the fear of the Lord for seventy-five minutes. When I was done preaching to them, I didn't say bow your heads and close your eyes. I said every person in this place if you are born again and you lack the fear of God stand up right now. Seventy-five percent of the people in that auditorium immediately stood to their feet. And it was the most amazing thing. As soon as they stood the presence of God came into that auditorium. I had been in that building for two hours and forty five minutes and hadn't felt a drop of God's manifest presence and as soon as they stood we didn't even pray a prayer yet and people were weeping all over the auditorium. The presence of God was like a wave, it lasted three or four or five minutes, then it lifted and the Holy Spirit whispered to me, "Son, lead them in a prayer of repentance." So I did and as soon as we said amen, another wave of His presence came in and now almost every person in the auditorium was weeping. It was amazing. It lasted three or four minutes then it lifted. There were a few minutes of silence and the Holy Spirit said, "Son, I'm coming one last time." Now I have no way to adequately describe this, but I'll try. Within seconds of Him saying I am coming one more time, the only way I can think of, is if you're standing on the end of a runway and a 777 jet is getting ready to take off on the runway right in front of you. That kind of a violent mighty wind came blowing into that auditorium. When it did thousands of Latinos started screaming but the wind was much louder. I was standing frozen and I got goose bumps on my goose bumps. I was petrified but a good petrified. There was such as awesome presence in that building for about a minute and a half. It then just gradually died out leaving people sobbing, collapsed in their chairs and weeping. So I thought to myself, "you can't make one wrong move in this atmosphere buddy." So, I realized God was through with me and I looked at the leader and said it's all yours.

So they whisked me out to the car and then they put the national singer in with her husband and she asks, "did you hear the wind, did you hear the wind?" And I said well it was probably a jet airplane right over the building. She looked at me with fire in her eyes and said, "What?! There was fire all around the building, what do you mean, jet?" Her husband calmed her down, then said to me, "sir there was no jet." I said how do you know? He said, "Because there were security men and police all around the outside of the auditorium, most of them not even saved and when that violent wind began to blow they sent messages in saying what is the sound of that violent wind coming from inside the building? Furthermore, I was at the

soundboard because my wife is a national singer. When that wind was blowing I was looking at the soundboard. It didn't come from our soundboard because the decibel meters were at zero. Not one ounce of that wind sound came from our sound system". I thought my God take me to my hotel room! I remember all I could do was stay up on the balcony of my hotel room until one thirty at night and worship Him in awe. The next morning we come in and people are receiving from God, getting healed, set free, it was amazing because God will not come into a place were He is not held with the utmost respect.

You see I've learned something. I've learned how to get into the presence of God more easily. What I started doing about a year and a half ago is I'd walk out to my prayer place, I wouldn't say a word. I just start meditating on the awesomeness of my Father, the awesomeness of my Jesus. Then all of a sudden bam! There is His presence. I thought Lord this is so easy. I used to struggle, why is it now so easy? Then one morning the Holy Spirit said: What did Jesus say to His disciples when He taught them to pray? Then I started reciting the Lord's Prayer - our Father, which art in heaven, hallowed be...hallowed be thy name... there it is. Jesus, you taught them. You don't come into the presence of God except with holy fear.

Turn with me in the Bible. (Leviticus 10:1) *"Then Nadab and Abihu, the sons of Aaron, each took his censor and put fire in it, put incense on it, and offered profane fire before the Lord, which He had not commanded them."* Some translations say "unauthorized", "strange", or "unholy" fire. But mine says, "profane" and since I'm preaching that's the one we're going with. Now at this time only six people were authorized to come into the presence of God: Moses, Aaron, Nadab, Abihu, Eleazar and Ithamar. But today, we are all authorized to come into the presence of God by the new and living way having our conscience sprinkled with the blood of Jesus. But at this time only six were authorized and these were two of them. Now the word profane means to treat what is sacred as common or to treat what is Holy as ordinary. Webster's dictionary gives it a one-word definition: Irreverent. So we have two men who are authorized to come into the presence of God but they come in with irreverence. Look at what happens, Leviticus 10:2-3, "So fire went out from the Lord and devoured them, and they died before the Lord. And Moses (their uncle) said to Aaron (their father), This is what the Lord spoke, saying: 'By those who come near Me I must be regarded as Holy; and before all the people I must be glorified.'" You have to understand this is what is called a "universal and eternal decree". Universal means it applies to every created being in the universe. Eternal means it's always been this way and it's always going to be this way. How many of you know the scripture has the 'should-be's and 'must-be's? How many of you know you would be wise to know what the 'must-be's are? This is a must be. God says you can't come into My presence without Holy fear. Some of you think well John that's the Old Testament we are living in the New Testament now.

Then let me tell you about Acts five, and a couple named Ananias and Sapphira. The reason most people don't understand chapter five is because unless you read Acts chapter 4 you'll never understand chapter five. What happens in four is that a man named Barnabus who is a Levite from the country of Cyprus sells his land and brings the money and puts it at Peter's feet. Now if you owned land in Cyprus back then you were very, very rich. This could be a million or maybe a couple million dollars and this guy brings it right to Peter's feet. Now this will get much attention because they are doing it openly, the offerings, and this brings much thanksgiving among the church. How many of you know we celebrate the gift of preaching, we celebrate the gift of teaching and we celebrate the gift of singing. Why don't we celebrate the gift of giving and administration and all the other gifts? We should celebrate giving because giving is a gift. The church had no problem with that, they were all celebrating this.

And then all of a sudden you have Ananias and Sapphira– whom I believe were the biggest givers in the church– yet all this attention is on this other guy Barnabas. This causes them to do something. It creates a reaction so they go out and sell their biggest plot. They say to themselves this is way too much for us to give, but we want to make it appear as if we are giving it all. They were more concerned with what people thought than what God thought. Listen to me - you will serve whom you fear– if you fear man you will ultimately obey man, if you fear

Lesson Four

God you will ultimately obey God. So Ananias brings the money, lays it at Peter's feet and Peter says is this what you got for the land? Ananias says yes it's everything. Immediately, BAM! God struck him dead. Three hours later here comes Ananias's wife. Peter says to her is this what you got for the land? She says yep. BAM! God struck her dead too. So the Bible says great fear came upon the whole church. All of a sudden they realize they had gone from laughing and celebrating to seeing that God is not only a God of love but He is also a Holy God. It takes the fear of God and the love of God to keep us on the path of life.

How many of you know every road has a ditch on both sides, right. So does the path of life. The first ditch is called legalism. How many of you remember the church was in a legalistic ditch, right? That's all these externals like wearing your hair up in a bun and your dresses down to the floor but you could have your hair up tight and your dress down low and still have a seducing spirit up to your eyeballs and that's not holiness, right? But then God gave the revelation to a man named Oral Roberts that God is a good God and then the Charismatic movement came and we found out that God our daddy loved us. And you know what the love of God did? It delivered us out of the legalistic ditch.

But you know what we did? We said I'm going to go so far from that ditch that I'm never going to fall in again and we went to the other side and fell into the other ditch. That ditch is called lasciviousness, which is an excessively fleshly lifestyle. So God gave us another force to keep us out of that ditch and that is called the fear of the Lord. What is the fear of the Lord? It is not to be scared of God. How can we be intimate with someone we fear? It has nothing to do with the spirit of fear; it has to do with the fear of the Lord. The fear of the Lord is when we venerate Him. We respect his presence. We honor Him. We revere Him and tremble at His Word. We love what He loves. We hate what He hates. What is important to Him is important to us, what is not so important to Him is not so important to us. How many of you know there are weightier matters to God? It says so in the book of Matthew chapter twenty-three so when we fear God we will obey even when we don't understand or see the benefit of it. Some Americans think that if they give, God will do something for them. That is the only way they'll obey. We've developed disciples that will only obey if you show them the benefit yet the fear of God means you tremble at His word and you obey whether you understand or not.

Go with me in the Bible to Psalms 25:14 please. *"The secret of the Lord is with those who fear Him."* Now can I ask you a question? How many of you have secrets in your life? All of us have secrets. There are good secrets. Not all secrets are bad. Who do you share the secrets of your life with, acquaintances or intimate friends? God is no different. God says I share the secrets of My heart with My intimate friends and My intimate friends are those who fear me. This verse in the New Living Translation is *"Friendship with the Lord is reserved for those who fear Him."* God is not everyone's friend. More specifically, God is not everyone's friend, even in the church. Now there are two men God called His friend in the Old Testament. Are there others? Absolutely. I believe Esther was; I believe David was.

But these two men's lives exemplify what it means to have a relationship or friendship with God. The first man is Abraham. Why is Abraham the friend of God? Because God comes to Abraham when he is his in old age and Abraham has Isaac whom he really, really loves. Isaac has been the number one thing in his life for sometime and God tells Abe to kill Isaac. God says "go three day's journey to mount Moriah and kill him." Now understand - this is the most important person in Abraham's life and God tells him to kill him. He didn't even tell Abraham his reasoning. He just says, "Go kill him". Now you know what my Bible says in the NIV translation? It says *"early the next morning."* Do you know how many people say you know The Lord's been dealing with me about this for several weeks now. Huh? Huh! You just showed your lack of the fear of God. Now God gives him three days. Do you know why He gave him three days? Because He wants to give him time to think it over in case he wants to turn back. It's real easy the night before when you heard the booming voice of God, but what about two and a half days later when you are looking at the mountain where you are going to put the most important person in your life to death just because God said to do it.

78

THE FRIENDS OF GOD

So Abraham goes to the mountain, ties Isaac up on the altar, lifts up the knife and is ready to put the most important person in his life to death, and the Angel of The Lord says, "Stop! For now I know you fear God." How did the angel know he feared God? Because he obeyed even when he didn't understand. He trembled at His word. Now watch this, you are going to like it. Abraham puts down the knife and looks up and there's a ram caught in the thicket. And out of his spirit comes this cry: Jehovah Jireh! The Lord Provides. God reveals a facet of His personality to Abraham that no one had ever known before because Abraham was God's friend.

Here's an example to help understand this. All of you this morning know me as John Bevere the preacher. Some may know me as John Bevere author. But there is an incredible lady, my wife, who knows me as lover, husband, father, friend, and sports men. You don't know me as lover, and you never will. She knows facets of me that you will never know. God revealed a facet of Himself that no one had ever known because Abraham was God's friend. He feared God. Look at the dynamic of the relationship between Abraham and God. God says one day you know what, should we destroy Sodom and Gomorrah without first talking to our friend Abraham about it? So God goes down and chats with Abe. God says, "Abe, we're thinking about blowing up these two cities what do you think about it?" Abraham says what!? My nephew Lot lives over there. Uh, Lord, alright, alright, uh, you wouldn't blow the place up if there were more then fifty righteous people there, would you? The Lord goes good point Abe. Abe says lemme think, uh, hold on, how about only forty-five? Would you do that? The Lord says good point. So he talks Him all the way down to ten and he thinks there's got to be ten– Lot's one– all I need now is nine. But there aren't nine! This is really something. Sodom and Gomorrah are buying, selling, trading, marrying and giving in marriage. What is that in today's vernacular? Life is good; the economy is great. Sodom is thinking if there is a God He certainly doesn't mind the way we live because they think they are the furthest things from judgment that could ever happen. They don't realize they are twenty-four hours away from being annihilated! This is what is scary! Even Lot who the Bible calls righteous doesn't even know it. He is as clueless as the world! God has to send two messengers of mercy, two angels to tell him. Even so when they do go out Lot's wife is a little too attached. She looks back and that's why Jesus said remember Lot's wife, speaking about the fear of The Lord in the New Testament. Here's a righteous man who knows what God is going to do even before He does it and even helps God make up His mind about doing it. And here is another righteous man who is as clueless as the world. Why? Because one man feared God the other man didn't. One man– Abraham– was the friend of God, the other man– Lot– was not, even though they are both righteous.

Moses is the other man God talked to face to face as a friend. Now let's talk about Moses and Israel. The Bible says Moses knew God's ways, Israel knew His acts. Now what does that mean? Let's put it in today's vernacular. Israel knew God by how He answered their prayers. Do you know how many Christians there are in America whose relationship with God is limited to how He has answered their prayers? Things like my daughter was sick, we prayed and God healed her, we had a need, we prayed and God met it, we sowed a seed and God brought a harvest. But Moses knew God's ways and many times even knew what God was going to do before He did it because God talked to Moses and Moses changed God's mind twice when God was angry. Do you know how hard it is to change someone's mind when they are angry? Yet the Bible says that God relented from what He was going to do because of what Moses said to God. Now turn with me in the New Testament to John 15:15. Jesus is speaking to the eleven (Judas has already left) and He said, "*No longer do I call you servants.*" The very fact that Jesus said I no longer call you servants is because at one time they were merely regarded as just servants. Why is there a time in our lives when even though we are his children and righteous yet He calls us mere servants? I'll tell you why: To protect us. He does not take delight in Ananias and Sapphira situations.

Let me give you a very weak example of this. It is weak but will illustrate the point. I worked for two ministry staffs in the 1980s. One was about 400 people and one about 150. When were launched into our own ministry in the 1990s I made a little policy that I was going to be all my employees' best

79

Lesson Four

buddy. First guy I hired in 1990, I was his best buddy. We played sports together, watched movies together, we'd do everything together and for the first year it was great until I had to bring some minor correction to him and when I did this, he looked at me from across the desk and he just railed on me. And immediately the Holy Spirit said to me, "you must release him." So I did, and wept like a baby when he left because I loved that guy so much. But the Holy Spirit said to me, "He will come back and be twice as faithful." Three months later he called me and said, "John God has never spoken to me like he has in past three months. I became too familiar with you and Lisa, I lost sight of the place God had placed you in my life. I treated your family as common and I have been so wrong." I said, "You're hired." He came back and I did not have problems with him in that area again.

Now I have a policy. I have about thirty employees and I will not share my heart and really open up the intimate things in my life until I know they are very firm in who they are and very firm in who I am because I don't want to hurt them like I hurt that young man. I do it for their good. I have nothing to hide. I love sharing with people but I know I am protecting them. Well this is what God said. God says I am not going to share my intimate things with you until you are very firm in who you are and very firm in whom I am– very firm in the fear of the Lord. That's why Jesus said no longer do I call you servants. At one time they were, but they had now endured. Now go back to that verse. (John 15:15) *"No longer do I call you servants, for a servant does not know what his master is doing; but I have called you friends, for all things that I heard from My father I've made known to you."* You share your ways with your friends what you are doing, right? Now look at the universal decree that Jesus makes for us. Look at verse 14: *"You are My friends if you do whatever I command you."* Notice the word "if" in that verse. "If" is a condition. It means you have to satisfy this in order to have that. Do you know what Jesus is saying there? He is saying not everyone in the church is His friend but only those who tremble at His Word and fear God. But, let me close by saying everyone in the church can be his friend, that's the invitation. Draw near to God, and He will draw near to you.

Video Session 5

WHAT HINDERS TRUE INTIMACY

Key Statement:
The fear of the Lord is the beginning (foundation) of knowledge
Prov. 1:7

"My son, if you receive my words, and treasure my commands within you, so that you incline your ear to wisdom, and apply your heart to understanding; yes, if you cry out for discernment, and lift up your voice for understanding, if you seek her as silver, and search for her as for hidden treasures; then you will understand the fear of the LORD, and find the knowledge of God."
Proverbs 2:1-5

1. The dictionary of biblical languages says that the Hebrew word for *knowledge* is: *Information of a person with a strong implication of a relationship to that person.*

2. This is not scientific knowledge or even _scriptural_ knowledge.

3. *W. E. Vine's Expository Dictionary* says it like this: "To have an _intimate experiential_ knowledge of God." And then it goes on to say, "Positively to know God is parallel _to fear Him_". The only way to _know_ God is first of all to _fear_ Him.

LEADER'S NOTES

(3–5 minutes)

Remind the group of a few key lessons by referring to these statements:

1. Intimacy with God is available to each one of us. This is God's passion.

2. We are to seek God for who He is and not what He can do for us.

Set this session up with the Key Statement. Then go through the questions, asking for and providing the answers.

Lesson Five

Leader's Notes

A Distorted or Clear Image of Him?

4. Without the fear of the Lord an __incorrect image__ is developed, shaped, and molded in our own __minds__ and __imaginations__.

Have a volunteer read this scripture aloud to the group, then go over the questions.

> "Now when the people saw that Moses delayed coming down from the mountain, the people gathered together to Aaron, and said to him, 'Come, make us gods that shall go before us; for as for this Moses, the man who brought us up out of the land of Egypt, we do not know what has become of him.' And Aaron said to them, 'Break off the golden earrings which are in the ears of your wives, your sons, and your daughters, and bring them to me.' So all the people broke off the golden earrings which were in their ears, and brought them to Aaron. And he received the gold from their hand, and he fashioned it with an engraving tool, and made a molded calf. Then they said, 'This is your god, O Israel, that brought you out of the land of Egypt!'"
> *Exodus 32:1–4*

Yahweh is the most sacred word in the whole Bible because it is the very name of God Himself. It is deemed so sacred the Hebrew writers did not even want to write the actual vowels themselves (YHWY—without the vowels). It is never used to describe a false god in the Bible.

5. The children of Israel never said it was Baal or an Egyptian god that delivered them out of Egypt. What did they do?
__They acknowledged it was God who delivered them from Egypt.__
__They did not deny the fact that it was God Almighty__
__(Elohiym).__

WHAT HINDERS TRUE INTIMACY

6. What had they done to the image of God?

- *They reduced God Almighty down to the image of a calf.*
- *They looked at the calf and in essence said "Behold Yahweh, who delivered us."*

7. Why did they fashion it after a calf?

They fashioned it after a calf because there were calves everywhere in Egypt. It was an image they were used to seeing that became a part of their life.

8. What happens when you reduce the glory of God to an image that is lower than what He really is?

- *You end up getting fleshly in your actions.*
- *You start thinking God does not see what you are doing anymore.*
- *You become deceived in your knowledge of Him.*
- *You change the image of His person.*

9. Before long, we actually end up:
- *Calling God Almighty by whatever name represents our own worldly image of Him*
- *Deceived and willfully worshiping the "calf" (image of God Almighty) we have fashioned for ourselves instead of the true God, Jesus who is Lord.*

10. This is a dangerous and at times subtle deception that can creep into any of our lives. How may you have reduced His glory into an earthly and worldly image?

LEADER'S NOTES

(10–20 minutes)

Discuss questions 9 and 10 with your group. Talk about ways we can be subtly deceived and find ourselves gravitating toward fleshly appetites as the children of Israel did with the golden calf.

Encourage people to share some of their own examples to question 10 but remind them not to get too personal in this public setting.

Lesson Five

Leader's Notes

Sample answers:
- *By regarding the Word of God simply as a motivational tool, not as God's Holy Word*
- *By picturing God as an American-type, democratic, CEO-style God that would have you only prospering, winning, and accumulating, as opposed to serving, giving, humbly witnessing and suffering for the gospel.*
- *By picturing God as a Hollywood God, where everything always works out the way you want.*
- *By relating to God as a father who spoils His child (you), worshiping Him as long as He tells you what you want to hear and gives you what you want to have.*

11. What happens when Christians lack the fear of the Lord? _____ *They gravitate toward fleshly appetites.* _____

12. Is this happening today? Are there those who have been delivered from the world by His saving grace who lack a holy fear and call on the Jesus they have formed in their imagination? Think of some examples, and list them here:

- *They are saved but go out and lie to get a business sale, and testify that God is blessing their business.*
- *They gossip about the pastor and others, yet say they are just telling everyone the truth.*
- *They commit fornication and other lewd acts, justifying their actions by saying they may be saved, but they still live in a body and have needs, too.*

 WHAT HINDERS TRUE INTIMACY

13. What is God's response to our fleshly appetites? Read Romans 8:5–7.
- *The flesh and its appetites are at enmity with God.*
- *Those who live by fleshly appetites are disobedient to His desires even though they call on His name and confess Him as Lord.*
- *Their lack of obedience stems from a heart that lacks the holy fear of God.*
- *Their misconduct is clothed in the deception of "knowing Jesus".*

14. What is the root of disobedience? It is the lack of _____*holy fear of the Lord*_____.

Key Statement:
Nothing can be hidden.

"Because, although they knew God, they did not glorify Him as God, nor were thankful, but became futile in their thoughts, and their foolish hearts were darkened. Professing to be wise, they became fools, and changed the glory of the incorruptible God into an image made like corruptible man—and birds and four-footed animals and creeping things. Therefore God also gave them up to uncleanness, in the lusts of their hearts, to dishonor their bodies among themselves, who exchanged the truth of God for the lie, and worshiped and served the creature rather than the Creator, who is blessed forever. Amen."
Romans 1:21–25

15. John tells the true story of meeting the man on the beach in Hawaii. How would you describe this man?

Sample answers: A hypocrite. Carnal. Saved but no fear of God. Well meaning, but deceived. No godly fruit.

LEADER'S NOTES

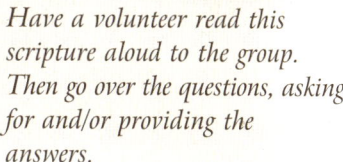

Have a volunteer read this scripture aloud to the group. Then go over the questions, asking for and/or providing the answers.

LESSON FIVE

LEADER'S NOTES

16. What was wrong with the man's lifestyle?

• *One minute he is talking about the island girls, the next, once he learns that John is a preacher, he suddenly gets religious.*

• *He uses profanity, yet hands out a tract and tells John how he witnesses of Jesus.*

17. Jesus said you'll know them by *their fruits*. The way to really know God intimately is to have *holy fear*, because that's when God reveals Himself.

18. If we don't have the fear of the Lord, then we have an image of Jesus that is shaped in our own *soul* and by the perceptions of *society*.

19. Many people today profess to be born again and say they serve Jesus. Paul says that although they know God, they do not glorify Him as God. They change the glory of the incorruptible God into an image made by corruptible hands. When we lose the fear of the Lord, we *lessen our spiritual common sense*.

When we lose the fear of God, we reduce Him down to our level and subconsciously think we can hide things from Him.

20. [x]True or [ ]False: Even a blatant sinner knows God is aware of his rebellion.

21. [x]True or [ ]False: Those with knowledge of God apart from His holy fear comfort themselves by saying, "The Lord doesn't see it" or "He understands."

22. [ ]True or [x]False: Leaders are exempt from this.

WHAT HINDERS TRUE INTIMACY

When you lose the fear of God, you believe in God's omnipresence and His omniscience, but deep within you've lost the awareness of His awesome majesty as Lord. When this happens, you begin to keep things secret from God and those around you.

23. A person who is deceived _believes with all their heart_ they are _right_ when in all _reality_ they are _completely wrong_.

24. They _believe with all their heart_ they are _obedient_ to Him and His Word when in all reality they are _walking in disobedience_.

"THEOLOGY 101"

Earlier in our journey we learned of omnipresence. *Omniscience* is another attribute of God and means God is all-knowing. Nothing happens anywhere of which He is ignorant. No one can hide his or her actions or thoughts from Him. It also means God has all wisdom in His plans and purposes. Some verses that speak of this are:

Psalm 139:1–4 (KJV): O LORD, thou hast searched me, and known me. Thou knowest my downsitting and mine uprising, thou understandest my thought afar off. Thou compassest my path and my lying down, and art acquainted with all my ways. For there is not a word in my tongue, but, lo, O LORD, thou knowest it altogether.

Acts 5:1–11: The story of Ananias and Sapphira.

LEADER'S NOTES

(5–10 minutes)

Optional: "Theology 101"

Lesson Five

Leader's Notes

Leaders:
Be prepared and give your own examples and ask the group to call out with some of their answers for questions A and B.

Here's a sample:

"I prayed for a job, but never got it, so I ended up with what I thought was 'second best.' Later I found out the whole division at the company I had wanted to work for was laid off permanently. God knew all of that and had a good purpose for me."

Revelation 2 and 3: Where God knows the actions and the inward spiritual condition of the churches.

A. What other verses can you think of that show God's omniscience?
_____
_____

B. How have you seen God's omniscience in your own life?
_____
_____

Key Statement:
We must all beware of self-deception.

25. [x]True or [ ]False: Iniquity is an offense against God whether it is intentional or not.

Self-Deception in the Men of Israel...

> "And the word of the LORD came to me, saying, 'Son of man, these men have set up their idols in their hearts, and put before them that which causes them to stumble into iniquity. Should I let Myself be inquired of at all by them?'"
> **Ezekiel 14:2–3**

> "Therefore put to death your members which are on the earth: fornication, uncleanness, passion, evil desire, and covetousness, which is idolatry. Because of these things the wrath of God is coming upon the sons of disobedience."
> **Colossians 3:5–6**

WHAT HINDERS TRUE INTIMACY

26. The apostle Paul says _____*covetousness*_____ is idolatry.

Webster's dictionary defines *covetousness* as "a strong desire of obtaining and possessing some supposed good."

27. Another way of defining covetousness would be "the desire for _____*gain*_____."

To sum it up, these men in Ezekiel 14 came to God with idolatry, which is covetousness or a desire for gain, in their hearts.

Self-Deception in the Prophet Balaam...

28. In Numbers 22, God specifically tells Balaam what to do, yet Balaam has his own desires and agenda, so he continues to petition God for it. In the end God gave Balaam what Balaam wanted. God answered Balaam according to the multitude of idols that were in Balaam's heart. What was it that Balaam wanted? _____*Money*_____.

29. Look at Numbers 22:32 in your Bible for an astonishing truth. It is almost funny, if it were not so sobering. The angel of the Lord says to Balaam, *"I have come out to stand against you because your way is_____perverse_____before Me."* Then the angel of the Lord goes so far as to say that he would have _____killed_____ Balaam and let the _____donkey_____ live!

Self-Deception in King Ahab...

In 1 Kings 22, King Ahab sought the advice of the prophets of Israel about going into battle. They all told the king what he wanted to hear and said, "Yes, you will be successful." Jehoshaphat, king of Judah, pointed

LEADER'S NOTES

Lesson Five

Leader's Notes

out that there was a different prophet who had not been consulted. Ahab said there was, but he hated him because he did not tell him what he wanted to hear. To which Jehoshaphat exclaimed, "Let not the king say such things." So the prophet Micaiah gives Ahab the truth, for which he was imprisoned. The Bible teaches that a lying spirit *from the Lord* (not from Satan!) filled the mouths of the prophets with the message Ahab desired. Ahab gladly listened to the false prophets and ended up killed in the battle.

We've seen the men of Israel in Ezekiel, the prophet Balaam, and King Ahab as examples of God's people who had come to the place where their own desires and strong covetousness within their heart brought self-deception and destruction into their lives.
Look at Ezekiel 14:4–5 for why this could happen.

> *"Therefore speak to them, and say to them, 'Thus says the Lord GOD: "Everyone of the house of Israel who sets up his idols in his heart, and puts before him what causes him to stumble into iniquity, and then comes to the prophet, I the LORD will answer him who comes, according to the multitude of his idols, that I may seize the house of Israel by their heart, because they are all estranged from Me by their idols."'"*

If time allows, have a volunteer turn to Romans 1:21-24 and James 1:22 and read them aloud.

- *Have the group offer ways in which these New Testament verses fit perfectly with the Old Testament scriptures.*

- *You could also ask for other passages that speak of these things.*

If we continue seeking God for the things within our own heart regardless of the will of the Lord, it is possible to have our hearts darkened to the degree that God gives us up to the lusts of our own hearts. Remember, self-deception is a sobering thing.
(See Romans 1:21–24; also James 1:22.)

Key Statement:
If we truly fear God, we will always come to Him with a neutral heart.

WHAT HINDERS TRUE INTIMACY

Approaching the Lord with strong desires that are not in line with His revealed will can prove to be unwise and dangerous. It can lead to the next level of deception, where God Himself will actually give us, or allow us, to have what we want.

Remember, according to Colossians 3:5–6, covetousness is idolatry, and we are to put to death desires that are not in line with God's will.

Why would God allow us to be given over to our own desires even when it could lead to dire consequences? Remember verse 5 in Ezekiel 14:

"That I may seize the house of Israel by their heart, because they are all estranged from Me by their idols."

In the video session John gives you the NIV translation, which puts it this way, *"I will do this to recapture the hearts of the people of Israel."*

30. What is God's goal?
<u>I will answer you according to the multitude of the desires of your heart because I want to recapture your heart.</u>

When we see how futile our idolatry and covetousness are, we will let go of them and come back to God's heart, realizing the only place to find true satisfaction is in the fear and the love of God.

LEADER'S NOTES

• *Provide the answer to this last question, by reading the question <u>and</u> the answer aloud to the group. Give them time to make sure they have it written correctly.*

• *Next, have the group read the question <u>and</u> the answer aloud WITH you. Have them do it more than once, encouraging them to add enthusiasm.*

• *Lastly, leave on a high note. Have the group read James 4:8 aloud with you (Draw near to God and He will draw near to you). Have them do it more than once, encouraging them to add enthusiasm.*

• *Finally, have them turn to one another and boldly proclaim it!*

Remind your group:
• *They should preview the next session and complete the personal discussion portions in their workbooks. If they would like, they may complete the entire section.*

• *Pray for the group before they leave. They may divide into groups and can pray for each other. Be led by the Spirit, but keep the focus on things that God may have brought to light from today's teaching.*

Lesson Five

Video Script for Lesson 5
What Hinders True Intimacy

Good Evening. Well we're back again and we're ready to do lesson number five on the Drawing Near Video Curriculum Series. Tonight we are going to begin in Proverbs chapter one. Now we learned in the last lesson that the fear of the Lord is the foundation for intimacy with God and I want to show you this again. Look in Proverbs chapter 1 verse 7, we read this, *"The fear of the Lord is the beginning"* or the starting place or the foundation of knowledge–now what kind of knowledge is He talking about? The answer is given in Chapter 2, verse 1. We read five scriptures here. *"My son, if you receive my words, and treasure my commands within you, so that you incline your ear to wisdom, and apply your heart to understanding; Yes, if you cry out for discernment, and lift up your voice for understanding, if you seek her as silver, and search for her as for hidden treasures; then you will understand the fear of the Lord."* Now watch this *"and find the knowledge of God"*.

Now we would say that we would find knowing God intimately. How do I know that? Because in the dictionary of Biblical languages we find out that the Hebrew word there for knowledge means this: *information of a person with a strong implication of a relationship with that person*. So we know the knowledge He is talking about is not book knowledge or head knowledge. It's not scientific knowledge; it's not even scriptural knowledge. It is information of a person with a strong implication of relationship to that person. Vine says it like this: to have an intimate experiential knowledge of God. And then Vine goes on to say: positively to know God is paralleled to fear him. So even W.E. Vine says the only way to know God is to first of all fear him.

Now without a fear of the Lord we really don't know God. An incorrect image is developed shaped and molded within our own soul and imagination. Go with me to Exodus 19 and I will show you this very clearly. Now I said this, this morning and I'm going to ask it again. When Moses delivered Israel out of Egypt where was their destination? Everybody should know; say it. The desert, right? Most people will say the Promised Land but Moses said to Pharaoh to let my people go that they might worship me in the wilderness, right? Why does Moses want to bring them into the Promise Land before first bringing them to the promiser himself? Because, if they go to the Promised Land without meeting the Promiser they will make the promises into idolatry and that is why God had to say to the priests in the book of Malachi I have to curse your blessings. You can actually take the blessings of God and make them idols. That's a scary thing isn't it? So what Moses said, because that's why Moses never desired to go back to Egypt. Moses had an intimate encounter with God at the burning bush and he said I've got to bring these people right to where I met with God because I want them to meet with Him. So he brings him to the mountain and he leaves them at the foot of the mountain. And look at Exodus 19, verse 3. This is what the Lord says, *"And Moses went up to God, and the Lord called to him from the mountain saying, 'Thus you shall say to the house of Jacob, and tell the children of Israel.'"* So this message is for everybody that came out, not just the priest. Of course we didn't have any priests, right? Verse 4 he said, *"You have seen what I did to the Egyptians, and how I bore you on eagles' wings* (now watch this) *and brought you to Myself."*

There is the whole reason you were born again, right there. It is so God can bring you to Himself. That's the whole reason He delivered you from the world– is to bring you to Himself. That was the reason He brought Israel out of out of Egypt was to bring them to Himself. Now God then tells Moses: Moses go down and get the people ready because in two days I'm coming down. Now how many of you know that is prophetic? A day with the Lord is a 1,000 years and a 1,000 years is a day. So what God is saying is after two days or after 2,000 years (hint, hint)– how long has it been since Jesus had

WHAT HINDERS TRUE INTIMACY

been raised from the dead? He said tell the people to sanctify themselves, and separate them unto me. What does sanctify mean? It simply means I delivered you out of Egypt and now you get Egypt out of you because I'm coming and I want you to be ready when I come.

But what happens is God comes down on the mountain and when He comes down the mountain you know what happens? The people draw back and they say, Moses we can't handle His presence, because look at Chapter 20, verse 18. *"Now all the people witnessed the thunderings, the lightening flashes, the sound of the trumpet, and the mountain smoking; and when the people saw it, they trembled and stood afar off."* Now isn't this amazing, these are the people who loved these miracles and even rejoiced when He split the Red Sea but now God comes down on the mountain and they're drawing back. Verse 19, *"Then they said to Moses, 'You speak with us, and we will hear; but let not God speak with us, lest we die.'"* Then Moses said to the people do not fear; do not be afraid of God. Remember we told you this morning that the fear of the Lord has nothing to do with being afraid of God. How can you have intimacy with somebody you're scared of? So Moses says, *"Do not fear; for God has come to test you, and that His fear may be before you, so that you may not sin."* So He said don't be afraid. God has come to see if His holy fear is in you.

Look at verse 21, *"So the people stood afar off, but Moses drew near the thick darkness where God was."* So the only one who was able to draw near was Moses himself. Why is that? In Deuteronomy chapter 5 you will notice. Don't turn there but several years later, four years later to be exact, Moses reviewed with Israel why they couldn't come to the mountain, why they couldn't come into God's presence. And God said to Moses the whole reason these people cannot come and be intimate with Me like you're intimate with Me is because they do not fear Me and Moses you do. So the Lord then says Moses you stand by Me and I'll stick with you but tell the people to go back to their tents. But there was another person God said to come here and hear me because God wanted to set up priesthood. Because God said hey these people don't want to come near Me and they can't because they don't fear Me so I've got to set up a family of men that are going to be priests that will come to Me for the people and that man of course was Aaron.

So the Lord says in Exodus 19 verse 24 *"Then the Lord said to him, 'Away! Get down and then come up, you and Aaron."* Aaron was invited to come up to the mountain with Moses to meet with God. However, if you read several chapters you are going to find out Aaron does not end up at the top, rather Moses ends up at the top and Aaron ends up back in the camp. The reason is that Aaron felt more comfort in presence of people than he did in the presence of God. He was more comfortable in church, you understand? It didn't say he went back to Egypt and went back to the church. Now I want you to notice what happens when God calls us into intimacy and yet we still know Him from afar and play church.

Go with me to Exodus 32, Exodus Chapter 32. Now we are talking about in this lesson what hinders true intimacy and you're going to see it right now– it's a lack of fear of the Lord. So now Aaron ends up back in the camp. Moses is at the top. God has called Aaron back but watch what we read in Exodus 32 verse 1, *"Now when the people saw that Moses delayed coming down from the mountain, the people gathered together to Aaron, and said to him, 'Come, make us gods that shall go before us; for as for this Moses, the man who brought us up out of the land of Egypt, we do not know what has become of him.'"* Now there is a lot in this one scripture. Let's break it down bit by bit. First of all notice they gathered together to Aaron, why is that? Because Aaron has a gift on his life called leadership. Leadership carries certain qualities. One of the qualities is it will draw people and it will draw people whether you've been to the mountain or not. Now does that explain why a person can have an 8,000-member church and he's never been to the mountain himself? So the people gather together to Aaron. Now watch this, and then they said to Aaron, come make us gods that shall go before us.

93

Lesson Five

Now I really believe the Hebrew translators got scared when they saw this word. You know what the Hebrew word is there for God? Elohim? Now let me tell you about Elohim. Elohim appears 2,606 times in the Old Testament. Now approximately 2,350 of these times it refers to God Almighty whom we serve. If you look in Genesis Chapter 1 you will notice the word Elohim appears thirty-two times in that one chapter alone. It appears in the first verse in the Bible *"in the beginning God created the heavens and the earth"*, literally reads this, *"In the beginning Elohim created the heavens and the earth."* Now roughly 250 times in the Old Testament it refers to a false god or an idol so whenever you see this Hebrew word you have to read it in context to see if it's talking about God Almighty whom we serve or a false god. So let's continue to do this because notice they didn't say as for God we don't know what became of Him, they said as for Moses we don't know what became of him. So Aaron says to them, gather all your gold and bring it to me. Look at verse 3, *"So all the people broke off the golden earrings which were in their ears, and brought them to Aaron. And he received the gold from their hand, and he fashioned it* (fashion it means form it or mold it) *with an engraving tool, and made a molded calf. Then they said, 'This is your god, O Israel, that brought you out of the land of Egypt!"* The Hebrew word there for God is again Elohim.

So now let's keep reading so we get the context. Look at verse 5, *"So when Aaron saw it, he built an altar before it. And Aaron made a proclamation and said, 'Tomorrow is a feast to the Lord."* Do you know what the Hebrew word for Lord is? Yahweh or Jehovah. Yahweh is the most sacred word in the whole Bible. It is the name of God. It is actually the name that the Hebrew writers wouldn't even write the vowels because they didn't want to write it out. It is the name of God and it is never used to describe a false god in the Bible. Do you realize what is happening here? They looked at that calf and said behold Yahweh who delivered us out of Egypt. Now listen carefully to me. They do not deny that it was God that delivered them out of Egypt. They don't say behold some Baal god who delivered us out of Egypt. They don't say behold some Egyptian god who delivered us out of Egypt. They looked at it and they acknowledge that God Almighty delivered them out. What they did was reduced His image down to a cow. Those calves were all over Egypt and that's what they were brought up in so they don't say look at Baal who delivered us, they say behold Yahweh. So once they reduced God down to this image then you know what the people do? Look at verse 6, *"Then they rose early on the next day, offered burnt offerings, and brought peace offerings; and the people sat down to eat an drink, and rose up to play."* So in other words they came to their church service the next day, they worshiped Yahweh who delivered us out of Egypt. So we're still talking about the Lord who delivered us out of Egypt but yet after they offered their offerings and had their service they rose up and began to indulge in the flesh the NIV says.

So now what happens is whenever the glory of God is reduced down to an image that is lower than what He is, people end up getting more fleshly, that's one of the things that happen. The other thing that happens is this– people reduce God down to a level being or lower and they now start thinking He doesn't see what they are doing anymore. They start making God more at their level and they do this deep in their subconscious. You see this with Cain. How many of you remember Cain? Cain and Abel are the two sons, the first two sons of Adam and Eve. Now Cain ends up bringing an offering to the Lord. He does not bring an offering to a false god he brings it to the Lord. However, he doesn't obey God. Now, let us go through this. A lot of people have a problem why does God reject Cain and not Abel. It's very simple. If you look at Adam and Eve when they were in the garden, when they sinned, what did they clothe themselves with? Fig leaves right? God comes into the garden says, " Uh, this is not my way. This is my way." And God kills an animal and clothes him with the skin of an animal. I believe it was a lamb. Thus showing them His acceptable sacrifice or what is obedience. Adam and Eve were ignorant, Cain and Abel weren't. Cain and Abel knew what God desired. So Abel brings the first born of the flock but Cain brings what? The first born of his fruit and God

WHAT HINDERS TRUE INTIMACY

said Abel this is not obedience, if you would just trade some of your fruit for one of your brother's flocks then I would accept you just like your brother. But instead Cain gets angry at God. Now what is the root of this disobedience? The Bible tells us it is lack of holy fear. Remember what Moses said to the children of Israel? God has come to test you to see that His fear is before you so that you may not sin.

The manifestation is obedience to God, obeying even when you don't understand it, obeying even when it hurts and even when it's not convenient. What is the root of disobedience? The lack of the fear of the Lord. Now I'm going to show you that this is the lack of the fear of the Lord because look what happens. God looks at Cain and says, Cain after he murders his brother. He says, "Cain where is your brother?" Listen to Cain's response." I don't know am I my brother's keeper?" Now he's talking to God like He's a human being. God comes to him and says, "Where is your brother?" "I don't know. Am I my brother's keeper?" Now if Cain had the fear of the Lord he would know exactly that God knew he just killed him because God is omniscient, omnipresent. What happens? He lost the fear of the Lord. He's reduced God down to a human being or even lower.

Now when people do this, you can look at them and say God is omniscient, He's all knowing, He's all present and they'll say yeah that's right. But deep down in their subconscious is where they lower Him. The apostle Paul says this is going to happen in the last days, in the days we're living in. I want to read a scripture to you and I want you to listen carefully to it. Paul says, in Chapter 1 of Romans, verse 21 through 23, I want you to listen carefully. Paul says, *"Because, although they knew God"*. Now He is speaking of the last days. *"Although they knew God, they did not glorify Him as God... and changed the glory of the incorruptible God into an image made like corruptible man."* So in other words they reduced His glory down to a level of their own. So this is the question that I have so many people today saying they are born again and that they serve Jesus and He's delivered me and saved me. But is it the Jesus at the right hand of the Father or is it a Jesus they made up just like them?

See, they acknowledged Jehovah delivered us from Egypt but they reduced His image down to a cow. We don't worship cows today in America we worship self, human beings, and corruptible men, so we have reduced His image down to make Him like us. I run into people constantly that will tell me that I'm born again– Jesus is my Lord– yet they live a very fleshly lifestyle. Just last year I'm in Hawaii and I was out praying early in the morning and you know how when people go to Hawaii especially from the Midwest and the east coast, they're up at 4:00 in the morning. So that's why I'm up in Hawaii and I'm down at the beach praying and this guy comes walking up to me and he's from New York. He comes walking up and says, "Hey man how are you doing?" I said, "I'm doing good." He said, "Man isn't this place great? He says the Island girls are wonderful, they're so great." He said "you know I was at this party last night" and all this just goes on and on and on. And so he's going on and there's profanity coming out of his mouth and "you know this" and I'm just sitting listening to the guy. He says, "Now what do you do?" I said, "Well I'm a preacher." Now listen as soon as I said that, he said, "Oh man praise God you are a preacher." Not kidding. He said, "You know what I'm part of this church in New York, I've been born again. Hey listen I've got a tract for you because I'm in this motorcycle group. You know we're all born again and we all go around we witness to people and I want you to have this tract." He's going on and on and I'm thinking how about the Island girls, let's talk about that. Obviously he had reduced Jesus down to an image and I don't think it was the one at the right hand of the Father. Now that's an extreme example.

This is why Jesus said you'd know them by their fruits. So you can see the way to really know God intimately is to have holy fear because that's when He reveals Himself and if we don't have the fear of the Lord then we've got an image of Jesus that is shaped in our own soul and in many times shaped

Lesson Five

by what society perceives Him to be.

So let me read this: when we lose the fear of the Lord we lessen our spiritual common sense for even a blatant sinner knows God is aware of his rebellion. Isn't that amazing? I mean some of the people I've met; sinners have got more fear of God than some people in church. Now watch this: those with the knowledge of God apart from His holy fear comfort themselves with this, Ezekiel 9:9. Are you ready for this? The Lord doesn't see it and if He does see it surely He understands. Now look at this. Even leaders are not exempt from this because God says this in Ezekiel 8:12, *"Son of man, have you seen what the elders (leaders) of the house of Israel do?"* They are saying the Lord does not see us. So you see what happens? They just think that God in their actual deep subconscious is just like another human being. I can hide this from God.

Go with me to James 1:22, I want to show you something. James 1:22, remember the manifestation of the fear of the Lord is to instantly obey? We tremble at His word. We love what He loves and we hate what He hates. James chapter 1 verse 22 we read this, *"But be doers of the word and not hearers only,* (watch this) *deceiving yourselves."* Now there is only one problem with deception, you know what it is? It's deceiving. That's the only problem with deception. A person who is deceived believes with all their heart they are right when in all reality they are wrong. They believe with all their heart that they are obedient when in reality they are in disobedience. How many of you remember King Saul? King Saul was told by the prophet– I want you to go utterly destroy all of the Amalekites. But he takes his armies and he goes, I mean it is not blatant rebellion, he just takes his armies and goes to kill tens of thousands of men, women and children but he saves one person the king because he wanted a trophy, a living trophy, in his palace and he saved some of the best sheep so that he can get favor with the people. Samuel comes out to the battle scene the next day. Saul runs up to Samuel and says, "Praise God Samuel: this is his exact quote, *"I will obey the commandment of the Lord."* Yet God the night before said to Samuel I regret that I set up Saul as king because he has turned back from obeying Me and has not performed My commandments. Now what has happened here? There is a deception. Saul believes he has really obeyed when in reality he hasn't. This is what happens when you lose the fear of the Lord– self-deception begins. Now this is one level of problem, but it will lead to the next level of deception, which is even worse.

The next level of deception is when God will actually give us what we want even if it's not His will. Did you get that? Go with me to Ezekiel the 14th chapter and I'm going to show you something and if this doesn't put the fear of God in you I don't know what will. Ezekiel the 14th chapter. Now remember James says if you don't obey the Word you deceive your own self. Self-deception is a very sobering thing. Ezekiel the 14th chapter, let's read from verse 1, *"Now some of the elders of Israel came to me and sat before me. And the Word of the Lord came to me, saying,* (now this is verse 3, Ezekiel 14) *Son of man, these men have set up their idols in their hearts."* What is interesting is, remember idols were usually something that were like statues or something else? But God doesn't say that here. In this book He says they've set up idols in their heart. *"And put before them that which causes them to stumble into iniquity."* Remember iniquity, it is an offense whether it is intentional or not against God. Then God says, *"Should I let Myself be inquired of at all by them?"* First of all let's talk about idolatry. Idolatry is not something we talk about much today because we really don't have a bunch of statues around here in America. In the New Testament Paul defines the root of all idolatry.

Colossians chapter 3 verses 5 and 6, listen to the scripture, *"Therefore put to death your members which are on the earth: fornication, uncleanness, passion, evil desire, and covetousness, which is idolatry."* So Paul says right there that covetousness is idolatry. If you want a definition of idolatry, it's covetousness. Now what is covetousness? Webster's defines it as this: a strong desire of obtaining and possessing some supposed good. Now I went to the Lord in prayer about this and I said God what is your definition of covetousness? As soon as I asked He spoke to my heart and He said, "John, covetousness is the desire for gain" What does the Bible say? Be content with such things that you have. Isn't that right because the Lord said I will never leave you nor forsake you. So covetousness is when we passionately desire something to gain. Now these men are coming to Ezekiel and they've got covetousness in their heart, a desire for gain.

Now listen to me. If you want to have intimacy with God there is something that you are going to have to understand: whenever you come to Him, your heart has got to be neutral. If you are leaning one way, like if you go to the Lord and say "should I do this", if you are leaning real strong that way, do you see the desire and the passion you have for gain rather than the passion you have to fulfill his will? Because let me tell you something the person who fears God has the heart to fear God, the desire to fulfill His wishes. Now I know this is heavy. The first four lessons were absolutely wonderful but you know what, I find that you have to get into this, in order to get people real intimacy. I'm like Lord, why are there so many Americas who are not telling people this? Folks we've got to talk about this, why aren't we telling people this? Because look what God says. Are you ready for this?

Look at verse 4 (Ezekiel 14), *"Therefore speak to them, and say to them, 'Thus says the Lord God: Everyone of the house of Israel who sets up his idols in his heart, and puts before him what causes him to stumble into iniquity, and then comes to the prophet, I the Lord will answer him who comes, according to the multitude of his idols."* Now can I read it to you out of another translation? In the New American Standard this is what God says, *"The Lord who will be brought to give him an answer in the matter and the view of the multitude of his idols."* It could read this way, *"I the Lord will be brought to give him an answer in the matter according to his covetousness desire."*

How about Balaam, remember Balaam? God tells Balaam clearly it's not My will. You shall not go when those guys come, and remember when they came from the King of Moab? The King of Moab sent messengers and said "Balaam could you come curse Israel". The first time they came, God said clearly you shall not go with them and you shall not curse the people. Then several weeks later he sends back more delegates with more honor and a lot more money. How many of you know Balaam wants that money because he likes it? So Balaam says hey guys let me pray about it again. So he goes and prays and you know what God says– not the devil– God. God says if the men come to call you, which they are going to do, the next morning you should rise and go with them. So God tells him now to go with them and the next morning he does exactly what God told him he could do the night before and now God is angry just because he is going. God gave Balaam what he wanted; he answered him according to the multitude of the idols that were in his heart, which was his covetousness for finances. God said, not the devil, it doesn't say a deceiving spirit came to him.

If you look in the books of the Kings over there (I don't know if its Chronicles or Kings, I think its Kings) you find out that King Ahab who was very covetousness wanted to go off and battle and he asked all the prophets of Israel "should I go" and everyone of them said, "Go." And then there was this real prophet and he said I don't like this guy because he always tells me the truth. His name was Micaiah and Micaiah came out and said you know what, you're going to be slaughtered. See all those prophets were giving him the answer according to the multitude of idols in his heart. But then Micaiah gave him the opportunity to get the real word of God. So this is what God says will happen: if you come to the place where you have such strong covetousness in your heart, He says I'll give you what you want. That is why it is so important, I always check my heart before I go before the Lord and I say, "Lord what is it you want me to do?" I make sure my heart is neutral and if it isn't neutral I start praying to God would you please make it neutral because how many of you know we can only do it by His grace? And I say Lord please deal with me, just root this thing out, root any kind of desire I have for my own personal gain. Root it out so that I can come and hear what Your wish and

Lesson Five

Your desire is. Jesus said so much about coming and following Him is denying yourself and taking up your cross and following Me. That speaks of death and your own desires. That means we will live now to serve and fulfill His desires but when we do that, we gain His life. Now that's a good trade. You understand when Indians used to trade they said "good trade". You understand? That's a good trade because I didn't have a whole lot to give but He gave me everything He's got.

Now God wants to bless His people. What He doesn't want is to have the blessings have a grip or hold on His people. So this is where religion and legalism really messed up. You can have everything and not be covetous of it. So it's all a matter of the heart. Look at what the Lord goes on to say (Ezekiel 14), watch this verse 5 He says, *"That I may seize the house of Israel by their heart, because they are all estranged from Me by their idols."* Now I want to read it out of another translation. In the NIV, He says, *"I will do this to recapture the hearts of the people of Israel."* God's got a goal. Do you know why He says He'll do this? I'll answer you according to a multitude of the matters of your heart. The ultimate reason is I want to recapture your heart. When you see how futile your idolatry and your covetousness is, He's saying you'll let go of it and you will come back to My heart and realize that this is the only place you are going to find true satisfaction: is in the fear and the love of God and having intimacy with me and that is what you are looking for.

TRUE WORSHIP

Video Session 6

TRUE WORSHIP

Key Statement:
Through intimacy with God, we are empowered to live a life of true worship.

1. God wants us not only to _obey_ but also to have the heart to _fulfill God's will_. We see this _repeatedly_ in the lives of those who walk with God.

2. Who were the three Old Testament saints John used as examples of those who walked in the fear of the Lord and obeyed Him?

- Enoch
- Noah
- David

3. _Enoch_ walked with God and he was _not_.

4. _Noah_ knew the _secret_ that God would destroy the earth with a flood. The rest of the world was unaware of it.

5. _David_ was a man after God's _own heart_ who would do all of _God's will_.

6. The fear of the Lord is not only when you _obey_, but also when you fulfill God's will completely and seek to _carry out His wishes_ as if they _were your own_.

LEADER'S NOTES

(3–5 minutes)

Remind the group of a few key lessons by referring to these statements:

1. Intimacy with God is available to each one of us. This is God's passion.

2. Recap last week's session with this statement: Deception awaits those who lack the fear of the Lord, intimacy awaits those who draw near in holy fear.

Set this session up with the Key Statement. Then go through the questions, asking for and providing the answers.

Lesson Six

Leader's Notes

A Religious Spirit vs. True Worship...

7. A religious spirit is one who uses God's Word to execute _his own will_. He does not carry out _God's Word_ with God's heart and interests but uses God's words to carry out _his own passions_ and _own interests_.

A religious spirit is the antithesis of the lives of men and women such as Abraham, Moses, Joshua, David, Esther, Daniel, and others who walked closely with the Lord.

8. What was the common denominator among those who walked in intimacy with God?

The very core of their intimacy with God is a genuine heart felt obedience to His desires.

9. What scripture verse in Jeremiah was God's cry to every person in the Old Testament that He had a covenant relationship with?

Jeremiah 11:7, "For I earnestly exhorted your fathers in the day I brought them up out of the land of Egypt, until this day, rising early and exhorting, saying, 'Obey My voice.'"

Have a volunteer read the scripture and then go over the following True and False questions.

"But the hour is coming, and now is, when the true worshippers will worship the Father in spirit and truth; for the Father is seeking such to worship Him. God is Spirit, and those who worship Him must worship in spirit and truth."
John 4:23–24

TRUE WORSHIP

LEADER'S NOTES

10. [x]True or [ ]False: God is seeking true worshippers.

11. [ ]True or [x]False: True worship is slow, beautiful church music.

"And Abraham said to his young men, 'Stay here with the donkey; the lad and I will go yonder and worship, and we will come back to you.'"
Genesis 22:5

12. [ ]True or [x]False: When Abraham went up the mountain to worship God, he was going there to sing songs of worship.

13. [x]True or [ ]False: When Abraham went up the mountain to worship God, he was going there to put the most important person in his life to death.

14. [x]True or [ ]False: True worship is a life of obedience.

15. [x]True or [ ]False: The first occurrence of worship in the Bible is Abraham going to sacrifice Isaac.

16. Do you remember? What was the other "first" that happened in the Bible as a result of Abraham's obedience to God? *(Hint: It was in an earlier lesson.)* God revealed Himself as Jehovah-Jireh, The Lord Who Provides.

Away with your hymns of praise! They are only noise to my ears. I will not listen to your music, no matter how lovely it is. Instead, I want to see a mighty flood of justice, a river of righteous living that will never run dry."
Amos 5:23–24, NLT

Lesson Six

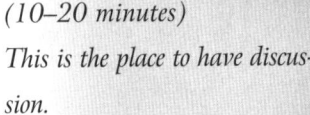

Leader's Notes

(10–20 minutes)
This is the place to have discussion.

• Ask a few volunteers to share their thoughts about this startling verse and about John's statement in the grey box.

• Before they give their answer, ask them questions 17-19.

If we are not living a lifestyle of obedience in the fear of God, our praise and worship songs and services can actually repulse God rather than bless Him. We look religious during church services, yet our hearts and lifestyles can be far from God.

17. Have you ever seen this verse (Amos 5:23) in the scriptures before?

Many of you have probably read or heard this scripture quoted, but not in the light that John has talked about it.

18. If so, did you ever think of it like this before?
The answers may be varied: yes, no or maybe.

19. Does this verse surprise you when you realize that God can be displeased with our church services and worship music?
The answers may be varied: yes, no or maybe.

20. Now that you see these truths, how does it change the way you think about what it means to worship God?

Chances are few people have actually encountered this verse, let alone thought about the way it is presented here.

TRUE WORTHIP

LEADER'S NOTES

He (God) said, "Son, I have these children that all week long I'm trying to get their attention. 'Hey, your neighbor needs help right now; you need to go over.' And they ignore Me. 'I'm busy, I'm busy,' and they suppress Me." He said, "I'll put in their hearts to witness to the person working next to them, at the perfect time, and they'll go, 'Yeah, yeah,' and they ignore Me. I'll tell them to give so much in an offering, and they'll go, 'Uh well, uh.' And they do this all week. Then they come into a service, and they want something out of me, mainly blessings. And they start saying, 'I love You, Lord.' And they call that worship." He said, "That is not worship; it's a slow song!"

—John Bevere

21. Do you find it inspiring or frightening that God looks to our whole life as an act of worship?

If they find it inspiring, ask why. Here are some sample examples:

- It gives you a goal to shoot for as you seek God.
- You are excited about what the Holy Spirit is showing you in your life to worship Him more actively and accurately.
- It is something new that you have learned, and you are excited to meditate and pray about.

• Once they have given their answers, ask them questions 21 and 22.

• The idea here is to get your group's heart and mind engaged in this highly relevant subject. You are trying to get them involved with this truth. Be sympathetic to people's answers, as this may be a brand-new concept to most of the group. Go through these questions, asking the Holy Spirit to encourage people through the discussion.

Lesson Six

Leader's Notes

If they find it frightening, ask why. Here are some sample examples:

- *It is strange and feels like a new set of rules.*
- *Now that you know about it, you actually have to seek to live it.*
- *It's just too hard. It's easier to tell yourself you can just go to church, sing a few songs, and call it worshiping God.*

Throughout your discussion of the above questions, be sure to constantly remind people:

- *This journey—intimacy with God—is not about rules or mechanical processes.*

- *Truth never brings bondage; it sets us free. The idea expressed here, namely that worship is a lifestyle not just once-a-week church attendance, will be daunting to many people.*

- *Make sure you drive home the point, the power to live a lifestyle of worship is more than an act of our will. It is through intimacy with God that He empowers us to please Him with our lives.*

22. Beyond what you think, what are some specific ways this truth will change the way you actually live your life?

Sample answers:

- *Instead of "just going to church" and calling it worship, I realize now that everything I do is to be an act of worship.*
- *God is omniscient and omnipresent. He knows everything and is everywhere, so He knows and sees all that I do, whether it really is a life of worship or not.*
- *It makes me more God-conscious. It makes me want to honor Him in all I do and not just in church services.*
- *It makes me want to pray and study more so I can be sure that God is pleased with my life and worship.*

Key Statement:
A heart of spirit and truth.

"Little children, let us not love [merely] in theory or in speech but in deed and in truth (in practice and in sincerity)."
1 John 3:18, AMP

TRUE WORSHIP

LEADER'S NOTES

"THEOLOGY 101"

God is looking for those who worship Him in spirit and truth (John 4:23–24). The ancient word for *truth* here (*aletheia*) signifies "the reality lying at the basis of an appearance; the manifested veritable essence of a matter." This cuts through appearances and shows us that true worship is found at the base level of a human being, which is the heart.

One level of communication is our words. However, a lifestyle of true worship will not only talk about serving God, but there will be action as well. We show our faith in part by our good works.

"And though I bestow all my goods to feed the poor, and though I give my body to be burned, and have not love, it profits me nothing."
I Corinthians 13:3

Action is a higher level than mere words when it comes to communicating our faith, yet our outward actions can be deceiving. We can perform glorious deeds with no love in our heart.

"If you are willing and obedient, you shall eat the good of the land."
Isaiah 1:19

Lesson Six

Leader's Notes

23. Notice this does not say if you are obedient, you will eat the good of the land. Willingness is also required and deals with your _attitude_. God says your _heart_ has to be in your obedience. This keeps you from _deception_.

The highest level of communication is the heart. This is what Jesus refers to as truth.

Key Statement:
When we are gut-level honest with the Lord, He will draw near.

"For the word of God is living and powerful, and sharper than any two-edged sword, piercing even to the division of soul and spirit, and of joints and marrow, and is a discerner of the thoughts and intents of the heart."
Hebrews 4:12

John uses an example from his own life of how God showed him that his thoughts, words and deeds needed an attitude adjustment. John was proud of the fact that God had shown him to stop complaining. But though he had stopped talking about his complaints, he was still complaining inwardly in his heart. God cut to the heart of the matter as He revealed this to John, and he repented.

John goes on to quote Psalm 62:8, *"Trust in Him at all times, you people; pour out your heart before Him; God is a refuge for us,"* and explains how God is seeking transparency in our worship. God wants us to come to Him and pour out our hearts in open honesty so He can work in us to accomplish His will. This results in a life of true worship.

TRUE WORSHIP

24. Can you think of times the Lord has blessed and challenged you in a similar way?

_____
_____
_____

LEADER'S NOTES

25. Gut-check time. Be humble, honest, and willing to let God search the thoughts and intents of your heart here. What things might you be saying and even doing that seem good and right, but when you really examine them with the help of the Holy Spirit and God's Word, they don't proceed out of a willing and obedient heart?

_____
_____
_____

Key Statement:
It all comes down to being willingly obedient.

"A little while longer and the world will see Me no more, but you will see Me. Because I live, you will live also. At that day you will know that I am in My Father, and you in Me, and I in you. He who has My commandments and keeps them, it is he who loves Me. And he who loves Me will be loved by My Father, and I will love him and manifest Myself to him."
John 14:19–21

26. To manifest means to bring out of the unseen into the _____seen_____, _the unheard_ into the _____heard_____, _the unknown_ into the _____known_____.

LESSON SIX

LEADER'S NOTES

27. It is when the Lord reveals Himself to our _____senses_____ and our _____mind_____.

Look at verse 21 in the Amplified translation (below). Then take John 14:19–21 with you into prayer and mediation. Journal what the Lord shows you about it for your life, personally.

"The person who has my commandments and keeps them is the one who [really] loves Me, and whoever [really] loves Me will be loved by My Father, and I [too] will love him and will show (reveal, manifest) Myself to him. [I will let Myself be clearly seen by him and make Myself real to him.]"
John 14:21, AMP

(10 minutes)

Ask for volunteers to share from their journaling if they are comfortable. If no one volunteers, that is no problem as this is very personal. Simply share from your own if you would like, or skip the question and encourage them to keep pressing into God.

28. Here's some help: Do you have His commandments? Do you know His Word? Do you keep His commandments? Are you trying to follow a set of rules, or do you keep His Word through the power of the Holy Spirit? Does Jesus manifest Himself to you? In what ways? What fruit is in your life in relation to this scripture?

_____
_____
_____
_____
_____

"Even so, every good tree bears good fruit, but a bad tree bears bad fruit. A good tree cannot bear bad fruit, nor can a bad tree bear good fruit. Every tree that does not bear good fruit is cut down and thrown into the fire."
Matthew 7:17–19

TRUE WORSHIP

"Either make the tree good and its fruit good, or else make the tree bad and its fruit bad; for a tree is known by its fruit."
Matthew 12:33

"But he who received seed on the good ground is he who hears the word and understands it, who indeed bears fruit and produces: some a hundredfold, some sixty, some thirty."
Matthew 13:23

29. Jesus said you would know a tree by its fruit. What does this mean?

Although people say all the time "God knows my heart," Jesus told us it was the fruit of a person's life that tells us what's really in a person's heart. Godly character and the fruit of the Spirit must be evident.

30. What fruit of your relationship with God do you have in your life?

Sample answers:
- *Peace, godly joy, and contentment*
- *Faithful tithing*
- *Keeping your thoughts pure*
- *Faithful service in the local church*

"But the fruit of the Spirit is love, joy, peace, long suffering, kindness, goodness, faithfulness, gentleness, self-control. Against such there is no law. And those who are Christ's have crucified the flesh with its passions and desires. If we live in the Spirit, let us also walk in the Spirit. Let us not become conceited, provoking one another, envying one another."
Galatians 5:22–26

LEADER'S NOTES

Lesson Six

Leader's Notes

Remind your group:

1. They should preview the next session and complete the personal discussion portions in their workbooks. If they would like, they may complete the entire section.

2. Pray for the group before they leave. They may divide into groups and can pray for each other. Be led by the Spirit, but keep the focus on things that God may have brought to light from today's teaching.

To finish the session, read the key statement aloud. Then have the group boldly read it with you.

Here is the classic Bible verse about good fruit. Remember, these are not just hollow words to be mentally assented to. Each of these words depicts a lifestyle that flows in intimacy with God. You can't just say you have love or joy; rather, love and joy and the other fruit are evident in your lifestyle.

31. What are some ways you might plant the seed of God's Word in your heart so He can search your heart and you can bring forth more good fruit?

Sample answers:

Regular devotions, Bible study (2 Tim. 2:15), etc.

"You don't have to drill a hole into the heart of a tree to know if its fruit is good or not. They can say all day long 'But God knows my heart,' but Jesus says look at their fruits."

—John Bevere

Key Statement:
Good fruit grows from those who draw near to Him in a life of willing obedience.

Video Script for Lesson 6
TRUE WORSHIP

Welcome back to the sixth lesson of Drawing Near life of intimacy with God. Tonight we are going to talk about true worship. I want you to open your Bibles with me tonight to John's gospel chapter 4 and we're going to have some fun, John's gospel the 4th chapter. Now, while you're doing that let me read this to you. We found out in the last lesson that deception awaits those who lack the fear of the Lord. You saw how Balaam was deceived and how Saul was deceived. Deception awaits those who lack the fear of the Lord while intimacy awaits those who draw near in holy fear. It gets me excited right there. Our evidence of this is unconditional obedience to the desires of God. Not only do we obey, but also we have the heart to fulfill His will. We see this repeatedly in the lives of those that walked with God. Who is the first person that we talked about after Adam that walked with God? It was Enoch. Now how many of you know in the Bible that it only says Enoch walked with God, and he had this testimony to please God. Why did he please God? To get a little more insight into Enoch we have to go back to the early church fathers.

There was a man named Clement of Rome, he was a companion of the apostle Paul. Clement of Rome was a very great man of God and he wrote in his writings, "Let us take for instance Enoch, who being sound, righteous in obedience was translated and death was never known to happen to him." So we can see the earmark of what pleased God was Enoch's obedience to the Lord.

What about Noah? Noah was the next man who walked with God. Remember the secret of God: destroying the earth with the flood was kept between Him and Noah for years and the rest of the world was unaware of it. What was the story of Noah? Out of the new living translation of Genesis chapter 6, verse 9 and 10 says this, *"This is the history of Noah and his family, Noah was a righteous man, the only blameless man living on the earth at the time. He consistently followed God's will and enjoyed a close relationship with him."* That's the new living translation. So you see Enoch and Noah, the earmark of their close walk with God was a life of obedience. Now, this is the antithesis of Balaam. Isn't that true? Balaam did not have the heart to obey God. If you look at David he was the man after God's heart. He was so close and intimate with the Lord he surpassed what any king did in his relationship with God and the fact that he moved into the prophetic. Listen to David's testimony. Acts 13:22, *"And when He had removed him, He raised up for them David as king, to whom also He gave testimony and said, 'I have found David the son of Jesse, a man after My own heart, who will do all My will.'"* So the fear of the Lord is when we not only obey but we fulfill all His will– we seek to carry out His wishes as if they were our own.

I'll never forget when I was in Canada. I was at a very large church and I was on the front row worshiping God. All of a sudden the Spirit of God asked me a question. Now I have learned that when God asks you a question He is not looking for information, okay? God will ask you a question because you don't know the answer. So all of a sudden the Spirit of God came on me in worship and He said, "Son do you know what a religious spirit is?" God was not looking for me to go, "Yeah it's this and this and this." When God said to me– do you know what a religious spirit is– I realized that even though I've written on it, I've preached on it, heard other people preach on it and read other people's writings on it, I didn't know what a religious spirit was. So as soon as the Lord said that, and here is a good hint for you, any time the Lord asks you something like that just say "no I don't know." So I said Lord I obviously don't know. What is a religious spirit? And I heard the Holy Spirit say this so quickly. He said a religious spirit is one who uses My word to execute his own will. He does not carry out My Word with My heart and interests.

LESSON SIX

He'll use his words to carry out his own passions and own interests. That's what Saul did. Saul went and attacked the Amalekites but he saved the best king alive and he saved the best animals so that they could offer them up to the Lord, but he's doing it all for his best interest and not for the heart God.

So this riveted me. If you examine the lives of Abraham, Moses, Joshua, David, Esther, Daniel and others in scripture who walked close with the Lord you find this common denominator in all of their lives folks, and that is this: in the very core of their intimacy with God was a genuine heartfelt obedience to His desires. God's cry to every person He has a covenant relationship in the Old Testament is this, Jeremiah 11:7 *"For I earnestly exhorted your fathers in the day I brought them up out of the land of Egypt, until this day, rising early and exhorting, saying, 'Obey My voice'."* This is what He said to them constantly– non-stop ever since the beginning– since He delivered them out of Egypt.

Now, in the New Testament Jesus tells us something most interesting. John 4 verse 23 Jesus says, *"But the hour is coming, and now is, when the true worshippers will worship the Father in spirit and truth: for the Father is seeking such to worship Him."* I'll never forget the time I was reading my Bible early in the morning and the Holy Spirit literally came on me and He screamed this in the inside of me. He didn't whisper He screamed. He said, "Son do you know what worship is?" And then he said this, "Worship is not a slow song." Now for those of you who aren't catching this, in case you haven't recognized, we have a charismatic bulletin. The method is they print theirs out; we memorized ours. We come into service and we have praise and then worship; for those of you who don't know the difference, praise is the fast ones and worship is the slow one.

This is my concept of worship: a slow song. And the Lord just nailed me. He said, "Son, worship is not a slow song." So I said Lord, you know I obviously do not know what worship is, what is it? I pushed my Bible back and I said what is it? And the Holy Spirit said, "It's a life" and then all of a sudden He starts using Lisa as an example. He says, "Son you get up at six o'clock in the morning and Lisa says, "Hey babe I need your help. I'm late getting the kids ready so can you help me get the kids ready?" " Oh, honey I'm really busy I've got some stuff to do, no no, I really can't help you." Then at nine o'clock she said, "Can you do this for me John? I really need you to go get me a Starbucks' coffee– I need to wake up this morning. Can you do this? "No babe, I'm busy, I'm sorry I can't do that." At twelve o'clock she says, "Honey, can you have lunch with me? I really want to spend some time with you" "Babe, I'm sorry." Three-thirty, "Honey can you go pick up the kids from school I really have so much going on?" "Oh babe, I'm sorry I really have something else I want to do." Five o'clock, "Can you help me get dinner ready?" "You know what, I really, really, really can't do it." She said after dinner, "Can you help me clean the kitchen up?" "You know babe I just can't." Then nine o'clock at night comes and you want something out of her, mainly sex. And you approach her and you go "Oh honey, I love you so much." He said, "What will she say to you?" I said, "She will say hit the road Jack." And then the Lord said, "And rightfully so. "He said why would she say that? I said because lovemaking began at six o'clock in the morning it just climaxed with the intercourse at night. He said that's right. He said, "Son I have these children and all week long I'm trying to get their attention. Your neighbor needs help right now, you need to go over, and they ignore Me. I'm busy, I'm busy and they suppress Me. He said I'll put in their hearts to witness to the person working next to them at the perfect time and they'll go "yeah, yeah" and they ignore Me. I'll tell them to give so much in an offering and they'll go, "well, huh". They do this all week and then they come into a service and they want something out of Me-- mainly blessings. They start saying "I love you Lord" and they call that worship. He said that is not worship, it's not a slow song!

Now let me make this clear. Go to the first place you find worship in the Bible. It is in Genesis 22. Now as an author I've learned something: whenev-

112

er I introduce a new term that somebody is not familiar with I've got to do one, two or three things– either define it when I introduce it, give an illustration that shows what it means or give an example that gives its definition in the example. If you go to Genesis 22 you'll find the first place you find worship in the Bible when Abraham looks at his servants and says Isaac and I are going up to that mountain and we're going to worship. I've got news for you; he is not going up there to sing a slow song. He was going up there to put the most important person in his life to death just because God said to do it. So it was obedience. So true worship is a life of obedience. That's why God said in the book of Amos, and this is out of the New Living Translation, chapter 5, verse 23 and 24, *"Away with your hymns of praise there are only noise in my ear, I will not listen to your music no matter how lovely it is and instead I want to see mighty flooded judgement, a river of righteous living that will never run dry."*

I was just at Hillsong two weeks ago preaching for Hillsong Church. Darlene Zschech has been a friend for a few years and three years ago when I first met Darlene, she and I, Lisa and her husband sat down and I said, "Darlene, I've got a question for you. How come I can go into a church and it's really tough to preach in that church, it's tough to minister in that church but they've got great praise and worship? They're musicians are wonderful and they're singers are great but then you get up and you preach on obedience you get a bunch of repents. You come back the next night and it's the same worshippers, the same songs and the presence of God. The place is like crazy." I said, "Have you discovered that? She said, "Absolutely. That's why sometimes in our practices we're on our face before God because the way I stress to all my team is a life of obedience and a life of true Christianity."

So that's why God said I don't want to hear your songs when you're not walking with righteous living because true worship is a life of obedience. Let's look at what Jesus says, *" But the hour is coming, when the true worshippers will worship the Father in spirit and truth; for the Father is seeking such to worship Him."* Now look at verse 24, *"God is Spirit, and those that worship Him must worship in spirit and in truth."* God said you've got to worship Me in spirit and in truth. We're going to talk about spirit a whole lot in the next coming lessons. In the later lessons in this series I want to talk about truth.

The word truth is the Greek word Aletheia. W. E.Vines defines it so beautifully. He says that Greek word means this: signifying the reality lying at the basis of an appearance, the manifested veritable essence of a matter. So what Vines is saying here is that true worship is found at the base level of the human being, which is the heart. True worship is found in the base level of human being, which is the heart. Now to understand what he is saying I've got to explain to you that there are three levels of communication. The first level and it is the lowest level is verbal. How do we know it's verbal? Look at Jesus' parable of the two sons. The father says to his two sons to go out and work my vineyards. The first son goes, "No way" but later on regrets it and goes out and does it. The second son says, "Sure dad I'll go work in your vineyards" but he doesn't do it. Jesus said which one did the will of his father? It wasn't the son who went okay I'll do it and didn't do it. It was the one that went no and ended up doing it. Why: because actions are a much higher form of communication than words. That is why we read in the book of James chapter 2 verse 15 and 16: suppose you see a brother or sister who need food and clothing and you say, "Well, goodbye and God bless you, stay warm and eat well, but then you don't give that person any food or clothing. What good does that do?" So again James says, "Well, God bless you, I love you but there is no love of God in your heart when you don't give him what he needs" because your actions spoke louder than your words. This is also what we find in 1 John 3:17. We read, *"But whoever has this world's goods, and sees his brother in need, and shuts up his heart from him, how does the love of God abide in him?"* In other words it's saying, you know a brother but if you don't give him what he needs your actions spoke much, much louder than your words. I really don't love you because actions are a higher form of communication than words.

Lesson Six

The Amplified Bible reads it like this, *"Little children let us not love merely in speech but in deed and truth."* So it talks about deeds. Now let me say this: actions, even though they are a higher level of communication than words, are not the highest level of communication because the highest level of communications is the heart. Corinthians says if I give my body to be burned and I give all my goods to feed the poor but I have not love that profits me nothing. Now listen, those actions– giving your body to be burned, giving everything you own to feed the poor– those certainly are very noble actions that would display love but Paul said you can give everything you've got to the poor and even give your body to be burned yet still not have love, which means you don't have it in your heart. That's the base level of a human being: the heart level. That's why a husband can do everything in the natural– could appear that he loves his wife but his wife knows deep down there's something wrong. He's got a mistress on the side. Every single time that has happened, you talk to a woman and she'll say, "I knew it, I just knew it deep down." Why, because she was picking up on the heart level of communication. She knew even when he was giving her nice gifts and saying nice things that it wasn't there. That's the highest level of communication: the base level of a human being. This is where Jesus said we worship the Father– that's the heart level. That's what John and Jesus both talked about, because John said little children let us not love merely in speech (speech being the lowest) but in deed (the next level) and in truth, the heart level.

The thoughts and the intents of the heart reveal the truth of our worship yet they cannot be discerned outside the Word of God. Let me say this, I believe God gave a prophetic scripture as well. It was something He required and the Old Testament saints really had a hard time with it but it's really speaking more to us than the Old Testament. God said to His people, if you are willing and obedient you would eat the good of the land. Notice He does not say if you are obedient each of you will get the land. Willingness deals with your attitude. God says your heart has to be in your obedience. That keeps you from deception. Saul was deceived; he really believed he obeyed but yet his heart wasn't in it. His heart was really for himself. You really want to know the difference between a believer and a non-believer? The real believer is selfless; the non-believer is selfish. An imposter in the church is one who serves only himself. You will notice it in the book of Jude that Jude says there will be impostors coming among us in the last days, that they have both been saved by the grace of God yet they feast among us but only serve themselves. That's a heart level thing. So God says if you are willing and obedient you will eat the good of the land.

God is always dealing with hard issues. That's why in the book of Philippians chapter 2 it says God is at work within you both to will and to do of His good pleasure. Willing deals with your heart. Let me just give you a personal example because this is what God is dealing with me about constantly. Sometimes people say, "You know John Bevere you preach a lot on hard issues." Well the reason I do is because God nails me and after God nails me I figure I should just nail you. Why does God nail us? Because He loves us. So when ever God deals with you and corrects you like that, you can just go, " Praise God, I'm His child because the person who does not feel that correction is a person who is not legitimately His child. That's why you need to rejoice whenever somebody is preaching the word of God and it goes right into your heart because only the Word of God can discern the thoughts and intents of the heart. Remember what I said to you earlier in one of the lessons: I said why does God hate complaining. Why does He hate complaining? Because it says to God: I don't like what You are doing in my life and if I were You I'd do it differently. It's a slam on His character and it's a lack of the fear of the Lord.

So I got to this place a few years ago where I made it a point not to complain. I cut my complaining out and I did not complain with my mouth. It is almost to the point where I was proud. One morning I was in this extended time where I was alone with the Lord in the mountains of Georgia and I wake up and I hear the Holy Spirit shout this on the inside of me: "I hear the complaining in your

heart". I just collapsed out of the bed. I'm just like, God forgive me because God is always dealing with us at the base level. Some people won't let Him deal with them at the base level. Let me tell you something: every decision of life should be made at the base level. You will have a choice. Ananias and Sapphira made a decision out of appearance. Remember we learned that this morning. They wanted to appear to giving it all. They did not make a decision based on the base level– they feared men more than they feared God. The fear of man is a trap– it is a snare and it will destroy you. It will cut off your intimacy with God because the only worshippers the Father is seeking are those who worship Him in spirit and truth. They worship and live for Him at the base level.

That's why when I go out to pray some mornings and I'm just sitting there praying away and praying, the heavens are just brass and all of a sudden I get gut-level and go "Lord, I'm really sorry. I was really ugly to Lisa last night; Jesus I'm so sorry" and then all of a sudden there He is. As soon as I got honest and gut level there He is. Anytime I go in there under pretense with the Lord forget it, heaven is just brass. I mean sometimes I have to get gut level honest– I've done this, I've done that, I've not done this, I've not done what You told me to do– I'm so sorry. And there He is. The Bible says in Psalms 62:8, *"Trust in Him at all times, you people; Pour out your heart before Him; God is a refuge for us."* What does pour out your heart mean? He's saying when you come to Me, pour out your heart and don't cover anything up; speak to Me from the base level of your heart. Live your life from the base level of your heart. If you do that you'll be successful with God.

Do you remember when John the Baptist was born? What did the angel say? He (John) shall be great in the sight of the Lord. It is one thing to be great in the sight of men it is another thing to be great in the sight of God. You can be great in the sight of men even in the church but not be great in the sight of God. How do you get great in the sight of God? By the integrity of your heart. You see, that's why I love Pastor Rob because he teaches entirely on integrity. Pastor Rob could have built a massive, massive church if he just eased up a little but he chose not to because he said I'm going to be honest with people and one day I'm going to face the Lord and I don't want their blood on my hands. Every good pastor or preacher says that. I said that one time. I was in Canada preaching to a bunch of people and preachers were there and I said "you know what, I'm going to tell the truth because I don't want people's blood on my hands. I don't want them to look at me at judgment screaming 'why didn't you tell me!'" And this pastor came up to me irate and said how dare you put that guilt trip on us. I said "guilt trip". Would you read this please and I opened up the Bible to the book of Acts to what Paul says, "I have not shunned and cleared you the entire gospel therefore I am innocent of the blood of all men." The man's a pastor and he says he's never seen that. I said yes sir, it's in there and then he softened and we had a very good conversation after that. Serve them from the base level and really love people.

I sometimes come with this cutting and I realize that's part of the call in my life. One time I'm at my tape table, a guy walks up to me and says I'm called to the ministry you're called to and I felt this "thing" on the inside of me and I thought something's really wrong here. I looked at the man and said you know how you are being prophetic? He said yeah and he's like ooh I'm going to get a revelation here. I said this is how you know you're being prophetic– the whole time you're bringing correction, rebuke or hard words– your heart is absolutely breaking because you love the people so much. And he looked at me and he goes, "God's got a little work to do in me." I said you took the biggest step right there because at least you know it. I went through nine years of training before God released me for what I've been doing in the last fifteen years. The thing the Lord told me was, "Son, before I released you for what I've called you to I've got to root you in My love so that you will always know that you are loving My people, that the motive of what you are saying is out of love.

Let's go to John's gospel the 14th chapter and we'll

Lesson Six

wrap up this session. John 14:19 says, *"A little while longer and the world will see Me no more, but you will see Me. Because I live, you will live also."* Now when He says you will see Me it means He is going to manifest Himself. Manifest means to bring out of the unseen into the seen, unheard into the heard, unknown into the known. It's when the Lord reveals Himself to our senses and our mind. Look at verse 20 and 21, *"At that day you will know that I am in My Father, and you in Me, and I in you. He who has My commandments and keeps them, it is he who loves Me. And he who loves Me will be loved by My Father, and I will love him and manifest Myself to him."* Now listen to this out of the Amplified Bible, *"The person who has My commands and keeps them is the one who [really] loves Me, and whoever [really] loves Me will be loved by My Father. And I [too] will love him and show (reveal, manifest) Myself to him– I will let Myself be clearly seen by him and let Myself be real to him."* Who is the one that Jesus said He would make Himself real to? The man that has His commandments and keeps them with His hearts passion and he fulfills His will. He does not use the word of God to execute his own desires such as Saul and Balaam did.

What does true worship really come down to? True worship comes down to a life of obedience. The apostle Paul in Romans 1:5 in the New International Version of the Bible says, *"Through Him and for His name's sake we received grace and apostleship. All people from among the Gentiles to the obedient that comes from faith."* True faith produces obedience and that's why James says show me your faith without your works and I'll show you I really have faith because I've got evidence. It's in obedience to the Master. When are we going to learn that Jesus said you're going to know them by their fruit? A good tree cannot produce bad fruit and a bad tree cannot produce good fruit. You don't have to drill a hole into the heart of a tree to tell if it's good or not. They can say all day long "but God knows my heart" but Jesus says to look at their fruit because out of the abundance of the heart is the base level. That is why you want the Word of God to be like a sword that discerns the thoughts and the intentions of your heart. Let Him do it. He's a skillful surgeon. He knows how to cut out, what will kill you, and leave you what you need.

WITH WHOM G

Video Session 7

WITH WHOM GOD DWELLS

Key Statement:
The power twins of the kingdom are the fear of the Lord and humility.

"But He gives more grace. Therefore He says: 'God resists the proud, but gives grace to the humble.' Therefore submit to God. Resist the devil and he will flee from you. Draw near to God and He will draw near to you. Cleanse your hands, you sinners; and purify your hearts, you double-minded. Lament and mourn and weep! Let your laughter be turned to mourning and your joy to gloom. Humble yourselves in the sight of the Lord, and He will lift you up."
James 4:6–10

1. This verse talks about believers who have gotten into the habitual patterns of disobedience because they lack the fear of the Lord. How can you break these habitual patterns of disobedience?

• *Submit to God*
• *Resist the devil and he will flee*
• *Cleanse your hands*
• *Purify your heart*

"For thus says the High and Lofty One who inhabits eternity, whose name is Holy: 'I dwell in the high and holy place, with him who has a contrite and humble spirit, to revive the spirit of the humble, and to revive the heart of the contrite ones.'"
Isaiah 57:15

LEADER'S

(3–5 minutes)

Remind the group of a few key lessons by referring to these statements:

1. Intimacy with God is available to each one of us. This is God's passion.

2. Recap last week's session with this statement: True worship is when we take His heart's desires on as our own.

Set this session up with the Key Statement. Then go through the questions, asking for and providing the answers.

Have a volunteer read Isaiah 57:15.

Leader's Notes

Ask for volunteers to share their answers. Consider writing down some of the answers, and then comparing them to what people have learned at the end of the lesson.

2. God is *not* looking for a place to visit. He is looking for a place to ___dwell___. God desires to dwell in those who have a ___contrite___ and ___humble___ spirit. Humility is ___essential___ if you are going to have ___intimacy___ with the Lord.

3. Before we continue the lesson, what is your definition of humility?
(Sample Answer) someone who doesn't brag, someone who is meek or mild-mannered, someone who doesn't make "waves."

4. Many in the body of Christ do not understand humility or the power associated with it. Humility is often viewed as being:
• *Weak*
• *Wimpy*
• *Soft Spoken*
• *Spineless*

"Likewise you younger people, submit yourselves to your elders. Yes, all of you be submissive to one another, and be clothed with humility, for 'God resists the proud, but gives grace to the humble.'"
<u>1 Peter 5:5</u>

Peter tells us to be clothed with humility. Humility is not a mystical word or a word that we can never know the meaning of. Further, it is essential that we understand what it means in order to have intimacy with God.

Key Statement:
God dwells with the humble.

5. What is the definition of humility? **First and foremost**, it is our ___instant obedience___ to God.

Abraham and Joseph are examples of men who had a dream from God. Their dreams took years to come to pass and were filled with seeming twists and turns. If they had not walked in humble obedience when God told them to do things they did not understand, their dreams would not have been fulfilled.

Oftentimes God will show you what to do in your life and then seem to throw a curve ball. He shows you the way you think it is going to go and then suddenly tells you to take a step in what seems to be the opposite direction. This is where true humility comes in.

6. True humility says I will obey God even __if it looks like I am going to destroy the very dream He told me I was going to__ fulfill.

"Trust in the LORD with all your heart, and lean not on your own understanding."
Proverbs 3:5

7. How have you seen this play out in your own life? What dreams have you had that God brought to pass because you humbly took a step of faith to obey Him even though you didn't understand?

_____
_____
_____
_____

8. Sometimes our God-given dreams happen almost in spite of ourselves. God will often perform His works on our behalf because He is good and is wooing us to learn to trust and obey Him. Can you look back in your life and see where this was ever the case?

(10 minutes)

For questions 7, 8 and 9, ask for volunteers to share and have an open discussion. Feel free to use your own examples to get things started.

LEADER'S NOTES

9. If so, what can you learn from the experience? (Perhaps you learned that the next time you should obey God instantly instead of waiting, or maybe you needed to learn to simply obey the Word and not your own desires.)

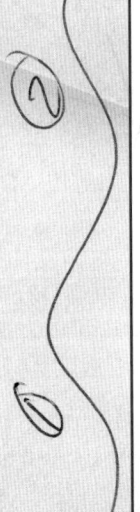

10. To walk in true humility means:
- I will ___obey___ even if I ___don't understand___.
- I will ___obey___ even if it looks like it's directly going against the ___goals___ that He placed in my ___heart___.
- Humility is my absolute and ___unconditional___ ___obedience___ to God.

11. In what ways did David show his humility and confidence in God?
- *David knew his ability came from God because it was the Lord who delivered him from the paws of the lion and the bear.*
- *He knew God would deliver him from the hand of the Philistine.*
- *David was not confident in himself but rather was utterly dependent on God.*

WITH WHOM GOD DWELLS

12. In what ways did Joshua and Caleb show their humility and confidence in God?
• *God sent twelve leaders to spy out the Promised Land. Ten of them came back with a report that appeared humble, but it was really unbelief.*
• *Joshua and Caleb were the only two that were truly humble. They believed and obeyed God.*

LEADER'S NOTES

who was more humble

13. **The second definition** of humility is this: complete and utter ___*dependence*___ on God. We know we ___*can't do anything*___ apart from Him.

> *There is nothing in us that allows us to claim that we are capable of doing this work. The capacity we have comes from God."*
> **2 Corinthians 3:5, TEV**

> "*Now I am glad to boast about how weak I am; I am glad to be a living demonstration of Christ's power, instead of showing off my own power and abilities."*
> **2 Corinthians 12:9, TLB**

> *Yea doubtless, and I count all things but loss for the excellency of the knowledge of Christ Jesus my Lord: for whom I have suffered the loss of all things, and do count them but dung, that I may win Christ."*
> **Philippians 3:8, KJV**

14. Paul had achieved many accomplishments before he met Christ, yet he says he counts it as dung. Then even after he did many great things in Christ, he said he needed to forget those things as well. Why? _____
Paul knew he couldn't do anything outside the grace of God.

Paul was mightily used of God yet under the inspiration of the Holy Spirit; he wrote and placed himself as the least of the apostles:

Lesson Seven

Leader's Notes

> *"For I am the least of the apostles, who am not worthy to be called an apostle, because I persecuted the church of God. But by the grace of God I am what I am: and his grace which was bestowed upon me was not in vain; but I laboured more abundantly than they all: yet not I, but the grace of God which was with me."*
> *1 Corinthians 15:9–10*

15. Those verses were written about A.D. 56. It may appear to be false humility, but it is not. Remember, Scripture was written under the direct inspiration of the Holy Spirit. Though in those verses it seems Paul is saying opposing things, he is actually able to separate himself from everything God had him do that was worth eternal value. He knew it __was done completely by the ability God gave__ him and had __nothing__ to do with what he had.

Between A.D. 56 and A.D. 63 Paul's ministry exploded. He established churches in Europe and Asia. Even from prison his ministry prospered. Now he places himself as the least of the believers:

> *"Of which I became a minister according to the gift of the grace of God given to me by the effective working of His power. To me, who am less than the least of all the saints, this grace was given, that I should preach among the Gentiles the unsearchable riches of Christ."*
> *Ephesians 3:7–8*

That passage of Scripture was written about A.D. 63, seven years after what Paul wrote in Corinthians and about four years before he was to be beheaded. Paul still was pressing into true humility.

WITH WHOM GOD DWELLS

A few years later, about A.D. 65, Paul goes a step further in his letter to Timothy, declaring himself the chief of sinners:

> *"This is a faithful saying and worthy of all acceptance, that Christ Jesus came into the world to save sinners, of whom I am chief."*
> *1 Timothy 1:15*

16. **The number three definition** of humility is "the way you _____*really see yourself.*"

As Paul faithfully served God, his ministry and influence increased more and more, up to and including his martyrdom. Yet the longer Paul lived, the more humble he became. He saw or viewed himself, not as a great apostle but as a humble, obedient servant of Christ, used by the Holy Spirit, to the glory of God the Father.

17. How did Paul manage to stay so humble yet so mightily used of God?

Sample Answer: He "prayed without ceasing." Remember our earlier lesson: God wants to "communicate" without ceasing!

18. What about the example Paul set for young Titus and Timothy?

Sample Answer: As Paul grew in fame and reputation, they must have seen how he also remained contrite before God. Paul was even willing to make tents and not burden others. Even though he was a great apostle, he set an amazing example.

LEADER'S NOTES

(5–10 minutes)

A discussion of the apostle Paul is always a great way to teach. Ask your group to offer some comments on questions 17 and 18.

LESSON SEVEN

LEADER'S NOTES

Key Statement:
"The humble He guides in justice, and the humble He teaches His way."
Psalm 25:9

In an earlier lesson we learned how Moses knew God's ways, while Israel knew only His acts. David was just a boy tending sheep, but God made him king and prophet. Paul had such intimacy with God that even the apostle Peter made mention of the fact that Paul's writings were hard to understand.

19. What were the characteristics these men had in common that God would entrust them with His ways? They were _unconditionally_ obedient to God, _utterly dependent_ on God, and kept a _humble view_ of themselves through their entire lives.

"The reward of humility and the reverent and worshipful fear of the Lord is riches and honor and life. Thorns and snares are in the way of the obstinate and willful; he who guards himself will be far from them."
Proverbs 22:4–5, AMP

The power twins of the kingdom of God are the fear of the Lord and humility.

20. What are the power twins of the kingdom of darkness? _Pride and rebellion (obstinate and willful)._

"This is the one I esteem: he who is humble and contrite in spirit, and trembles at my word."
Isaiah 66:2, NIV

WITH WHOM GOD DWELLS

"He who kills a bull is as if he slays a man; he who sacrifices a lamb, as if he breaks a dog's neck; he who offers a grain offering, as if he offers swine's blood; he who burns incense, as if he blesses an idol. Just as they have chosen their own ways, and their soul delights in their abominations, so will I choose their delusions, and bring their fears on them; because, when I called, no one answered, when I spoke they did not hear; but they did evil before My eyes, and chose that in which I do not delight."
Isaiah 66:3–4

"He has no use for conceited people, but shows favor to those who are humble."
Proverbs 3:34, TEV

[handwritten annotation: Trust in Self / Trust in God]

The fear of the Lord and humility are coupled with pride and rebellion in Isaiah 66. People were so caught up in religious duty that when God Himself called, they weren't even listening (vv. 3–4). But in verse 2, God says that "the person I regard is humble and contrite in spirit, and trembles at My word." The Hebrew word (nabat) literally means "this is the person I will pay special attention to."

As God sent the great prophet to call the young shepherd boy David to be king, so God pursues those who walk in the fear of the Lord and humility!

LEADER'S NOTES

Remind your group:

1. They should preview the next session and complete the personal discussion portions in their workbooks. If they would like, they may complete the entire section.

2. Pray for the group before they leave. They may divide into groups and can pray for each other. Be led by the Spirit, but keep the focus on things that God may have brought to light from today's teaching.

LESSON SEVEN

Video Script for Lesson 7
WITH WHOM GOD DWELLS

In lesson number seven, I want to talk to you about who God dwells with. Let's read in James Chapter 4 verse 6, *"But He gives more grace. Therefore He says: 'God resists the proud, But gives grace to the humble'."* God resists the proud but gives grace to the humble. Now watch this, *"Therefore submit to God. Resist the devil and he will flee from you. Draw near to God and He will draw near to you. Cleanse your hands, you sinners."*

He's speaking to believers not unbelievers because fifteen times He said my brethren in this book. He is talking about believers that have gotten into habitual patterns of disobedience; they lack the fear of the Lord. All that we talked about so far wrapped up in here. Verse 10, *"Humble yourselves in the sight of the Lord, and He will lift you up."* Now, did you notice He talks about humility before James 4:8 and He talks about humility right after James 4:6. In other words: draw near to God and He will draw near to you is sandwiched between two scriptures talking about humility and for a good reason. Notice He says He will lift you up. Where is He going to lift us up? Look at Isaiah 57 and we're going to find out why James says humble yourself on both sides of drawing near to God. Isaiah 57:15, *"For thus says the High and Lofty One Who inhabits eternity, whose name is Holy: 'I dwell in the high and holy place, With him who has a contrite and humble spirit, To revive the spirit of the humble, And to revive the heart of the contrite ones.'"* Notice He does not say visit. So God says I dwell in the high and holy place with him who is humble. Humble yourself in the sight of the Lord that He may lift you up where God dwells.

Humility is absolutely essential if you are going to have intimacy with the Lord. Many in the body of Christ (and I mean many) do not understand humility or its power. They often view humility as being weak, wimpy, soft spoken and spineless. Unfortunately that's their image of humility. But can I say this: many times the truly humble are mistaken for being arrogant. Consider David. David comes to the battle scene. His three oldest brothers, his oldest being Eliab, are at war with the Philistines. They are in Saul's army. David comes to the battle scene and finds them all in a new strange battle position hiding behind rocks shaking. David looks at his brother's, his oldest brother Eliab, the rest of the soldiers and he looks up at Goliath. He looks at his brothers and he goes who is this uncircumcised Philistine? Big brother Eliab turns to his little brother David and says in 1 Samuel 17:28 in the NIV, *"I know the pride and the insolence of your heart."* Now, let me ask a question: who is full of pride? Go back one chapter earlier and the senior prophet comes to Jesse's house and says there's a king among one of your sons and Jesse thinks it has to be Eliab, my oldest son. After all he is 6'6", weighs 275 lbs., 6% body fat, can bench press 415 pounds, he's quarterback for Notre Dame's football team, majoring in political science and is head of the speech and debate team. It has to be Eliab, right? So Elab comes strutting out there and what does God say to Samuel? "Don't even look at him, I rejected him." Now there is only one reason God rejects and that's pride. So the very thing Eliab has in him, he accuses David of because David is confident in God.

Let me really prove to you that we do not know what humility is. I'm going to submit to you tonight that we do not really know what it is. Can I prove it to you? It will take me three minutes to prove to you that we do not know what humility is. Go with me to Numbers chapter 12 and I will prove to you we do not know what humility is. Number's 12 look at the 3rd verse, *"Now the man Moses was very humble, more than all men who were on the face of the earth."* Wow, what a statement! Now that is a statement you would love to have somebody say about you but you wouldn't dare say it, but can I ask you a question? Who wrote numbers 12, verse 3? Moses. You have to be really humble to write that you're the most humble man in the whole earth. Can you imagine a preacher standing up in front of a conference and all these other preacher's there and he goes, "Ya'll, I'm humble let me tell you about it." I mean we'd laugh him out of the build-

ing, right? But how much different is that than what Jesus in Matthew 11:28-29, *"Come to me, all you are weary and burdened, and learn from me for I am gentle and humble in heart and you will find rest in your souls."* Jesus said come and learn from Me, I am humble."

Can I make a statement? We have made Humility such a serious mysterious woo woo word, we don't even know what it is. Peter says that we are to clothe ourselves with humility. How in the world are we supposed to clothe ourselves with humility if we've made it into this weird, mystic word and we don't even know what it is? So let me define humility. We're going to learn the definition of humility. First and foremost it is our instant obedience to God. That is why we read in James 4:7 therefore submit yourself to God right after He talks about being humble. Now let me give you an example of this. How many of you know the Lord will always show you what He is going to do in your life? How many of you have a real good idea of the call of God that's on your life and what you're going to be doing in year's to come? Put up your hands real, real high. How many of you know God does that with people? He says I know the thoughts I think towards you, thoughts of good not of evil to give you a future and a hope. So what is hope? Hope is the clear picture of what He is going to do. God will show us what He is going to do because He did it with Abraham. He said Abraham you are going to be the father of a multitude. How many of you know Abraham had to wait twenty-five years for that to even begin to happen but after twenty-five years of waiting he got Isaac. They can see now how it's going to come to pass. Isaac's going to grow up, marry a girl, they're going to have kids, they're going to have kids and they're going to have kids and here come the nations and kings that God said would come from my loins. But then one night God says go kill Isaac. Now wait a minute... when God shows you things He's going to do in your life it's like you're here and He show's you what He's going to do and its over there. And this is what the Lord will do. He'll say you know what, I'll give you a few steps that look really nice and then all of a sudden He goes "wham" and you go "ah", and He goes "wham" and you go "ah." Why? You think all I've got to do is walk over here and it's fulfilled but you take two steps, you're the king's armor bearer and then you're eating at the table with his sons. His son becomes your best friend; the king gave you his daughter for a wife and "wham" the king wants to kill you.

You get a dream that you're going to be your brother's leader and they're going to bow down to you and "wham" you're thrown into a pit: creatures in training. So what does God do? He shows you the way and you think it's going to go that way and all of a sudden He tells you to take a step directly opposed and go kill your son. You know what the Bible says? Trust in the Lord with your whole heart and lean not on your own understanding. True humility says I will obey God even if it looks like I am going to destroy the very dream He told me I was going to fulfill. Proverb 3:5, *"Trust in the Lord with all of your heart, and lean not on your own understanding."* Humility means I will obey whether I do or don't understand. I will obey if it looks like it's directly going against the goals that He placed in my heart and the hope He placed in my heart. Number one: it is our obedience to God. It is our absolute, unconditional obedience to God.

Humility is defined as our complete and utter dependence on God. We know we can't do anything apart from Him. David knew this because David appeared arrogant yet he knew his ability came from God. I mean even his older brother said I know the pride and insolence of your heart, right? Listen to what David says in the 1 Samuel 17:37, *"The Lord, who delivered me from the paw of the lion and the paw of the bear, He will deliver me from the hand of this Philistine."* David knew his confidence was in God– not in himself– he was utterly and completely dependent.

You see this very same thing, in Joshua and Caleb. Now how many of you remember God sent twelve leaders of Israel to spy out the Promised Land. Ten of them came back and ten of them looked humble because they said we assessed the situation and we realized they are trained warriors, they are giants over there and we are a bunch of slaves. After all we are protecting our wives and our children. Joshua and Caleb stand up and Caleb in particular goes what are you doing? There's our meat, let's go get them. You are so full of yourself it's all about you isn't it? You're not taking into consideration your wife and children and our wives and our children, you're just full of yourselves. Can I ask a

Lesson Seven

question? Who was full of themselves? God said hang the ten and Joshua and Caleb were the only two that went in.

See if you go through the book of Samuel you'll find it over and over with David. David inquired of the Lord, David inquired of the Lord and David inquired of the Lord. David knew he couldn't do anything unless he had God's ability. That's why he constantly sought the Lord before he made moves. Saul on the other hand, he was real charismatic he said I "felt" compelled and Samuel said you just lost your kingdom.

Let's talk about Paul's life. I want you to notice his utter dependence on the Lord. Listen to what he says in the 2 Corinthians chapter 12 verses 9 and 10. Paul says, *"Now I am glad to boast about how weak I am, I am glad to be a living demonstration of Christ's power, instead of showing off my own power and abilities."* Listen to what he says in 2 Corinthians Chapter 3 verse 5 in today's English version. He says, *"There is nothing in us that allows us to claim that we are capable of doing this work, the capacity we have comes from God."* Paul knew he couldn't do anything outside of the grace of God. Number three is the way we really view ourselves, write that down, that's another definition of humility. If you look at Paul, Paul says when he was in the book of Philippians chapter three, he says you know if anybody can have more confidence in the flesh it should be me and he starts listing his accomplishments and achievements prior to him meeting Jesus. He says I was circumcised the eighth day of the stock of Israel, of the tribe of Benjamin; I was the Hebrews of Hebrews, which meant he had a Doctorate in divinity and that gave him status. He said concerning the law I was blameless; I was a Pharisee political leader not only a religious leader. So he had some achieved status and some accomplishments prior to meeting Jesus but he said all of that I counted as dung, rubbish or really poop is what he is saying. How many of you know that when we get born again that everything we accomplish prior to meeting Jesus is rubbish? But he didn't stop there because he says now I haven't already attained. He said the only way I can press into the high calling is to forget those things, which are behind.

Well listen, you don't have to work at forgetting your poop. When you flush that commode that's the last time you ever think about it. You are not going through the day going, "You know what?" It's not like eleven o'clock going, "Man that load this morning was wonderful." I have to keep eating this All-bran, this was great." But I have to forget it, and I have to put it behind me. He's not talking about what he did prior to meeting Jesus; he's not talking about his failures like some people preach out of that scripture. He's saying now what I've got to forget is everything God has done in me and through me because if I remember what God has done in me and through me I'll start seeing myself as above other people.

Let me show you Paul's life. Go with me to 1 Corinthians, the fifteenth chapter I want to show you this. Now let me say this, while you're turning there. 1st Corinthians was written in the year 56 AD. Let me give you the timeline so you can understand this. Paul was beheaded between 66 and 67 AD. That means this was written ten years prior to his being beheaded. If I had to do a contemporary "somebody" that we know in our generation it would be Lester Sumrall. How many of you know who Lester Sumrall was? Lester Sumrall was probably one of the greatest men of God in the 1900's. I met him when he was seventy-three years old. He went home to be with the Lord when he was eighty-three. I met him ten years prior to him going home to be with the Lord. When I met him he came to my church and I was his host. I picked him up at the airport and let me tell you something– I was shivering, shaking while I was driving that man of God. You understand, I had such respect and the whole body of Christ had such respect for that man. This is where Paul is when he writes this. He's already got churches all over Eastern Europe and Asia. He's got more fruit than anybody and look what he says about himself, ten years before he goes home to be with the Lord. Look at chapter 15, verse 9, *"For I am the least of the apostles, who am not worthy to be called an apostle, because I persecuted the church of God".* You look at all the apostles and he said I'm bottom of the barrel of every single one of them.

Now how many of you know what false humility is? It's saying the right thing but it's not what you mean at the base level of the heart. It's like, "oh it really wasn't me" but inside you're going: take a good look. Right? You know what to say but inside

you're saying something else. How many of you know false humility is a lie, it's deception? How many of you know that you can't lie when writing scriptures? If that's not the way Paul really saw himself the Holy Spirit never would have let him put it in there. He said I am the least of all the preachers'. Then he goes on to say in verse 10, *"But by the grace of God I am what I am, and His grace toward me was not in vain; but I labored more abundantly than they all, yet not I, but the grace of God which was with me."* Paul was able to separate himself from everything God had him do that was worth eternal value because he knew it was done completely by the ability God gave him and nothing to do with what he had.

Let me give you an illustration. Back in the early nineties God told me to write. I will never forget 1992. The Spirit of God spoke to me one day, he said,"Son I want you to write." I about choked and laughed at the same time. I said, "Write? I hate writing. I hate English, that's why I became an engineer." I flunked the SAT in the verbal. I got 370 out of 800. So I was said Lord you have the wrong guy so I did nothing for ten months. Well ten months later two women from two different states within two weeks of each other came to me and gave me the exact same prophetic word. Do you know what the word was? John if you don't write what God has given you to write then He is going to give the message to somebody else and you will be judged. When the second woman from the state of Texas said it two weeks after the first, the fear of God hit me and I said, "I better write."

Now when I started writing I started writing on tablets like Dr. Sumrall did but you know what I found happened? When I made the decision to obey thoughts started coming to my mind I hadn't thought of preached or heard in my whole life before. They would come by revelation and they were coming so fast I couldn't keep up. So what I did was I bought a laptop computer and I started making myself learn how to type 50-60 words a minute and I could semi keep up. Now let me tell you this has happened many, many, many times. I've been in my hotel room writing like crazy and finally I just can't stand it anymore so I jump out of my chair and I just walk back and forth and I go "Man, that is so good. Oh that is so good." Now how can you be so arrogant? It's very simple:

nobody on the face of this earth knows more than this guy where those books came from. I know who wrote those books. I was just the first guy to get to read them. You understand what I'm talking about? Now those books are in the millions, they are in 26 languages all over the world and I know who wrote them– I know whose they are– I was able to separate myself from the grace. That's simply what Paul is saying here, and that's why he is able to say I'm bottom of the barrel of the preacher's but I've got more labor than all of them. I've got more fruit than all of them but I know it wasn't me it was the grace of God in me.

Now go with me to the book of Ephesians, chapter 3. This book was written in the year 60 AD. Well it's quite interesting– half of the Bible scholars say 62 AD and the other half say 64 AD. I say a very simple solution to that– shoot an arrow in the middle, 63. There are some good things to compromise on, okay. So if it's 63 and Corinthians was written in 56 that means this was written seven years after Corinthians or three years before he is beheaded. So this would be like Lester when he was 80-years-old. Now how many of you know that our ministry and our lives are like an exponential curve? Is that too technical for some of you? An exponential curve means it starts out real slow and then it goes right up fast because the Bible says we are like trees planted by the rivers of water and we bring forth fruit in our season. I remember when Lisa and I planted our first orange tree in Florida when we lived there. Well you know the story: one year no fruit, two years no fruit, three years no fruit, the fourth year we had one orange. Addison, Austin, Lisa and I harvested our one orange. We danced back into the kitchen and cut it four and ate our harvest. I'll never forget it. The fifth year we had twelve oranges. The sixth, well you know the story, we had a hundred, the seventh year hundreds. Are you following me? It's an exponential curve.

This is what it is with Paul in those next seven years, from 56 to 63 his ministry exploded. Now he's got churches, not only in Eastern Europe and Asia but Western Europe and the whole known part of the world. But listen, his ministries even explode when he's in prison. It's amazing at the multiplication of what God's doing in his life. Now it is absolutely clear who the man is. Let me show you what he says seven years later, three years before he

is beheaded. Watch this. Ephesians Chapter 3, verse 7 Paul says, *"Of which I became a minister according to the gift of the grace of God given to me by the effective working of His power. To me, who am less than the least of all the saints, this grace was given, that I should preach among the Gentiles the unsearchable riches of Christ."* Seven years earlier he claims himself to be least of all the preachers. Seven years later, three years before he is beheaded, now he says I'm bottom of the barrel of the whole church: look at every single person in the church and I am below him or her.

How many of you remember what false humility is? It's a lie: it's knowing the right thing to say, or the politically correct jargon. How many of you know you can't write a lie when you're writing scripture? The only way the Holy Spirit would have let him write that is if that is really the way he saw himself. What is he doing? He is pressing into true humility because he knows in true humility is where you're going to know the Lord because God dwells with the humble. If you go a couple years later in the year 65 or 66 you'll find out he writes two letters to a young man named Timothy and you know what he says in one of those letters? First chapter the 15th verse he said Christ Jesus came into the world to save sinners of whom I am chief, not I was chief, I am chief. And he's the guy that had the revelation of being a new creature. So he goes from the bottom of the barrel of all the preachers, to the bottom of the barrel of everybody in the church, to the bottom of the barrel of all humanity. What is he doing? He's pressing into true humility.

The third definition of humility is the way you really see yourself. Do you see yourself wise in your own eyes, wise in your own opinions? You know what I noticed: Jesus never gave opinions. They tried to get Him to give opinions but He wouldn't give them. Did you ever notice that? I looked at my wife just recently and said, "Lisa I'm not giving opinions. I mean I have to Email on my computer right now and they want an opinion for a huge magazine. I said I'm not giving it. I said I'll give the word the Holy Spirit places– the Rhema, word of God– I'll give that but I'm not giving my opinion. Who am I to give an opinion?" I am a servant; I am a vessel, a representative of Him, that's the way we all should be. When you begin to live like that you begin to live like Samuel where God said not one of your words will fall to the ground because you're only going to speak what you hear Him saying. That's what Jesus said, I only speak what I hear my Father speak and that's humility. You are utterly dependent on Him and you do not see yourself above other people so you think you can give your opinion so you will not take on an attitude of being wise in your own eyes, or wise in your own opinions.

Now go with me to Psalms 25 again where we were in one of the earlier lessons when we talked about the fear of the Lord. Psalm 25, verse 9 says, *"The humble He guides in justice, and the humble He teaches His way."* We read in an earlier lesson Moses knew his way, Israel new his acts. Moses knew what God was going to do many times before He even did it because God showed Him the ways. God says I teach the humble my ways. Now let me ask something here: could this be why Moses knew God better than anybody in his generation is because he was the humblest man in the whole earth? Could this be why David went beyond being a king into a prophetic realm and no other king could do it and he really wasn't even supposed to do it? He called himself this poor man when he had stockpiles of silver. He wasn't talking about financially he was talking about being humble. Could this be why Paul knew Him so intimately that finally it blew Peter away and Peter wrote a letter and said the intimacy level that Paul has with Jesus is mind blowing, some of his letters are hard to understand. Why: because he pressed into the true humility. The longer Paul lived the more humble he became. The lower he saw himself God says I dwell with those people.

So what is humility again? Humility is your unconditional obedience even when it looks like you are going directly against what God has promised you. Number two it is your absolute and complete utter dependence on Him. Number three is the way you really see yourself. In the scriptures, the power twins of the kingdom of God are the fear of the Lord and humility, just like the power twins of the kingdom of darkness are pride and rebellion. I can read to you from Proverbs 22, verses 4 and 5 out of the Amplified, *"The reward of humility and the reverent and worshipful fear of the Lord is riches and honor and life. Thorns and snares are in the way of the obstinate and willful; he who guards himself will be far from them."* Notice how He couples the fear of the

Lord and humility and pride and rebellion because the fear of the Lord and humility are the power twins of the kingdom. God says in Isaiah chapter 66 to His people, as they were obeying Him, they were bringing animal sacrifices and He said, your animal sacrifices that you are giving me even though I told you to do it in the book of Numbers are like breaking a dog's neck and killing a man. The people said why is that? He said because when I called nobody answered. You were so busy trying to get my approval in your actions you weren't even listening when I was whispering in your heart to do something, when I had spoken to you from My word to do something. And then God said to those people this is the person that I pursue. In Isaiah 66:2 He actually says this is the person that I regard or this is the person that I will look upon that word. That Hebrew word literally means: this is the person that I will pay special attention to, I will give My attention to and I will highly esteem this person. God said, *"On him who is poor and of a contrite spirit, and who trembles at My word."* Notice what He says about the person who is humble and the person who fears God. God says that is the person I'm chasing. That's why God sends a prophet all the way to a guy's house when there is a little boy watching sheep, because God said, "I'm pursuing him. When you walk in the fear of the Lord and humility God will chase you.

Tommy Tenney is a good friend of mine. I think he's got the greatest title of a book of any contemporary author, "The God Chasers" but let me say this: it is one thing to chase God but it is an entirely different thing to have God chasing you. That's what God was doing with David because he was humble and he feared God.

INTIMACY WITH THE HOLY SPIRIT

Video Session 8

INTIMACY WITH THE HOLY SPIRIT

Key Statement:
The Holy Spirit is the most ignored person of the Trinity.

"Or do you think that the Scripture says in vain, 'The Spirit who dwells in us yearns jealously'?"
James 4:5

1. Read James 4:5 again. Who does that scripture says yearns to dwell in us? __*The Spirit*__.

2. Jesus is seated at the right hand of the Father in heaven and He sent the __*Holy Spirit*__ to dwell __*in*__ us.

One of the reasons that we do not have intimacy with the Holy Spirit is that we have been taught a distorted image of the Holy Spirit. We have preached Him to be a "mystical" person of the Godhead.

3. One of the first impressions we think of for the Holy Spirit is __*a dove*__. The Holy Spirit is described as a dove in the Gospels, but just because He descended upon Jesus "like a dove" does not make the Holy Spirit an actual dove.

LEADER'S NOTES

(3–5 minutes)

Remind the group of a few key lessons by referring to these statements:

1. Intimacy with God is available to each one of us. This is God's passion.

2. Recap last week's session with this statement: The power twins of the kingdom are the fear of the Lord and humility.

Set this session up with the Key Statement. Then go through the questions, asking for and providing the answers.

133

Lesson Eight

Leader's Notes

(10 minutes)

Have a volunteer turn to each of the scriptures you give them for each of these answers and read them aloud.

4. The Holy Spirit is a person of the Godhead. He:

- *Has a mind (Rom. 8:27)*
- *Has a will (1 Cor. 12:11)*
- *Has emotions (Rom. 15:30)*
- *Speaks (Heb. 3:7; 1 Tim. 4:1)*
- *Teaches (1 Cor. 2:13)*
- *Can be grieved (Eph. 4:30)*
- *Can be insulted (Heb. 10:29)*
- *Can be lied to just like any human (Acts 5)*

"Then God said, 'Let Us make man in Our image, according to Our likeness."
Genesis 1:26

"You send forth Your Spirit, they are created."
Psalm 104:30

5. God did not say, "Let Me make man in My image." He said, "Let __Us__ make man in __Our__ image." Man was made in the image of the __Father__, the __Son__, and the __Holy Spirit__. It was the Spirit who was sent to create.

Key Statement:
The Role of the Holy Spirit is communion.

"All the saints greet you. The grace of the Lord Jesus Christ, and the love of God, and the communion of the Holy Spirit be with you all. Amen."
2 Corinthians 13:13–14

6. __Grace__ is attributed to the role of __Jesus__ in our lives.

INTIMACY WITH THE HOLY SPIRIT

7. _Love_ is attributed to the role of _God_ in our lives.

8. _Communion_ is attributed to the role of the _Holy Spirit_ in our lives.

Communion can be broken down into five basic definitions to help you understand the role of the Holy Spirit in your life. We will look at these one at a time.

FELLOWSHIP: The Holy Spirit is your constant companion...

Webster's dictionary describes fellowship as "companionship, company, the quality or state of being comradely."

The Holy Spirit was Paul's comrade through all his journeys. He would reveal things to Paul and direct his path in each city that he went to. There was interaction going on between the two (Acts 16:6–7; 20:22–23).

The Holy Spirit spoke to Philip in the middle of the desert and told him to overtake the chariot, and Philip ministered and brought the man to the Lord (Acts 8:29).

The Holy Spirit spoke to Peter and told him that three men were seeking him and that he should arise and go to them (Acts 10:19–20).

9. The New Testament servants of God were very aware of the Spirit of God's constant _companionship_ with them.

LEADER'S NOTES

LESSON EIGHT

LEADER'S NOTES

SHARING TOGETHER: The Holy Spirit reveals intimate things...

Social intercourse is the exchanging of thoughts and feelings. With our closest friends we share the deep and intimate things of our heart.

10. What happens when you do that? You make yourself ____vulnerable____.

11. Why does this type of relationship with the Holy Spirit make the fear of the Lord so important? Because the Holy Spirit is not going to ____share____ the ____deep____, intimate ____secrets____ He has with people who do not ____fear____ Him.

God desires to reveal and share deep and intimate things to you through His Spirit.

PARTNERSHIP: The Holy Spirit is your partner...

> *"For it seemed good to the Holy Spirit, and to us."*
> **Acts 15:28**

12. This awe-inspiring verse clearly shows a ____partnership____. It shows two ____views____.

Earlier in our journey we looked at another excellent example of interaction between God and His people. Remember God discussing Sodom and Gomorrah with Abraham. In Exodus 32:9–14 we see similar interaction between God and Moses.

13. In the Old Testament some men and women walked very closely with God, yet what is it about the New Testament that makes our relationship with God potentially even better?
The Holy Spirit Himself dwells within us.

Intimacy With The Holy Spirit

"Therefore take heed to yourselves and to all the flock, among which the Holy Spirit has made you overseers, to shepherd the church of God which He purchased with His own blood."
Acts 20:28

Leader's Notes

"THEOLOGY 101"

14. In Acts 20:28 there is a wealth of biblical truth. One of the most important is that it references all three persons of the Godhead. Pick out and identify the respective roles of the Father, Son, and Holy Spirit within the verse, and write them below:

- The Holy Spirit empowered them as overseers
- God is the Father and we as the church body belong to Him
- Jesus is the one who purchased us with His own blood

15. **As a student of Scripture**, you always want to be looking for these types of things as you daily read the Word of God. What are some other verses that you can think of that clearly show all three persons of the Trinity? If you can't think of any, now is a good time to get out your Bible and do a study.

Examples:
- *Matthew 3:16–17: The Holy Spirit descends on Jesus and the Father speaks*
- *John 14:16, 26*
- *Matthew 28:19*
- *2 Corinthians 13:14: the Apostolic Benediction*
- *Jude 20–21*

Helpful Hint:

There is a book called a "concordance" that shows every word in the Bible and gives you an easy reference on how to look it up. These are available on the Internet or in any Christian bookstore.

Lesson Eight

Leader's Notes

16. What was the Holy Spirit's partnership with the apostles as described in Acts 20:28?
    He made them overseers

17. What does 1 Corinthians 3:9 call us? We are God's
    fellow workers

CLOSE MUTUAL ASSOCIATION: You are to be known by your association with the Holy Spirit...

John describes examples of several men and women of God he personally knew who walked closely with God. Where those people were, the Holy Spirit was also. In fact, you could say these people were associated with the Holy Spirit. The idea of mutual association means it is two-sided. The dictionary defines it as "the feelings of each toward the other."

18. It is really a simple principle. When you are strongly associated with someone, you begin to take on his or her thoughts and feelings. Their attitudes and values tend to become yours. Like all things on your journey, it brings you back to our flagship scripture, James 4:8: "Draw *near to God and He will draw near to you*."

The more closely you become associated with God, the more people will see your partnership with Him.

INTIMACY: The Holy Spirit desires intimacy with you...

19. Intimacy speaks of *communication* which is the avenue of a strong friendship. "... *the intimate friendship of the Holy Spirit, be with you all*" (2 Cor. 13:14, THE MESSAGE). It all comes down to *friendship*, which is the end goal of communion.

INTIMACY WITH THE HOLY SPIRIT

LEADER'S NOTES

"THEOLOGY 101"

Two Word Studies

A.) There are two Greek words that are translated into the word "another" in the New Testament. The word *allos* means "another word of the same kind." The word *heteros* means "another word of a different kind."

In the video, John uses the example of fruit to help you understand this distinction. Another example could be a ball. Suppose you give someone a football, and they lose it and then ask you for another ball. If you gave them another football, you have given them a ball of the same kind they lost. But if when they asked for another ball you gave them a baseball, you have given them a ball of a different kind.

B.) The Greek word *parakletos* means "advocate" or "one called alongside to aid another." It was commonly used to describe a lawyer in a courtroom. It is only found in the New Testament in John 14:16, 26; 15:26; and 16:7, speaking of the Holy Spirit, and in 1 John 2:1, speaking of Jesus.

Key Statement:
Jesus sent a helper who was like Himself: the Holy Spirit.

"If you love Me, keep My commandments. And I will pray the Father, and He will give you another [allos] Helper [parakletos], that He may abide with you forever—the Spirit of truth, whom the world cannot receive, because it neither sees

Lesson Eight

Leader's Notes

Him nor knows Him; but you know Him, for He dwells with you and will be in you. I will not leave you orphans; I will come to you."
John 14:15–18

"My little children, these things I write to you, so that you may not sin. And if anyone sins, we have an Advocate [parakletos] with the Father, Jesus Christ the righteous."
1 John 2:1

- The word used for "another" in John 14:16 is *allos*—meaning *another of the same kind.* The word used to describe the Holy Spirit (helper) is *parakletos*.

- In 1 John 2:1 we see the word *Advocate* to describe Jesus. This is the same Greek word *(parakletos)* used in John 14:16 to describe the Holy Spirit.

20. Jesus is saying He is going to give the Holy Spirit as another helper—one who __is just like Jesus Himself__.

"Nevertheless I tell you the truth. It is to your advantage that I go away; for if I do not go away, the Helper will not come to you; but if I depart, I will send Him to you."
John 16:7

21. Oftentimes people say, "Oh, if only I could have been there to talk to Jesus." Yet Jesus said it would be better if He went away. Why is it actually better for us that Jesus would depart?

- *Jesus had physical limitations in His time on earth.*
- *He was one man; He could only speak with people one at a time or in groups.*
- *The Holy Spirit is available to all believers at the same time at all times*

INTIMACY WITH THE HOLY SPIRIT

The Three Levels of Relationship:

Level 1

22. What did Jesus say to Thomas about believing?
Those who believe without having to see are more blessed.

23. What did Jesus mean by this?
You could know Him better by the Holy Spirit than by seeing Him physically present.

24. What is the first and lowest level of relationship?
Physical.

25. Who was it that said Paul's letters were hard to understand?

Peter, "As also in all his epistles, speaking in them of these things; in which are some things hard to be understood, which they that are unlearned and unstable wrest, as they do also the other scriptures, unto their own destruction" (2 Pet. 3:16, KJV).

26. Why is that such an amazing statement coming from Peter?

Peter was physically present with Jesus for three and a half years; Paul was not. Paul didn't even get saved until after the Crucifixion.

27. How did Paul know such deep things of God if he didn't walk and talk with Jesus as did the other apostles?
He knew Jesus by the Holy Spirit.

LEADER'S NOTES

Lesson Eight

Leader's Notes

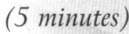

(5 minutes)

Have a volunteer turn to Galatians 1:11-17. Before having this scripture read aloud, tell the group to listen carefully for the secret, which is the answer to how Paul knew God so deeply.

Ask volunteers for the answers.

- *Paul didn't receive it from man but through the revelation of Jesus Christ.*

- *He did not confer with flesh and blood.*

(10 minutes)

Ask for volunteers to share their answer.

- *Ask your group if they find this verse hard to believe and if any have testimonies of how they are doing in the Drawing Near journey so far. Here are some questions to ask:*

28. Can you support your answer with scripture?

"But I make known to you, brethren, that the gospel which was preached by me is not according to man. For I neither received it from man, nor was I taught it, but it came through the revelation of Jesus Christ. For you have heard of my former conduct in Judaism, how I persecuted the church of God beyond measure and tried to destroy it.

And I advanced in Judaism beyond many of my contemporaries in my own nation, being more exceedingly zealous through His grace, to reveal His Son in me, that I might preach Him among the Gentiles, I did not immediately confer with flesh and blood, nor did I go up to Jerusalem to those who were apostles before me; but I went to Arabia, and returned again to Damascus."

Galatians 1:11–17

"Oh, there is so much more I want to tell you, but you can't bear it now. When the Spirit of truth comes, he will guide you into all truth. He will not be presenting his own ideas; he will be telling you what he has heard. He will tell you about the future. He will bring me glory by revealing to you whatever he receives from me. All that the Father has is mine; this is what I mean when I say that the Spirit will reveal to you whatever he receives from me."
John 16:12–15, NLT

29. What does John 16:12–15 mean to you today?

Like Paul, although we never walked and talked with Jesus physically, we can have intimacy with God through the Holy Spirit.

INTIMACY WITH THE HOLY SPIRIT

The Three Levels of Relationship:

Level 2

30. What is the second level of relationship?
_____*Soulish*_____.

In 1 Samuel 18 we see that King Saul's son Jonathan had become a great friend to David. Their souls were knit together. A soulish relationship is stronger than a carnal or physical relationship, but it will never compare to the spiritual relationship we can have in God.

The Three Levels of Relationship:

Level 3

31. The highest level of relationship is ____*spiritual*____.

"But God has revealed them to us through His Spirit. For the Spirit searches all things, yes, the deep things of God. For what man knows the things of a man except the spirit of the man which is in him? Even so no one knows the things of God except the Spirit of God. Now we have received, not the spirit of the world, but the Spirit who is from God, that we might know the things that have been freely given to us by God."
1 Corinthians 2:10–12

"Therefore, from now on, we regard no one according to the flesh. Even though we have known Christ according to the flesh, yet now we know Him thus no longer."
2 Corinthians 5:16

32. How can we know the deep things of God?
_____*The Holy Spirit shows us*_____
_____.

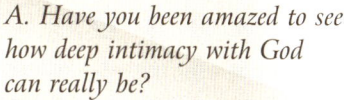

A. Have you been amazed to see how deep intimacy with God can really be?

B. As you are going through the sessions, is it becoming easier to believe in the work of the Holy Spirit?

C. Does it encourage you to know that Jesus and the Holy Spirit are always available to help you draw near to God in intimacy?

143

Lesson Eight

Leader's Notes

33. Our physical bodies are not redeemed, but they will one day _____perish_____ and we will get a new, incorruptible body. Our souls are being renewed; our spirits are redeemed. Our bodies are not capable of knowing God to the depths we can know Him in our _____spirits_____. Until our bodies are glorified, we have to know Jesus in the _____spirit_____.

> "The grace of the Lord Jesus Christ, and the love of God, and the communion of the Holy Spirit be with you all. Amen."
> **2 Corinthians 13:14**

34. What is special in this verse? (*Hint: Remember earlier in the lesson what was said about being a student of scripture.*) <u>You may get many answers, but the answer you are looking for is that the Trinity is contained in this single verse. This verse is the Apostolic Benediction.</u>

- Point out that the grace and love and communion of the Trinity is for ALL!

- Tell your group this brings us back again to our flagship scripture and the purpose of our journey. Have them recite aloud James 4:8.

- Finally, with boldness and authority as the leader of the group, have them place their hands on one another's shoulders, and lead them in prayer for one another, pronouncing over them the Apostolic Benediction that they would grow in "the grace of the Lord Jesus Christ, and the love of God, and the communion of the Holy Spirit through their Drawing Near journey."

Remind your group:

1. They should preview the next session and complete the personal/discussion portions in their workbooks. If they would like, they may complete the entire section.

2. Pray for the group before they leave. They may divide into groups and can pray for each other. Be led by the Spirit, but keep the focus on things that God may have brought to light from today's teaching.

INTIMACY WITH THE HOLY SPIRIT

Video Script for Lesson 8

INTIMACY WITH THE HOLY SPIRIT

Oh boy do I love this one; it's called Intimacy with the Holy Spirit. Let's look at our flagship scripture, James 4 verse 8 we read, *"Draw near to God and He will draw near to you."* We have said what James is saying here is: we are the ones who determine the level of intimacy with the Lord, not God. James gets specific because how many of you know in an earlier lesson I taught how passionate the Lord is about drawing near to you? In fact, He is more passionate about drawing near to you than you are to Him but I want to go to the specific person of the Godhead who is passionate. Look at verse 5, "Or do you think that the Scripture says in vain, 'The Spirit who dwells in us yearns jealously'?" The word "yearns" means to long for intensely and consistently. What does He yearn for– our companionship. Notice He says the Spirit who dwells in us. Notice He does not say Jesus who dwells in us because Jesus isn't here, He's at the right hand of the Father millions of miles away in the throne room. Do you not remember what the angels said when Jesus was taken up? They said in Acts 1:11, *"Men of Galilee, why do you stand gazing up into heaven? This same Jesus, who was taken up from you into heaven, will so come in the like manner as you saw Him go into heaven."* Has He come back in the same way in the clouds? Who has been the one that's been here? The Holy Spirit.

I want to say this: the Holy Spirit is probably one of the most ignored person's in the church. Think about it. How many times would you ride in a car with somebody sitting in the passenger seat of the car, you ride twenty minutes with them and you don't say one word to them? Not even, " Hey, how are you doing?" or "What do you plan on doing today" or even "good-bye". Yet how many times do we ride twenty minutes in the car and we do not say one word to the Holy Spirit? I mean if you ever have a problem with rejection, especially with family members, go talk to Him about it because He understands.

Now one of the reasons why we do not have intimacy with Him is our warped image of Him and the reason is because we've preached Him to be such a mystical person. The Bible clearly shows that He has a mind in Romans 8:27; that He has a will in 1 Corinthians 12:11; that He has emotions in Roman 15:30; that He speaks in Hebrews 7; in fact He speaks explicitly in 1Timothy 1; He teaches 1 Corinthians 2:15; He can be grieved in Ephesians 4:30; He can be insulted in Hebrews 10:29 and He can be lied to just like any other human being in Acts chapter 5.

Now the reason we don't communicate with Him is because of our warped impression of Him. Usually one of the first things we think of is a dove. Now can I make a statement here? Yes, in all four gospels it says the Spirit of God descended upon Jesus like a dove, but can I say something? We have statements such as this: she ran like the wind and he's as strong as an ox but does that make her into the wind and him into a four footed beast? Just because He descended upon Jesus like a dove doesn't make Him a dove. Some people have this image of the Holy Spirit and that He is this flighty bird. The Holy Spirit is a person. I said He's a person. In fact Genesis 1:26 says, *"Then God said, 'Let Us make man in Our image, according to Our likeness'."* It was the Father, the Son and the Holy Spirit. God did not say let Me make man, He said let Us make man. I know that because Job 33 verse 4 says, *"The Spirit of God has made me."* I also know from Psalms 104 verse 30 it says, *"You send forth your Spirit, they are created."* Let me ask you this: how in the world could Mary be impregnated by the Holy Spirit? Doesn't it usually take two beings of the same image to create a normal offspring? Let me read to you out of the New Living Translation in Matthew 1:18, *"While she was still a virgin she became pregnant by the Holy Spirit."* Later on it was said to Joseph her husband, what is conceived in her is from the Holy Spirit (Matthew 1:20 in the New International Version).

So I hope you are seeing He is a person and in fact He is a most wonderful person. For this reason Paul says in 2 Corinthians, chapter 13 verse 14, *"The grace of the Lord Jesus Christ, and the love of God, and the communion of the Holy Spirit be with you all."* Now

Lesson Eight

notice He directly attributes communion with the Holy Spirit not Jesus or the Father. You see the love of God there and that's the Father; you see the grace of our Lord Jesus Christ and that's our Lord and savior Jesus. But then you see Him attributing communion or fellowship directly with the Holy Spirit. I have studied this verse and I have studied that word "communion" for years and out of all the research that I have done I was able to bring it down to five basic definitions. The first one is fellowship. Paul said may the fellowship of the Holy Spirit be with you. Webster's dictionary defines fellowship as this: companionship or company. It is also defined as this: the quality or state of being comradely. Now can I ask you something? Have you ever met comrades who do not interact? They keep each other informed don't they? Well, it's the same way with the Holy Spirit– He's our comrade. He wants to have companionship with us. This is seen in what Paul says in Acts 20, verse 22-23 in the New Living Translation. Listen to these words carefully, *"And now I am going to Jerusalem, drawn there irresistibly by the Holy Spirit, not knowing what awaits me except that the Holy Spirit has told me in city after city that jail and suffering lie ahead."* So you notice the Holy Spirit is repeatedly talking to him. He said the Holy Spirit– He didn't say that Jesus told me this. Now don't get me wrong, the Holy Spirit is called the Spirit of Christ. Jesus said when He comes He will reveal the things of mind. He will take what is mine and show it to you. He always seeks to glorify Jesus and Jesus glorifies the Father. But notice Paul says the Holy Spirit told me in city after city. Does that sound like there's some interaction going on between them in city after city?

You see this also with the other apostles in the Bible, the evangelists and the disciples. The Holy Spirit speaks to Philip right in the middle of the desert and says, *"Go near and overtake this chariot"*, that's Acts chapter 8:29. Peter in Acts 10:19,20 the Spirit said to him, *"Behold, three men are seeking you. Arise therefore, go down and go with them, doubting nothing; for I have sent them."* We read this in Acts 16: 6 and 7, *"Now when they had gone through Phrygia and the region of Galatia, they were forbidden by the Holy Spirit to preach the word in Asia. After they had come to Mysia, they tried to go into Bithynia, but the Spirit did not permit them."* Notice it was the Holy Spirit. The point I'm trying to make here in the New Testament is; servants were very aware of the Spirit of God's constant companionship with them. People ask me all the time, "don't you get bored in hotel rooms" and I say "no" because to be very honest with you I have a companion and his name is the Holy Spirit.

Last year I was in Paris and had nothing to do for the whole day. I didn't have to preach until 8:00 o'clock at night and they said, "Do you want to go to the city?" I said, "No I really don't" and do you want to know why? There was an absolutely gorgeous garden right across the street from my hotel and I walked out into that garden and had communion with the Holy Spirit. I didn't want to go do and see all that stuff because I'd seen it all. I wanted to have intimacy and I wanted to have time with the Holy Spirit because I love it.

Number two, this word communion means this: sharing together or social intercourse. Social intercourse is exchanging thoughts and feelings. Now listen to me carefully. In my inner circle of friends, the greatest times I've had are when we begin to share the deep and intimate things of our heart. How many of you know when you do that you make yourself vulnerable? That's exactly what Paul is talking about here. He is saying may that kind of intimacy be between you and the Holy Spirit, where you can share each other's thoughts so intimately and deeply. That is why the fear of the Lord is so important because the Holy Spirit is not going to share the deep intimate secrets that He has with people who do not fear Him.

In the Old Testament it cries out, *"Can you search out the deep things of God?"* That is Job 11:7. In the New Testament listen to what the apostle Paul said, *"God has revealed them to us through His Spirit. For the spirit searches all things, yea the deep things of God."* So in other words the Holy Spirit is saying: I long to reveal to you the deep things of God.

Number three, this word communion means: partnership or joint participation. The most beautiful scripture that exemplifies this is Acts 15:28. Listen to what the apostle's wrote in a letter, *"For it seemed good to the Holy Spirit, and to us."* Do you see the partnership there? They distinctly show His view and their view. Now this is seen in the Old Testament when God comes down and talks to Abraham about His plans for Sodom and

Gomorrah. He chats with Abraham and says, "Now Abraham I'm thinking about blowing up the cities" (like I said in an earlier lesson). What do you think about this? And Abraham was able to interact and they discussed the plans and out of the new joint decision they decided if there are more than ten righteous people they were not going to blow up the city but there wasn't.

You see it with Moses constantly. Moses is interacting with God and even gets God to change His mind twice because Moses was His close friend. We read in the Old Testament, *"So the Lord changed his mind about the harm, which he said he would do to his people"* in Exodus 32:14 because of Moses words. They were partners yet Moses and Abraham didn't have the continuous companionship that we are afforded in the New Testament. The Bible says we are to dwell with Him. Jesus said abide in me.

There is clear evidence the Holy Spirit's role as our senior partner in Acts 20. I want to go over there to Acts 20:28. Paul says to the elders of Ephesus, *"Therefore take heed to yourselves and to all the flock, among which the Holy Spirit has made you overseers, to shepherd the church of God which He purchased with His own blood."* Do you notice that Paul talks about all three persons of the Godhead there? He talks about the church of God the Father, he talks about being purchased by His own blood Jesus and he talks about the fact that it was the Holy Spirit that made them overseers. Do you see the partnership? What does Paul say in 1 Corinthians, 3:9? " He says, *"For we are God's fellow worker's."* It's a little more blunt in the King James. He says we are laborers together with God. In other word's we are co-laborers. We both labor together there is a partnership.

Now number four is this: close mutual association. Let me give you an example of this. Over the years I have had the privilege of taking care of men and women of God. Back in the 1980's my job was to take care of every guest speaker that came to our church but there was one man who really impacted me and it was Dr.Cho. I remember when Dr. Cho came to preach in our church. He got into my car and when he got into my car the presence of God got into my car. I remember I am sitting there driving and tears were running down my cheeks when I was driving him to service. I was very respectful and I did not carry on conversation unless they initiated it because I knew they were getting ready to preach. But finally I couldn't stand it anymore and I said, "Dr. Cho, God is in this car." He looked at me, smiled and he said, "Yes I know." Now why was that? I'm going to tell you why. It was, because Dr. Cho frequently talks about the Holy Spirit being his senior partner. He's preaching about the Holy Spirit all the time and he communes with the Holy Spirit in his language constantly so there is a close mutual association. There are some preachers that talk about the Holy Spirit, and when they do, they manifest, they are closely associated.

One such person was a lady named Jeannie Wilkerson. Jeannie Wilkerson was a lady who I would like to call my spiritual grandmother. I met Jeannie Wilkerson back in the 1980's. I remember the first time I met her was when she came to preach for my pastor's wife at the women's conference. She got into the van and literally my jaw must have dropped down to my lap the whole time. When she got into the van, God got into the van and she didn't talk about God. She talked as if somebody who really knew Him. I had gone through Bible school and listened to all kinds of tapes and here this woman was saying things that were blowing my mind.

I mean here I am, a young man and I've really been studying, but you could never get that in a Bible school. That woman spent twenty years in a prayer meeting in her basement with several other women and you know what, I'm going to tell you something– when she prophesied, the hair on my arms would stand up. I remember the day she died, I cried like a baby because she was like my grandma. But that woman knew God– she knew the Holy Spirit– and whenever you were around her you felt the presence of God.

I remember I was in a church in the Midwest section of the United States about a year and a half ago on a Sunday morning. I preached on the Holy Spirit. I was supposed to be done preaching by 8:30 but I didn't get the microphone until 8:45. The reason is the Holy Spirit came in so strong that we were all over the floor because people were getting healed and people were getting ministered to. The Pastor who can bench 500 pounds comes up to me with tears running down his cheeks saying,

Lesson Eight

"John, I have pastored this church eight years and have never felt the presence of God like I am tonight." I said do you want to know why? He said, "Why?" It is because we talked about Him this morning and when you talk about Him He manifests. He who honors me I will honor God said. Just as I am talking right now, do you notice the presence of God getting thicker in here? But now He doesn't draw attention to Himself, He points your heart to Jesus. You'll fall in love with Jesus more when you get around Him and you commune with Him and you fellowship with Him. So what does close mutual association mean? It means this: when people get around you and you acknowledge Him and you walk with Him, when you have that kind of intimacy with Him, they'll know about Him.

Fifth definition of the word communion is intimacy. This word best describes communion. It really sums up the previous four categories that I just talked about. Now, one of Webster's definitions of communion is this: intimate fellowship or rapore. It speaks of communication: intimate communication. Intimacy can only be developed by communication, which is the avenue of a strong friendship. One version of the New Testament reads in 2 Corinthians Chapter 13:14. *"May the intimate friendship of the Holy Spirit be with you all."* That's in the Message Bible.

So it all comes down to friendship: this is the end goal of communion. We read in Isaiah 40:13,14 in the New American Standard, *"Who has directed the spirit of the Lord? Or as His counselor has informed Him, with whom did He consult and who gave Him understanding and who taught Him in the paths of justice and taught Him knowledge and informed of the way of understanding?"* Well, the answer to that is nobody because He's God. When you know something of great value what do you want to do? You want to share with them, with your close friends. Do you realize how passionately He wants to share with you what He knows? It is sad to say but there are many people today who want a relationship with Jesus apart from the Holy Spirit, but how different is that than the Jews? Remember the Jews looked at Jesus who was the one on the earth then and said: God is our Father, Abraham is our father, Moses is our teacher, who are you? They wanted a relationship with God the Father apart from Jesus.

Do you know there are people today in the church that want a relationship with Jesus apart from the Holy Spirit?

Now go with me to John 14 and I'll try to wrap this up in the next few minutes, but you've got to see this. John's gospel the 14th chapter, look at verse 15. Jesus said, *"If you love Me, keep My commandments. And I will pray the Father, and He will give you another Helper, that He may abide with you forever."* Now isn't it interesting that Jesus talks about obedience and then He talks about the Holy Spirit being given to those that obey? How does that differ from Acts 5:32? Peter says God gives the Holy Spirit to those that obey him. Why haven't we preached that? He said in John 14:16, *"And I will pray the Father, and He will give you another Helper, that He may abide with you forever– the Spirit of truth, whom the world cannot receive, because it neither sees Him nor knows Him; but you know Him, for He dwells with you and will be in you."*

There are two Greek words that are used or translated into the word "another" in the New Testament. The first one is Allos and the second one is Heteros. The word Allos means another word of the same kind. The word Heteros means another of a different kind. Let me give you an example: if I give you a banana and you eat that banana, and I look at you and say would you like another piece of fruit and I give you another banana, I have given you another piece of fruit of the same kind. But if I give you a banana and I say to you would you like another piece of fruit and I give you a peach, I have given you another piece of fruit of a different kind. Do you see the difference? The Greek word that Jesus uses here is not Heteros, another of a different kind; He uses the word Allos, which is another of the same kind. He is saying He's going to be just like Me. He says I'm going to give you another Helper. Helper in the Greek is the word Parakletos. It actually means: one who summons to another side to aid him. It was used to describe, an advocate or a lawyer in a courtroom by the Greeks. This word Parakletos is only used one other place in the whole New Testament and that's in 1 John 2:1 where it says, *"...we have an Advocate with the Father, Jesus Christ the righteous."* Jesus is called Parakletos there. In other words when He says I'm going to give you another one just like Me He is actually saying He's called alongside to help

# Intimacy With The Holy Spirit

you just like I am.

Now how many of you have met Christian's that have constantly said, "Oh I wish I could have walked the shores of Galilee with Jesus. Oh, the questions I would have asked them." I don't think so because you have been ignoring the One who is just like Him that is with you in your midst. Jesus made this statement in John 16:7, *"Nevertheless I tell you the truth."* Now stop and think about this. He's talking to the disciples, the apostles. He says guys; I'm telling you the truth. Now wait a minute, He's been with them for three and a half years and He's never told one lie. Everything He has ever said has always come to pass. He looked at a tree, cursed it and the next day it's dead. He looks at the wind and says "be calm" and it's calm. He says go find the colt and they go and find the colt. Are you getting this? Everything He's ever told them has come true. He never lied to them once but He has to preface this statement with: I'm telling you the truth. In other words, what I'm about to say is so mind blowing you may think I am lying but I'm not. Isn't this is amazing? Look at what He says, *"Nevertheless I tell you the truth. It is to your advantage that I go away; for if I do not go away, the Helper will not come to you; but if I depart, I will send Him to you."* If Jesus was still here do you know what we'd have to do if we wanted to inquire of Him or talk to Him? We'd have to catch a plane and fly to Tel Aviv. Then we'd have to rent a car and drive out to the countryside of Galilee. He would be easy to find because there would be thousands of people around Him but then we'd have to wait a few weeks before all the thousands could get through asking Him their questions. We'd finally get to the center and we'd be ready to ask our questions but Peter who is so outspoken is asking all kinds of questions. Then John and James, the sons of thunder, would have their questions and Thomas has got his doubting questions. You're sitting there trying to get a word in edgewise but they're talking, and you know He does need to sleep a few hours a night, take care of his personal needs and He does need to eat once in awhile.

But you know what's amazing? Jesus said the Holy Spirit is going to be just like Me. Just like the disciples were able to ask Him questions, but they can only ask them one at a time, this is going to be much better because fifteen thousand people can have a conversation with the Holy Spirit about fifteen thousand different things any time, day or night. And I've got news for you: Jesus was willing to speak if you asked Him a question. He did not neglect your question if you had a sincere heart. He said He is going to be just like Me, which means He will teach you, He will talk to you, He will show you things. How many of you remember in the scripture when Thomas said unless I put my hands in His side and my finger in His holes I won't believe it. So Jesus comes a week later and Thomas is with Him. I love what Pastor Ted, my pastor says: "Jesus I love the way He does things. The door is locked, the windows are barred and bam, He's there. He scares the living daylights out of him and the first thing He says is, 'Don't be afraid.' It's almost like He's having fun with him. You know He's got a sense of humor." So He shows up and says don't be afraid. Come here Thomas, put your fingers in My hand, put your hand in My side; don't be doubting, believe. And Thomas collapses on the floor and goes, "My Lord and my God." Then Jesus says this to him, "Thomas you believe because you saw, how much more blessed are those who do not see and believe." What He is saying is this: Thomas you can't know Me to the level that you can know Me by knowing Me in the natural and as you can know Me in the spiritual.

Paul went to a level I alluded to in the last lesson but I'm really going to go into it now. Paul went to a level in his knowing intimacy with Jesus. His relationship with Jesus was so deep that Peter finally cannot stand it and he writes a letter that says, "This guy Paul, his relationship with Jesus is so deep that some of his letters are hard to understand." Now Peter is the guy who walked with Jesus three and a half years in the flesh and yet Paul goes to a deeper knowledge. Why? Because Jesus said I've got more things to show you and you can't bear it. However, the Spirit of God can show you that. To really understand it, you have to understand that there are three levels of relationships. The lowest level is that of the physical, and sad to say that is how most people get married. You know what happens? They see each other (wow she's gorgeous or he's a hunk) and the physical characteristics hide up the soul in the spiritual level. The next level of relationship is soulish. That's the level that David and Jonathan were connected on. Remember what David said, "Jonathan your love to

Lesson Eight

me was better than any woman." He never knew Jonathan carnally but he knew Jonathan better than any of his wives because their relationship was on the soulish level. This is the level that marriages were first birthed by, was long distance and many times are stronger because the physical didn't get in the way. They got real hooked up and connected in the soul. This is also why and I'll go to a perverted level and say this is why people can leave marriages for people that they met on the Internet. I will never forget I walked back to my tape table one night and there is a father who has two little babies in his arms, two babies clinging to his legs and another two kids running around. He's got this really sad look on his face and I said, "Sir, are you okay?" He said, "No I'm really not, my wife who I had six children with just left me for a man she met on the Internet." I said, "Timeout here, did she ever meet him?" He said, "No." I said, "Does she even know what he looks like?" He said, "I don't think she did." She left those six children for that man she met on the Internet because that soul connection was so strong.

The highest level of relationship is Spirit. For this reason Paul makes this statement: we have not received the spirit of the world, but the Spirit who is from God. Paul said the deepest things of the man, is known by the spirit of the man, even so the deepest things of God, should be revealed by the Spirit of God. This physical body which includes my brain which is not redeemed– our spirits are redeemed, our souls are being renewed– but our bodies will one day perish and we will get incorruptible for corruptible. Listen to me carefully: this body is not capable of knowing God to the depths that I can know Him in my spirit. So what Jesus is saying to Thomas is this: if I was to reveal Myself to you physically you couldn't go to the level that you can go with Me if you go in the Spirit because your body is not redeemed. Paul is able to go to that depth because he wasn't constantly relying back to when he walked with Jesus in the flesh. That actually was hindering Thomas and that's what Jesus was saying, "Thomas, that is going to hinder you if you keep relying on that. You have to know me by My spirit."

One day we will have a glorified body and the Bible says we will behold Him and we will be able to know Him on that level in that body because it's a redeemed body and it can go to that depth but until that happens we've got to know Him in the Spirit. That's why Paul says, "May the intimate communion of the Holy Spirit be with you" because it's the Holy Spirit and He's the one that reveals Jesus to us.

THE PROMISE OF THE FATHER

Video Session 9

THE PROMISE OF THE FATHER

Key Statement:
The promise of the Holy Spirit is for everyone.

"That if you confess with your mouth the Lord Jesus and believe in your heart that God has raised Him from the dead, you will be saved. For with the heart one believes unto righteousness, and with the mouth confession is made unto salvation. For the Scripture says, 'Whoever believes on Him will not be put to shame.'"
Romans 10:9-11

If you say with your mouth that Jesus is Lord and believe in your heart that God raised Him from the dead, you will be saved. That is not make-believe or new popular jargon; it is what the Bible says in the tenth chapter of Romans. Whoever believes in Him will not be ashamed. **(See Appendix A for more information on how to be saved.)**

In college John became a Christian, yet in his testimony he says that there was a void in his life. He knew he was saved and would go to heaven, but when he read the Bible, he felt like he was in a cloud. He felt distant from the Lord.

1. As he began to search the Scriptures, what did he realize? He was ___*missing an aspect of his walk and he needed another encounter with the Lord.*___

LEADER'S NOTES

(3-5 minutes)

Remind the group of a few key lessons by referring to these statements:

1. Intimacy with God is available to each one of us. This is God's passion.

2. Last week's session: The Holy Spirit desires intimacy with each of us.

Set this session up with the Key Statement. Then go through the questions, asking for and providing the answers.

Note: At the end of this session there will be an opportunity to lead people in prayer for the infilling of the Holy Spirit, so seek to gently but boldly prepare people for that time as you go through the session

• *There is a lot of Scripture in this session, so if you are short on time, you may have to simply refer to the verse quickly as opposed to reading it all.*

• *Don't let discussions disintegrate into wars over doctrine. The minute it begins to happen, tell people you "respect their positions, but this is not the time for a doctrinal debate." Then get back to the journey.*

Lesson Nine

Leader's Notes

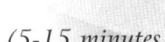

(5-15 minutes)

A GREAT TIME FOR A DISCUSSION.

Ask if anyone in the group can identify with John's experience.

• Have they been a Christian, but felt "dry" or "in a cloud" when they read the Bible?

• Have they wondered about a further encounter with God, as John called it?

• Have they heard about this subject before?

• If no one volunteers, then consider sharing your own experiences that were similar to John's, to get things started.

2. Can you identify with John's experience either now or in the past? Being a Christian, but feeling something is lacking even though you are serving God and reading the Bible?

___

3. Have you ever felt "in a cloud" or "distant" from God when reading the Bible? Or what words would you use to describe your experience?

___

4. During this time, in what ways did you search for more of God?

___

5. The encounter John speaks of is called the ___baptism___ or the ___infilling___ of the Holy Spirit.

> *"And being assembled together with them, He commanded them not to depart from Jerusalem, but to wait for the Promise of the Father, 'which,' He said, 'you have heard from Me; for John truly baptized with water, but you shall be baptized with the Holy Spirit not many days from now."*
> ### Acts 1:4–5

6. In Acts 1, Jesus has been raised from the dead and is speaking to His disciples. What did He command the disciples to do? He ___commanded___ them ___not___ to ___depart___ from Jerusalem but ___wait___ for the ___Promise___ of the Father. Notice this was not a request but a command.

THE PROMISE OF THE FATHER

7. What does the word *baptize* mean?
   To immerse, submerge or to make overwhelmed.

In Acts 2 we see the story unfold...

"When the Day of Pentecost had fully come, they were all with one accord in one place. And suddenly there came a sound from heaven, as of a rushing mighty wind, and it filled the whole house where they were sitting. Then there appeared to them divided tongues, as of fire, and one sat upon each of them. And they were all filled with the Holy Spirit and began to speak with other tongues, as the Spirit gave them utterance. And there were dwelling in Jerusalem Jews, devout men, from every nation under heaven. And when this sound occurred, the multitude came together, and were confused, because everyone heard them speak in his own language."
                    Acts 2:1–6

8. In verses 5 and 6 we see the Holy Spirit got the attention of the whole city of Jerusalem. Multitudes gathered when they heard the wind. At this point they were all __*confused*__. What did Peter do next?
   He preached

9. Look in your Bible at Acts 2:14. What did Peter say to the men of Judea and Jerusalem? "Let this be __*known*__ to you, and __*heed*__ my words."

10. What Old Testament prophet did he quote?
    Joel

As Peter himself is filled with the Spirit, he preaches and points the people to Jesus. Let's break down the following scriptures:

LEADER'S NOTES

Have someone read Acts 2:14.

Point out that Peter is telling the people to take his words seriously, and we are to take the Word of God seriously on this journey.

Tell the group that this journey contains God-things that will challenge them to grow in their intimacy with Him. Remind them here that intimacy is God's will for them personally, and today James 4:8 will offer real opportunity to them. They should listen and be ready to draw near to God in this very session!

LESSON NINE

LEADER'S NOTES

"'Therefore being exalted to the right hand of God, and having received from the Father the promise of the Holy Spirit, He poured out this which you now see and hear.'...Then Peter said to them, 'Repent, and let every one of you be baptized in the name of Jesus Christ for the remission of sins; and you shall receive the gift of the Holy Spirit. For the promise is to you and to your children, and to all who are afar off, as many as the Lord our God will call.'"
Acts 2:33, 38–39

11. What was the Promise that both Jesus (Acts 1:4–5 above) and now Peter refers to?

[ ] The Promise of water baptism
[ ] The Promise of Jesus
[X] The Promise of the Holy Spirit

12. What distinguishing characteristics accompanied the outpouring of the Holy Spirit? The outpouring was both ___*seen*___ and ___*heard*___. Remember this as we continue today's session.

13. Who was the promise to?

[ ] You
[ ] Your children
[ ] All who afar off
[ ] As many as the Lord will call
[X] All of the above

14. Does that promise include you? [X] Yes [ ] No
Why? *Because it says "as many as the Lord God will call." If you are saved, it is because He has called you.*

THE PROMISE OF THE FATHER

A JOURNEY THROUGH THE NEW TESTAMENT CHURCH

LEADER'S NOTES

There are four other occurrences of people being filled with the Holy Spirit in the Book of Acts. What are the two things John wants us to make note of?

15. It is a __*separate experience*__ from receiving Jesus Christ as Lord and Savior.

16. People around them __*saw*__ and __*heard*__ the manifestation of being filled with the Holy Spirit.

Samaria...

"Then Philip went down to the city of Samaria and preached Christ to them....But when they believed Philip as he preached the things concerning the kingdom of God and the name of Jesus Christ, both men and women were baptized."
Acts 8:5,12

17. What happened when Philip preached the gospel?

[ ] The people revolted
[ ] The people stoned him
[x] The people believed and were baptized

"Now when the apostles who were at Jerusalem heard that Samaria had received the Word of God, they sent Peter and John to them."
Acts 8:14

18. Why did the apostles send Peter and John to Samaria?

[ ] Because there was trouble
[x] Because the people had received the Word of God and became saved

155

Lesson Nine

Leader's Notes

"Who, when they had come down, prayed for them that they might receive the Holy Spirit."
Acts 8:15

19. If the people in Samaria were already saved, why did they need the apostles to come down to receive the Holy Spirit?

[ ] Because they were faking salvation
[x] Because this verse is speaking of the baptism or infilling of the Holy Spirit, which they had not yet received

"For as yet He had fallen upon none of them. They had only been baptized in the name of the Lord Jesus."
Acts 8:16

20. Acts 8:16 confirms again:

[ ] The people in Samaria had been saved
[ ] There are two separate experiences being described here
[ ] Neither
[x] Both

"Then they laid hands on them, and they received the Holy Spirit."
Acts 8:17

21. [x] True or [ ] False: These people had already believed Philip concerning the kingdom of God and the name of Jesus Christ and had been baptized, yet subsequent to their salvation the apostles are laying hands on them so they can receive the Holy Spirit.

22. How could these people be saved since no one can say that Jesus is Lord but by the Holy Spirit (1 Cor. 12:3)?

At the moment of conversion, the Holy Spirit indwells us, but we are not filled with His presence until we ask the Father in Jesus' name (Luke 11:13).

THE PROMISE OF THE FATHER

In John 14:17 Jesus says the world cannot receive the Spirit of truth. It is the children of God who ask the Father to fill them with the Holy Spirit.

> "Then they laid hands on them, and they received the Holy Spirit. And when Simon saw that through the laying on of the apostles' hands the Holy Spirit was given, he offered them money, saying, 'Give me this power also, that anyone on whom I lay hands may receive the Holy Spirit.'"
> Acts 8:17–19

Again, what are the two things we are looking for in each of the passages to study?

23. The infilling or baptism of the Holy Spirit is a __*separate experience*__ from receiving Jesus Christ as Lord and Savior.

24. People around them __*saw*__ and __*heard*__ the manifestation of being filled with the Holy Spirit.

In Acts 8 we've seen the first thing we are watching for. When Philip preached, the people were saved. When the apostles came, they were filled with the Spirit. This shows a *separate experience.*

25. But what evidence do you find that the people around them saw and heard the manifestation of the Holy Spirit? Simon __*saw*__ that through the laying on of the apostles' hands the __*Holy Spirit*__ was given.

As we look at the other verses in Acts, we will see that each of them was accompanied by speaking in tongues. It would make sense that what Simon saw was the same because it is congruent with what happens with the other infilling experiences.

LEADER'S NOTES

LESSON NINE

LEADER'S NOTES

The apostle Paul...

A man named Saul had been converted on the road to Damascus. When God sent a believer named Ananias to Saul, Ananias said to him, "Brother Saul, the Lord Jesus, who appeared to you on the road as you came, has sent me that you may receive your sight and be filled with the Holy Spirit" (Acts 9:17).

26. Here again we're looking for our two principles. Immediately we see the first. On the road to Damascus Saul had recognized Jesus by calling Him "Lord." What other evidence do you see in this verse that Saul had become a believer? _Ananias addresses Saul as "Brother Saul."_ So we see that Saul was already saved and then subsequently was filled with _the Holy Spirit_.

> *"I thank my God I speak with tongues more than you all."*
> **1 Corinthians 14:18**

> *"I wish you all spoke with tongues."*
> **1 Corinthians 14:5**

In those verses we see that the apostle Paul (his name was changed from Saul in Acts 13:9) also spoke in tongues. Again, it would make sense that this happened when Paul was filled with the Holy Spirit when Ananias prayed for him, just like in Acts chapter 2.

Cornelius and his household...

A Roman officer named Cornelius and his family were Gentiles. The Jewish people wanted nothing to do with the Gentiles in regard to religious or social matters (Eph. 2:12). Yet God supernaturally answers Cornelius' prayer and sends Peter to preach to him. What happens next astonishes the Jews who were with Peter.

THE PROMISE OF THE FATHER

"While Peter was still speaking these words, the Holy Spirit fell upon all those who heard the word. And those of the circumcision who believed were astonished, as many as came with Peter, because the gift of the Holy Spirit had been poured out on the Gentiles also. For they heard them speak with tongues and magnify God."
Acts 10:44–46

27. Why were the Jews with Peter astonished?
Because the gift of the Holy Spirit was poured out on Cornelius and his family, who were Gentiles.

28. How did they know the Holy Spirit had been poured out?
They heard them speak with tongues and magnify God.

This verse clearly shows the evidence of the Holy Spirit's outpouring was hearing the people speak with tongues and magnify God. The New Living Translation says, "…the gift of the Holy Spirit had been poured out upon the Gentiles, too. And there could be no doubt about it, for they heard them speaking in tongues and praising God" (vv. 45–46).

LEADER'S NOTES

"THEOLOGY 101"

Acts 10 is the only incident in the Bible where the people actually got saved and received the gift of the Holy Spirit at the same time. The reason for this can be seen within the verse itself. Remember, it was not even believed that Gentiles could be saved, let alone filled with the Holy Spirit. In verses 9–17 God went so far as to give Peter a supernatural vision three times to convince him about this.

Lesson Nine

Leader's Notes

29. When Peter obeyed God and went to preach to these Gentiles, how would he and the Jews with him know that they were truly saved? The answer is in verse 46.
God not only saved them but He also filled them with the Spirit and because the Jews heard them speak with tongues and magnify God. This convinced them that God would indeed save Gentiles.

This encounter changed the world.

Ephesus...

30. When the apostle Paul and his team came to Ephesus and found some disciples, what was the first question he asked them? Paul said to them.
"Did you receive the Holy Spirit when you believed?" (Acts 19:2)

These people were disciples, yet they answered Paul that they had not even heard there was a Holy Spirit. Paul asked them what they were baptized into, and they answered, "The baptism of John." Paul preached to them the baptism of Jesus and they were baptized in the name of the Lord Jesus. (Acts 19:4–5)

31. What happened next in verse 6, after they were baptized?
Paul laid hands on them. The Holy Spirit came upon them; and they spoke with tongues and prophesied.

Here again we see these disciples were filled with the Holy Spirit after they were saved. We also see they immediately began to speak in tongues and prophesied.

THE PROMISE OF THE FATHER

When Will Tongues Cease?

The Bible says tongues will cease. Let's find out when:

"Love never fails. But whether there are prophecies, they will fail; whether there are tongues, they will cease; whether there is knowledge, it will vanish away. For we know in part and we prophesy in part. But when that which is perfect has come, then that which is in part will be done away.
1 Corinthians 13:8–10

32. Tongues will cease when that which is ___perfect___ has come.

Some say the perfect has already come in the form of the Bible. Therefore, the early disciples needed tongues and gifts, but we don't because we have the Bible. However, verse 12 says that now we see dimly but then—referring to when the perfect has come—face to face and that we shall know just as we are known. This is plainly referring to the time when that which is perfect has come. That perfect time is when we see Jesus face to face and we will know Him just as He knows us.

"For now we see in a mirror, dimly, but then face to face. Now I know in part, but then I shall know just as I also am known."
1 Corinthians 13:12

33. That time is obviously ___not___ now. It is speaking of the time when we will be with the Lord in our glorified bodies. That is when the perfect will come.

34. What is the other thing that will vanish away when the perfect has come? ___Knowledge___.

35. If the "perfect" had already come in the form of the Bible, revealed knowledge would have ceased as well as

LEADER'S NOTES

Lesson Nine

Leader's Notes

tongues, it is obvious knowledge has not ceased. These verses are saying tongues and knowledge will pass away, but not until we see Jesus __face to face__ and we __know Him__ as we are known.

Tongues Are For Everyone...

36. Even though tongues have not ceased, some say that not all will speak with tongues. The reason people say this is because they do not understand that there are __four__ different tongues the New Testament speaks about. Two are for __public__ ministry, and two are for your __private__ walk with God.

What are the two categories of tongues for public ministry?

37. Tongues as __a sign to the unbeliever__ (1 Cor. 14:22).

38. What are these tongues? They are when the Holy Spirit __transcends__ your intellect, empowering you _to speak, preach, or teach in any language of this earth of which you have had no previous knowledge_. This only happens as the Holy Spirit __wills__.

39. Tongues for __interpretation__ (1 Cor. 14:5)

40. What are these tongues? They are tongues that are __heavenly languages__ that we have __no knowledge__ of on earth. They must be __interpreted__ not translated.

What are the two categories of tongues for private ministry?

41. Tongues for __intercession__. (Rom. 8:26-28)

THE PROMISE OF THE FATHER

42. What are these tongues? The Holy Spirit ___*helps us*___ in our distress. He prays through us when we ___*don't*___ even know what we should pray for or ___*how*___ we should pray.

43. Tongues for ___*personal prayer*___, which results in ___*personal edification*___ (1 Cor. 14:4).

44. What are these tongues? These are for our ___*personal prayer*___ time. They result in ___*personal edification*___.

We are not to interpret the Word of God by our experiences (or traditions); rather we must allow the Word of God to dictate our experiences. It is certainly God's will for you to be filled with the Spirit. As shown in the Bible, the infilling of the Holy Spirit will be accompanied with tongues. Look at some other straightforward things the apostle Paul says.

> "Now concerning spiritual gifts, brethren,
> I do not want you to be ignorant."
> **1 Corinthians 12:1**

> "I wish you all spoke with tongues."
> **1 Corinthians 14:5**

> "Do not forbid to speak with tongues."
> **1 Corinthians 14:39**

Only you know the reasons you are on this Drawing Near journey, but God is offering you the way to draw nearer to Him right now, from the truths you have just studied. Could the gift of tongues be the next step on your journey with God? Don't hesitate or be nervous. Be bold. Step out in faith believing God will give the Holy Spirit to those who ask!

LEADER'S NOTES

Go over this last section briefly with your group, building toward an invitation:

LESSON NINE

LEADER'S NOTES

- Finally, with boldness and authority, ask if there is anyone who needs to accept the Lord.

- Then ask for those who want prayer to be filled with the Spirit, with the evidence of speaking in tongues, to raise their hands. You can use Appendix B and/or use the video clip of John to lead them in prayer. Be bold, and tell your people to expect the Lord to come in power as He answers their faith. Spend the time it takes to minister as necessary.

1. They should preview the next session and complete the personal/discussion portions in their workbooks. If they would like, they may complete the entire section.

2. Pray for the group before they leave. Remind those who spoke in tongues for the first time to keep praying daily, and they will grow in their faith.

Remember what the apostle Peter said—the promise is for YOU. If you have not received the infilling of the Holy Spirit, turn to Appendix B and/or if you have the DVD, go to lesson 9 and enter code 545 when the icon appears on your screen.

Be filled with the Holy Spirit today, and continue further than you ever imagined in your journey to intimacy with the Lord! Draw near to God. Trust Him to draw near to you!

THE PROMISE OF THE FATHER

Video Script for Lesson 9
THE PROMISE OF THE FATHER

In the next several lessons we are going to talk about the reality of having intimacy with God and how it works. I am going to lay the foundation in this lesson so that you will be propelled into the next lesson which is one of the most important ones that I teach on, but this one is called "The Promise of the Father." I was born again in January of 1979 and I went several months without being filled by the Holy Spirit and for those several months I realized that there was a void in my life. I knew I was saved and that I had received Jesus Christ as my Lord. I knew I was born again and on my way to heaven and yet when I would read the Bible I felt like I was in a cloud. I would feel distant from the Lord even though I knew He was my Savior and I had received Him in my heart. So I began a search and I started reading the scriptures. Then one day I realized that another encounter with the Lord was missing in my life and that encounter is called the baptism or the infilling of the Holy Spirit and that is what I want to talk about tonight.

Jesus has already been raised from the dead and He is speaking to his disciples. Look what He says in Acts 1:4, *"And being assembled together with them, He commanded them not to depart from Jerusalem, but to wait for the Promise of the father, which, He said, you have heard from Me; for John truly baptized with water, but you should be baptized with the Holy Spirit not many days from now."* The first thing we need to notice is that Jesus said you will be baptized. The word baptized comes from the Greek word Baptiso, which means to immerse, submerge or to make overwhelmed. Now that in no way means just a little dab; it means a complete submersion, an infilling or to be full. He looked at the disciples and He commanded them not to leave. How many of you know that we are not to take His commands lightly? They are not a suggestion, they're not a recommendation– it's a command– it is the Promise of the Father.

What is the Promise of the Father? Joel spoke about it in Joel 2:28, *"And it shall come to pass afterward that I will pour out my Spirit on all flesh; your sons and your daughters shall prophesy, your old men shall dream dreams, your young men shall see visions. And also on My menservants and on My maidservants I will pour out My Spirit in those days."* What these guys did not realize was that they were only ten days away from this promise being poured out. When Jesus was raised from the dead it says in 1 Corinthians 15 that He appeared to five hundred believers. The thing that I find so interesting is that ten days later after He was taken into heaven there were only 120 left in the upper room. Why is that? I believe God waited until he had 120 people that said if we rot we are not leaving because the Master said wait. I believe God waited until He had 120 that had totally and completely given Him their lives, were dead to their own desires, wishes and wills and God said this is the people I can pour out my Spirit upon. Watch what happens ten days later, Acts 2:1, *"When the Day of Pentecost had fully come"*… now you must realize Pentecost was a Jewish feast. It does not have anything to do with the fact that it is just singularly related to being filled with the Holy Spirit. *"When the day of Pentecost had fully come, they were all with one accord in one place. And suddenly there came a sound from heaven, as of a rushing mighty wind, and it filled the whole house where they were sitting. Then there appeared to them divided tongues, as of fire, and one sat upon each one of them. And they were all filled with the Holy Spirit and began to speak with other tongues, as the Spirit gave them utterance."*

When the Holy Spirit came in His initial entrance into the earth there was a roar, a rushing mighty wind. You know what I find to be interesting: anything the devil does is perverted to the way God does it. If you look at the Holy Spirit when He comes, He comes with a roar. Every person that was filled with the Holy Spirit could see and hear the evidence that they had been filled with the Spirit of God but whenever the Spirit of God leaves, He leaves quietly. Remember Samson: he said I will get up and go against the Philistines like

Lesson Nine

I had done before but the Bible says he knew not that the Spirit of God had departed from him. So when the Spirit of God comes He comes with a roar and when He leaves He leaves silently. When the enemy comes into a person's life and possesses a person the demonic forces come in silently but when they leave they leave with a roar. You will see it all throughout the gospel: manifestations of roars. People would scream out as demons came out from people and so I think that's a very interesting point.

Now the wind blew and that initial entrance of the Holy Spirit got the attention of the entire city of Jerusalem. There were many from all the nations of the world that were devout Jews who had come to Jerusalem to celebrate the feast of Pentecost. When they heard the wind they all started coming out into the streets. They gathered to the area where the upper room was and they looked at the disciples who were speaking the wonderful works of God in all these different languages. Now they're confused because these are uneducated men but they are speaking perfectly in our languages from these different nations and so they said, "what ever could this be"? Peter stood up and started preaching to them about Jesus. He begins to preach a magnificent message out of the book of Psalms or the book of Joel that he had never studied before, and that's what happens when you get filled with the Holy Spirit: you begin to prophesy. Prophecy means you speak under divine inspiration. It's the most wonderful way to speak. Peter is just ripping along and look at what he goes on to say in Acts 2:32, *"This Jesus God has raised up, of which we are all witnesses. Therefore being exalted to the right hand of God, and having received from the Father the promise of the Holy Spirit, He poured out this which you now see and hear."* The Promise of the Father you are now seeing and hearing. Verse 38, *"Then Peter said to them, Repent and let every one of you be baptized in the name of Jesus Christ for the remission of sins; and you shall receive the gift of the Holy Spirit. For the Promise is to you and to your children, and to all who are afar off, as many as the Lord our God will call."* I remember when I saw this. I said I'm one of those that the Lord our God has called. That means this promise is for me. I want to say this again because you have to get this: Peter said it *"is to you and to your children, and to as many as are far off as our Lord God calls."* I want to ask you: are you as far off as one of those that are far off that the Lord God has called? We're a long way from Jerusalem and it doesn't matter how many generations, because we're one of them. That means this Promise is to every single one of His children.

Now what I want to do is to quickly go through the other four incidents in the book of Acts. There are only five incidents in the book of Acts where we read people are getting filled with the Holy Spirit. I want to go through the other four very quickly and there are two things that I want you to notice. First of all: it is always a separate experience from being born again, except for one time. There is a reason for that one time and I'll share it with you later. Number two: whenever the Holy Spirit came on people and they were filled, people around them saw and heard the manifestation of being filled with the Holy Spirit. We are going to look for those two things. The first place is Acts 8:5, *"Then Philip went down to the city of Samaria and preached Christ to them. And the multitudes with one accord heeded the things spoken by Philip, hearing and seeing the miracles which he did. For unclean spirits, crying with loud a voice, came out of many who were possessed; and many who were paralyzed and lame were healed. And there was great joy in that city."* Verse 12, *"But when they believed Philip as he preached the things concerning the kingdom of God and the name Jesus Christ, both men and women were baptized."* They believed what he preached concerning the things of the kingdom of God. What did he preach? He preached Christ to them so they believed and were baptized in the name of Jesus. Does that make them saved? When you believe what a person's preaching under the name of Jesus, you confess Him as Lord and you're baptized, does that make you saved? Yes. Jesus said go into the world and preach the gospel– to every creature that believes and is baptized shall be saved. He who does not believe shall be condemned. So they are now saved.

Now look at verse 14, *"Now when the apostles who were at Jerusalem heard that Samaria had received the word of God,* (That were born again not by corrupt-

THE PROMISE OF THE FATHER

ible seed but by incorruptible seed the Word of God, which lives and abides forever) *they sent Peter and John to them, who, when they had come down, prayed for them that they might receive the Holy Spirit. For as yet He had fallen upon none of them. They had only been baptized in the name of the Lord Jesus. Then they laid hands on them, and they received the Holy Spirit."* Do you see it is a separate experience from being saved? Verse 18, *"And when Simon saw that through the laying on of the apostles' hands the Holy Spirit was given, he offered them money."* Now it does not directly say that they spoke in tongues and prophesied here, however there is a sorcerer who when he "sees" that they received the Holy Spirit, offers money. That means he obviously saw them doing what they did in the book of Acts, chapter 2: they were speaking in tongues and prophesying. So even though it doesn't directly say it, we can see it that there is evidence because the guy is offering money. We see here again it is a separate experience and that they could see and hear the fact that they had been filled with the Holy Spirit.

Saul of Tarsus is on the road to Damascus to destroy Christians and he has an encounter with the Lord. He falls down on his face and he says *"who are you, Lord?"* The Lord said, *"I am Jesus, whom you are persecuting."* Then Saul says, "Lord what do want me to do?" Acts 9:6, *"So he, trembling and astonished, said, Lord, what do you want me to do?"* Right there Saul said, "Jesus you are my Lord." Notice what happens if you continue to read: Saul goes into the city of Damascus and he fasts and prays three days and three nights. Then we have a man named Ananias who God speaks to. He is a disciple in Damascus. God says to Ananias in Acts 9:10, *"Now there was a certain disciple at Damascus named Ananias; and to him the Lord said in a vision, 'Ananias'. And he said, 'Here I am, Lord.' So the Lord said to him, 'Arise and go to the street called Straight, and inquire at the house of Judas for one called Saul of Tarsus, for behold, he is praying. And in a vision he had seen a man named Ananias coming in and putting his hand on him, so that he might receive his sight.'"* Ananias has a little chat with the Lord about him because he is a little resistant to it. Then we see in verse 17, *"And Ananias went his way and entered the house; and laying his hands on him he said,* (that again confirms that Saul is saved on the road to Damascus) *Brother Saul, the Lord Jesus, who appeared to you on the road as you came, has sent me that you may receive your sight and be filled with the Holy Spirit."* Once again you see it is a separate experience. Now somebody can say that it doesn't say that Paul spoke in tongues here, but if you look over in Corinthians the 14th chapter Paul said, I speak in tongues more than you all and I wish you all spoke in other tongues. When did Paul start speaking in tongues? It would be the same as Acts 2, when they received the Holy Spirit on the day of Pentecost.

In Acts 10 we have the Gentiles and we have a man named Cornelius who is a Roman officer. Cornelius is a man who gives alms constantly and he fears God. An angel of the Lord appears to him and says Cornelius, your prayers and your giving has come up as a memorial before God. Then he says, Cornelius, I want you to send for a man named Peter. He told him where he was, Cornelius sends for Peter and then Cornelius gathers all of his friends and his family, Peter comes up to his house and he starts preaching. Now I think this is an amazing thing: Peter gets about three paragraphs out of his mouth and look what happens in verse 44 of Acts chapter 10, *"While Peter was still speaking these words, the Holy Spirit fell upon all those who heard the Word. And those of the circumcision who believed were astonished, as many as came with Peter, because the gift of the Holy Spirit had been poured out on the Gentiles also."* How do they know it? Verse 46, *"For they heard them speak with tongues and magnify God. Then Peter answered, Can anyone forbid water, that these should not be baptized who have received the Holy Spirit just as we have?"* I want to read this to you out of the New Living Translation, *"The Jewish believers who came with Peter, were amazed that the gift of the Holy Spirit had been poured out on the Gentiles too. And there could be no doubt about it because they heard them speaking in tongues and praising God."* So what was the evidence to the Jewish believers that these guys had received the Holy Spirit? They saw and heard them speaking with other tongues. This is the only account where you do not have them getting filled with the Holy Spirit, after getting saved. I believe there's a reason for that. The Jews would have nothing to do with the Gentiles and the Jews didn't even believe

Lesson Nine

the Gentiles could really be saved, so I believe that it took God having to do a supernatural thing to get these Jews attention. Think about it. When a person says I receive Jesus as my Lord in my heart there is no outward manifestation, but when the Holy Spirit comes on somebody there is an outward manifestation. So God says I'm going to have to get it through these Jew's head because they are a little bit thick on this thing and that I am reaching out to the Gentiles too. The same gift of the Holy Spirit will be poured out onto the Gentiles as well as the Jews and to as many as call upon the Lord.

In Acts chapter 19 is the final one. Acts 19:1 and 2, *"And it happened, while Apollos was at Corinth, that Paul, having passed through the upper regions, came to Ephesus. And finding some disciples he said to them, 'Did you receive the Holy Spirit when you believed?'"* Why did they ask questions like that with such urgency? Because Jesus commanded them– it wasn't an option. He said don't go preach the gospel in all the world until you're endued with power. Now remember: the purpose of receiving the Holy Spirit is power to give evidence of His resurrection. The benefit of being filled is being able to speak in tongues. Continuing in verse 2, *"So they said to him, We have not so much as heard whether there is a Holy Spirit. And he said to them, Into what then were you baptized? So they said, "Into John's baptism. Then Paul said, "John indeed baptized with a baptism of repentance, saying to the people that they should believe on Him who would come after him, that is, on Christ Jesus. When they heard this, they were baptized in the name of the Lord Jesus."* They are saved because they are baptized in the name of Jesus. Look at verse 6, *"And when Paul had laid hands upon them,* (they had just been baptized and after they were baptized he laid hands upon them) *the Holy Spirit came upon them, and they spoke with tongues and prophesied."* They could see and hear the evidence or that the fact that they had received the Holy Spirit.

Tongues are not a complicated thing: all God means when He talks about tongues in the Bible is a language that you are not familiar with. If you look at a person and say, "What is your mother tongue?" you're just asking what is the tongue that your mother taught you when you were a child. I'm going to refer to it as tongues as well. I don't want you to get hung up on it, but that's what it means. It has been something that has been fought in the church and the reason it has been fought is because you are about to discover how important it is. First of all let me tell you a couple of things that a lot of people use to try to say we don't need tongues. The first thing people will say today is this: the Bible says that tongues will cease when that which is perfect has come. Now I would like to address that question because I find that these kinds of questions show people's faith, and the only way you can receive the Holy Spirit is by faith so let me eradicate the questions that destroy people's faith.

Let's go over to Corinthians and I will show it you that this is a very incorrect interpretation. 1 Corinthians 13:8, *"Love never fails. But whether there are prophecies, they will fail; whether there are tongues, they will cease; whether there is knowledge, it will vanish away. For we know in part and we prophesy in part. But when that which is perfect is come, then that which is in part will be done away."* They are saying the perfect has come because the perfect is the Bible and since we have the Bible, we don't need tongues or prophesy anymore. I am going to show you that the perfect that has come is not the Bible because if you keep reading it says in verse 11, *"When I was a child, I spoke as a child, I understood as a child, I thought as a child; but when I became a man, I put away childish things. For now we see in a mirror, dimly, but then face to face. Now I know in part, but then* (when the perfect comes) *I shall know just as I also am known."* Paul says the two indicating factors of when the perfect comes is when I am looking at Him and His resurrected body face to face– when I see His eyes blazing like laser beams and His face shining like the sun– that's when the perfect is. The other thing He said, you'll know the perfect is come when you know Him as He knows you. Do you know Him as well as He knows you? No. You will know it when you are in your glorified body looking at Him face to face and worshiping him. That means that tongues has not ceased, the knowledge has not vanished away and prophecy has not failed.

Now somebody else will say: the Bible says do all speak with tongues? That means just a few people

get the privilege of speaking in tongues. Let me bash that one. Go with me to 1 Corinthians 12 and I will show you where they get that. Paul says in verse 28, *"And God has appointed these in the church: first apostles, second prophets, third teachers, after that miracles, then gifts of healings, helps, administrations, variety of tongues. Are all apostles? Are all prophets? Are all teachers? Are all workers of miracles? Do all have gifts of healings? Do all speak with tongues? Do all interpret?"* The reason they say that about tongues is because they do not understand that there are four tongues that the New Testament teaches about. Two of the tongues are for public ministry. Public ministry is when you minister to one person or to a group of people. Two of the tongues deal with public ministry and two deal with your private walk with God. Let's talk about the four categories of tongues and you are going to understand why Paul said "you all speak with tongues."

The first one is this: tongues as a sign to the unbeliever. 1 Corinthians 14:22, *"Therefore tongues are for a sign, not to those who believe but to the unbelievers."* These tongues occur when the Holy Spirit transcends our intellect, empowering us to be able to speak, teach, preach or sing in any language of this earth, which we have had no previous teaching or learning about. This only happens if the Spirit wills. Let me give you an example. Last year I was preaching in a very large church, one of my staff members was at the meeting and I remember during this meeting there was a particularly wonderful anointing to preach. There was a flow. My staff member that was at this meeting is an intercessor and she was sitting in one of the last rows because she just really felt the burden in her heart to pray while I was preaching. She was praying in what she thought to be her prayer language: unknown tongues. After the meeting was over this distinguishingly dressed man stands up who was sitting in a row in front of her and said, "Your French is very good; in fact you even have perfect accent." She looked at him and she said, "I don't speak French." He said, "Ma'am, I'm a French instructor. I know somebody when they are speaking French; you were speaking perfect French." She said, "Sir, I don't speak French." He said, "Ma'am not only were you speaking French but– what he said was very, very intriguing to me was– you would pray for him while he was preaching and you would start speaking a scripture in your prayer and as soon as you got done speaking the scripture, he would say, "turn to that scripture in the Bible." What was this? This was a sign to that French teacher that what I was preaching that night was the work of God. It made her excited. It was a sign to an unbeliever. This is exactly what happened on the Day of Pentecost. Those untrained men were speaking in languages they had never been trained in before.

For language number two tongues are for: interpretation. 1 Corinthians 12:10, *"To another the working of miracles, to another prophecy, to another discerning of spirits, to another different kinds of tongues, to another the interpretation of tongues."* These are the tongues in which our heavenly languages that we have no knowledge of them on the earth and they must be interpreted, not translated. This is when we will begin to speak out in a public assembly a language of heaven that gives an interpretation. This is what Paul meant when he said in 1 Corinthians 14:5, *"I wish you all spoke with tongues (speaking of a private language) but even more that you prophesied; for he who prophesies is greater than he who speaks with tongues, unless indeed he interprets, that the church may receive edification."* Let me give you an example of this. I was in Singapore getting ready to speak to one of the largest churches in the nation. It was a packed house that night and the first time I had ever been at the church. I remember we had just gone through a beautiful praise and worship time. We were just getting ready to come up and begin to exhort the people from the scripture when all of a sudden this man starts speaking in an unknown language from the balcony. When he did my hair started standing up on my arms. God's presence hit that place and the most amazing thing was it was a large auditorium yet you could hear that guy like he had a microphone. It was almost like heaven had amplified his voice. Once he spoke in that tongue the interpretation came and the interpretation was exactly what I was going to preach on that night. I sat there in awe because they had never heard me before; they didn't realize the kind of flow of the ministry I had. Here this guy is giving the interpretation of what I am about to preach, I stand up

and preach and it was an absolute edification thing for the whole church because they saw that the word that God had placed in me was what He wanted spoken that night.

You will see these two tongues distinctly identified in 1 Corinthians 14:22 & 23, *"Therefore tongues are for a sign, not to those who believe but to unbelievers; but prophesying is not for unbelievers but for those who believe. Therefore if the whole church comes together in one place, and all speak with tongues, and there come in those who are uninformed or unbelievers, will they not say that you are out of your mind?"* So that's talking about the tongue where we speak in a heavenly language because they were all speaking in tongues on the Day of Pentecost. At the same time they didn't say they were "mad" because they understood their language, but if we are all speaking in the tongue that needs to be interpreted and somebody that is an unbeliever comes in, he'll think you are crazy.

The next one is tongues for intersession, this is personal. Romans 8:26-28 says, *"Likewise the Spirit also helps us in our weaknesses. For we do not know what we should pray for as we ought, but the Spirit Himself makes intercession for us with groanings which cannot be uttered (or be expressed in words). Now He who searches (knows) the hearts knows what the mind of the Spirit is."* This says the Spirit leads believers in harmony with Gods own will. We don't know what's happening right now with a family member that is three states away but the Holy Spirit does. I'll never forget when this happened. I used to have a fraternity Bible study when I was in college. A bunch of sorority and fraternity kids came one night and there was a girl sitting in there. She had been taught her whole life that tongues had passed away. I started just preaching these scriptures to them that night and she said, " My goodness, this is in the Bible! I've been lied to all my life. She believed that night and she spoke in tongues along with a bunch of other ones.

The next morning I'm in my Fraternity and I get woken up by the intercom, "John Bevere, you have a visitor in the lobby." It's 6:30 in the morning and I come out there a little bit tired. Here is this sorority girl beaming and she says, "John, I've got to tell you what happened." I said, "What happened?" She said, " At five O'clock this morning I was woken up by the Lord. I just felt like I should pray in tongues." So she started praying in tongues. And she said, "I kept remembering you saying to ask to pray that you may interpret" so while I was praying in tongues I said in my mind "Lord, what am I saying, who am I praying for?" She said the Lord showed me that there was a man, and she knew it was a life threatening thing; the Lord showed me I was praying for an older man and his life was in danger." And she said, "About five to six o'clock, I got a release and I had joy so I just stopped praying. Two minutes later my roommate, who is also a Christian, got an emergency phone call that her grandfather just had a massive heart attack at five o'clock in the morning. They stabilized him right before six o'clock. How would she have ever known to pray for him if she had not had the gift of tongues? The Holy Spirit knows what we need to pray and how we need to pray.

Turn to page 226 and read Appendix B "How to Be Filled With the Holy Spirit".

The last tongue is tongues for personal prayer, which results in personal edification. 1 Corinthians 14:4, says, *"He who speaks in a tongue edifies himself."* And this is what I am going to go into for the next lesson: I am going to talk about the language of intimacy.

Video Session 10

The Language of Intimacy

Key Statement:
Because God desires His interaction with you to be deep and rich, He has made a way for you to fellowship with Him on His level.

"For he who speaks in a tongue does not speak to men but to God, for no one understands him; however, in the spirit he speaks mysteries."
1 Corinthians 14:2

1. What kind of tongue is this referring to?
   The tongue of your personal prayer language.

2. Who is doing the speaking? ____*You are*____.

3. Who is being spoken to? ____*God*____.

4. What is being spoken? ____*Mysteries*____.

"THEOLOGY 101"
These "mysteries" are not mysterious!

"Study to show thyself approved unto God, a workman that needeth not to be ashamed, rightly dividing the word of truth"
2 Tim. 2:15 KJV

LESSON TEN — LEADER'S N...

...pirit desires inti-m... ...n each of us.

2. Go over the last session with a brief reminder: There are four different kinds of tongues.

Set this session up with the Key Statement. Then go through the questions, asking for and providing the answers.

At the end of this session, provide another opportunity to lead people in prayer for the infilling of the Holy Spirit.

• Note: Don't let discussions disintegrate into wars over doctrine. The minute it begins to happen, tell people you "respect their positions, but this is not the time for a doctrinal debate." Then get back to the journey.

You are finding on this journey that theology is about knowing God Himself. And what is more exciting than to dig a little and find God's treasures? In a moment we will look at what Paul meant in 1 Corinthians 14:2. First, let's talk about the Bible itself. The Word of God is full of things that are "mysteries" to most people, but understanding these truths is available to you as a diligent student. In today's instant gratification society, many people are sadly put off by the word *theology* because it implies work or strenuous thought or religion.

In John's books and videos, he frequently refers to W. E. Vine, an expert in Greek New Testament words who spent a lifetime as a scholar to bring people more understanding of the scriptures. *Vine's Expository Dictionary of New Testament Words* is one of the many tools available today for the believer who is serious in his journey with God. The book title may sound intimidating, but it is written for the average reader and serves as a concordance, dictionary and commentary all at once! It is full of insight and is readily available at bookstores.

5. The word *mysteries* is the Greek word *musterion*. In the New Testament it denotes not the mysterious, as with the English word, but that which being outside the range of unassisted natural apprehension can be made known only by _____*divine revelation*_____ and is made known to those who are illuminated by _____*the Holy Spirit*_____. In the ordinary sense, a mystery implies knowledge _____*withheld*_____, but in this scripture it means truth _____*revealed*_____.

If you were to speak with the president of the United States, you would have a difficult time understanding things at his level because he knows things you have no way of being informed of. For you to understand him, you would need a way for him to come down to your level of understanding.

6. How does this parallel our fellowship with God? *When you walk into the King of the universe's office (God), and you only pray according to your own understanding (your native language), then God must come down to your level of understanding. Therefore, you would never experience higher levels of intimacy.*

7. So God says, "I'm going to __make a way__ for My children to come in and talk to Me on My level." God's way is through __tongues__.

8. How does God provide for the fact that when we pray in tongues, we cannot understand what we are praying? *We are to pray for the gift of interpretation. "Therefore let him who speaks in a tongue pray that he may interpret. For if I pray in a tongue, my spirit prays, but my understanding is unfruitful" (1 Cor. 14:13–14).*

9. How is praying in tongues a blessing in the spiritual war we are involved in? *The enemy (Satan) does not understand it all.*

10. What is the number one reason we want to be able to communicate with God through speaking in tongues? *Intimacy. To be intimate with Him.*

Key Statement:
Tongues are how we receive God's counsel.

LESSON TEN

LEADER'S NOTES

11. What does God give us when we are intimate with Him? ___His counsel___.

"The spirit of a man is the lamp of the LORD, searching all the inner depths of his heart."
Proverbs 20:27

12. When God speaks to us, He speaks to our ___hearts___ not our ___heads___.

"Counsel in the heart of man is like deep water, but a man of understanding will draw it out."
Proverbs 20:5

13. What is counsel? ___Wisdom___ applied to a ___specific___ situation.

14. Why do you go to a counselor? You need ___advice___.

15. Where is the counsel you need? In your ___heart___, but it is like deep water and needs to be ___drawn out___.

16. How is it drawn out? Jesus said, *"He who believes in Me, as the Scripture has said, ___out of his heart will flow rivers of living water___. But this He spoke concerning the Spirit, whom those believing Him would receive"* (John 7:38–39).

Have a volunteer read 1 Corinthians 2:7–14 aloud, slowly.

"But we speak the wisdom of God in a mystery, the hidden wisdom which God ordained before the ages for our glory....But God has revealed them to us through His Spirit. For the Spirit searches all things, yes, the deep things of God. For what man knows the things of a man except the spirit of the man which is in him? Even so, no one knows the things of God except the Spirit of God. Now we have received, not the

THE LANGUAGE OF INTIMACY

spirit of the world, but the Spirit who is from God, that we might know the things that have been freely given to us by God. These things we also speak, not in words which man's wisdom teaches but which the Holy Spirit teaches, comparing spiritual things with spiritual. But the natural man does not receive the things of the Spirit of God, for they are foolishness to him; nor can he know them, because they are spiritually discerned."
1 Corinthians 2:7, 10–14

There is a lot in this passage from 1 Corinthians. Put your heart and mind into this. Read these verses and hear John's examples about:

- Reading the Bible
- Writing books
- Marrying the right person
- Business deals
- Family members

17. Sum up how God can help you through praying in tongues:
There are many things in life that we do not know the answers to. But through speaking in tongues in our private prayer time, we can draw out counsel from the Holy Spirit for all things. The mysteries will be revealed as we are intimate with God.

18. The number one thing people need help with is ____direction____ for their lives.

19. What is God's provision for this? *"If any of you ____lacks wisdom____, let him ____ask____ of God, who gives to ____all____ liberally and without reproach, and it ____will be____ given to him"* (James 1:5)

LEADER'S NOTES

LESSON TEN

LEADER'S NOTES

(5 minutes)

For questions 21 and 22 ask for one or two volunteers to share their examples how God has blessed or changed them through praying in tongues.

You may also want to share your story or examples you know of in your church.

20. Remember in earlier sessions we learned that God is omniscient and omnipresent. He is all knowing and everywhere. He knows all things that you need to know to serve Him and be blessed. As you are worshiping God and praying in tongues, God will bring His wisdom to your mind, from deep down in your spirit. What types of things "come bubbling up" from the heart?
Sample answers: People to pray for, things to do, things NOT *to do, ideas, creativity, etc.*

21. Have you ever experienced this type of thing before? [ ] Yes [ ] No

If not, it is God's will for you, and you can be filled with the Spirit!

22. If your answer is yes, what are some examples of things God has done for you as you received information, strength, or peace that you or others needed?

_____
_____
_____
_____
_____

Key Statement:
Praying in tongues gives us strength by building our inner man.

"He who speaks in a tongue edifies himself."
I Corinthians 14:4

176

THE LANGUAGE OF INTIMACY

"But you, beloved, building yourselves up on your most holy faith, praying in the Holy Spirit."
Jude 20

23. What does the word *edify*, a house, and our bodies have to do with praying in tongues?
The Greek word edify means "to build a house." We are the temples of the Holy Spirit (2 Cor. 6:16), the building of God. When we pray in the Spirit, we are enlarging our ability to contain His presence and power in our lives.

24. Praying in tongues promotes __spiritual growth__ and develops __character__ in believers.

"Of whom we have much to say, and hard to explain, since you have become dull of hearing....But solid food belongs to those who are of full age, that is, those who by reason of use have their senses exercised to discern both good and evil."
Hebrews 5:11, 14

25. What are the five "spiritual senses"?
- *Taste (Ps. 34:8)*
- *Touch (2 Cor. 6:17)*
- *Smell (2 Cor. 2:14–16; Eph. 5:2; Phil. 4:18–19)*
- *Sight (Ps. 36:9)*
- *Hearing (1 Kings 18:41–42; Luke 14:35)*

26. What do gemstone experts, wine tasters, musical conductors, and athletes have to do with praying in tongues?

These are people who have learned to train their physical senses. God says the mature in the Spirit are those people who have trained their spiritual senses.

LEADER'S NOTES

You may want go over these briefly and have a volunteer read each scripture.

Lesson Ten

Leader's Notes

(10 minutes)

Have the people break into small groups to agree together in prayer as they lift up whom and how to share this message with.

• Tell them to pray that God opens doors of utterance and softens hearts to the message.

• Encourage them to consider asking this person to church or the next Drawing Near session.

• They may also want to give them a copy of John's book or tapes on Drawing Near. These are easy ways they can open doors and minister.

• Remind them to pray in the Spirit for these people and to speak boldly when they do minister.

27. Why is this so very important to our intimacy with God?
In the natural world, if you can't hear, taste, touch, smell, or feel, there is no way to communicate with you. Someone could yell, scream, hit, and do all kinds of things, but you wouldn't even know it. It is the same with God; if we don't have our spiritual senses developed, God cannot get things communicated to us. We will be "dull of hearing."

28. The reason God gave us the ability to speak in tongues is to enhance our ___*intimacy*___ with Him. When we pray in the Spirit, we build up our ___*inner man*___ and become ___*sensitive*___ to what God wants, what God loves, and what God needs us to do. We ___*hear*___ His voice more ___*easily*___.

• Do you know someone who is saved but not yet filled with the Holy Spirit with the evidence of speaking in tongues?

• Do you know someone who has heard about this but doesn't know how to be filled with the Holy Spirit or does not understand it is God's will?

• Do you know someone who speaks in tongues but doesn't understand all the spiritual benefits of it?

THE LANGUAGE OF INTIMACY

Take some serious time to pray in the Spirit. Ask God to show you:

- Who
- How to share the message you've learned in last week and today's session.

29. Put their name below and the time you will take the opportunity to minister to them as the Lord leads you.

Who: _____
_____

How: _____
_____

When: _____
_____

Leader's Notes

- *Finally, with boldness and authority, ask for those in your group who want prayer who have not yet been filled with the Spirit, with the evidence of speaking in tongues, to raise their hands. You can use Appendix B and/or use the video clip of John to lead them in prayer. Be bold, and tell your people to expect the Lord to come in power as He answers their faith. Spend the time it takes to minister as necessary.*

Remind your group:

1. They should preview the next session and complete the personal discussion portions in their workbooks. If they would like, they may complete the entire section.

2. Pray for the group before they leave. Remind those who spoke in tongues for the first time to keep praying daily, and they will grow in their faith.

Lesson Ten

Video Script for Lesson 10
The Language of Intimacy

In the last lesson we learned that there are four different kinds of tongues. The first tongue is the tongue that is a sign to the unbeliever. The second one is the tongue for interpretation– that is when we speak a heavenly language. It is also called diverse tongues. That's when we speak a language of heaven and it must be interpreted not translated. The third tongue is tongues for intercession. The fourth one is tongues for edification and that's where we are going to begin.

Lets read 1 Corinthians 14:2, *"For he who speaks in a tongue does not speak to men but to God."* Does that confirm to you that there are different kinds of tongues? Can I ask a question: on the Day of Pentecost whom were the apostles speaking to? They were speaking to men from nations all around in their own languages. They weren't speaking to God; they were speaking to men because that tongue was a sign to the unbeliever. When somebody gives a tongue in a church service that needs to be interpreted they are not speaking to God, they are speaking to the church. Paul says right here he who speaks in a tongue does not speak to men, he speaks to God. This is your tongue of your personal prayer language. Why do we need to speak in tongues? Let's keep reading this verse, *"For he who speaks in a tongue does not speak to men but to God, for no one understands him; however, in the spirit he speaks mysteries."* Mysteries is a Greek word. W.E. Vines defines this word mysteries as: it denotes not the mysterious as with the English word when we say mystery we think mysterious, but that which being outside the range of unassisted natural apprehension can be made known only by divine revelation and is made known to those who are illuminated by the Holy Spirit. In the ordinary sense a mystery implies knowledge withheld, its scriptural significance is truth revealed.

Why does God give us the ability to speak with tongues? Let me give an example. If I walked into the oval office of the President of the United States office today, would I be able to speak with the President of the United States on his level? No, because he knows things about the security of the United States, the national security codes, and things that are happening that I am just not aware of. In order for us to really have fellowship he has to come down to my level of understanding. The same is true when I walk into the King of the Universes' office. When I walk into the King of the Universes' office and the only way I know how to pray is by my understanding English then He's got to come down to my level of understanding. We can never have higher levels of intimacy. So God said I'm going to make a way for my children to come in and talk to Me on my level. Now this is going to get better and better. Somebody says "but when I speak in tongues I don't know what I'm saying." That's why Paul says in I Corinthians 14:13,14, *"Therefore let him who speaks in a tongue pray that he may interpret. For if I pray in a tongue, my spirit prays, but my understanding is unfruitful."* Paul says let him pray that he may interpret.

The Bible says in Psalms 42:7, *"Deep calls unto deep at the noise of Your waterfalls."* That is a prophetic scripture because Jesus said later on that when we receive the Holy Spirit, out of our bellies shall flow rivers of living water. God has given us a way to be able to have intimate communion and fellowship with Him at His level. This is absolutely exciting! How many of you know that there were things that God wanted to hide from the enemy? People that are in war together have a language called codes. In World War II they had codes and they spoke in a language that the enemy couldn't pick up. The Bible says the same thing: if the principalities and the powers had known the wisdom of God they would not have crucified the Lord of Glory. That deals with Jesus being crucified. But how many of you know there are things that God does not want the enemy to know? When we start speaking in

that heavenly language the enemy doesn't understand it, and then all of a sudden a barrage of angel's show up and just blow up the thing the enemy was planning for somebody. It's that language of intimacy and one reason why He gave it to them but the number one reason God gave us the ability to speak in tongues was for intimacy.

Do you realize there is so much that He knows and wants to reveal to us right now? If you want to be somebody that God reveals His secrets and His mysteries to, then you need to be somebody that is faithful of what He gives you. God won't share the deep intimate things of your life with somebody that He knows is going to go blabbing it to everybody. I learned that God would give mysteries and share deep and intimate things and secrets with people that will not blab it wrongly. I learned this the hard way. Back when I was first starting in the ministry I was in a part of the world where there was a very famous Evangelist and I was preaching at this pastors church. He asked if I wanted to meet this famous Evangelist. I said absolutely. This man of God was really well known and I remember meeting him at dinner one night. When I met him at dinner the pastor was there, this man of God, his wife and my wife. I just started pouring out everything the Lord had ever shown me and it was the revelation contest. You know what I'm talking about. And so I'm saying the Lord showed me this, and the Lord showed me that all throughout the whole dinner. He's saying it too and so it looks like it's a good conversation from the outside. We drive back to the hotel and my wife and I are exhausted and I said, "Lisa something is not right inside here; I need to pray." She said, "Are you sure John, you're exhausted." I said I have to pray. I remember she went to bed and as I started walking out to the balcony, the moment my foot touched the balcony the Holy Spirit shouted this the inside of me: "Well the king showed all the treasures tonight didn't he?" And I went, "Oh my God". Then I remembered when Hezekiah wanted to impress some people and he showed them all the treasures and the prophet came and rebuked him and it cost him greatly. God said to me right then, "Son, I do not reveal things to you for you to go spout off and impress people with what you know. I reveal things to you because I can trust you with them. That means you don't speak it unless I put an unction on you to speak it." I said, "Yes sir, I've learned my lesson." If God's going to share with you secrets you've got to be trustworthy. The number one reason why we want to be able to communicate with God and speak in tongues is to be intimate with Him and when you are intimate with Him you know that He'll give you His counsel.

Proverbs 20:27 says, *"The spirit of man is the lamp of the Lord, searching all the inner depths of his heart."* God speaks to us is in our spirits not in our heads. God speaks to us in our hearts and the way I liken it is this: when revelation comes to us it is like trapped air in a seam bubbling up into your mind. You hear it and it's almost like you sense it deep from within but it bubbles up to where you can recognize it with your mind. Proverbs 20:5 we read this, *"Counsel in the heart of man is like deep water. But a man of understanding will draw it out."* What is counsel? It is wisdom applied to a specific situation. You go to a counselor because you need advice. All the counsel you're ever going to need is in your heart, but it's like deep water, and only the person who has understanding knows how to draw it out. How does he draw it out? Jesus said, "He who believes in Me as the scripture has said, out of his heart will flow rivers of living water. Counsel in the heart is like deep water. He spoke this concerning the spirit whom those believing on Him would receive. So we see that in Proverbs the counsel or wisdom that we need for a specific situation is like deep water but the man of understanding draws it out.

Go with me to 1 Corinthians 2:7 and it says, *"But we speak the wisdom of God in a mystery, the hidden wisdom which God ordained before the ages for our glory."* Mystery means unrevealed truth. Continue with verse 12, *"Now we have not received, not the spirit of the world, but the Spirit who is from God, that we might know the things that have been freely given to us by God. These things we also speak, not in words which man's wisdom teaches but which the Holy Spirit teaches, comparing spiritual things with spiritual."* Paul says that we

Lesson Ten

speak the wisdom of God in mystery and then goes on to say we have been given the Spirit of God. Why? So that we can know the things freely given to us by God and we speak these things not in words which men of wisdom teaches, but which the Holy Spirit teaches. Now remember counsel, wisdom in the heart of the man is like deep waters. Jesus said out of his belly shall flow rivers of living water. Paul is talking about the wisdom that we are speaking is what the Holy Spirit gives us.

1 Corinthians 14:2, *"For he who speaks in a tongue does not speak to men but to God, for no one understands him; however, in the spirit he speaks mysteries."* How often I have come to places where I've read scriptures and I say, "That doesn't make any sense." Usually when I get a scripture that doesn't make any sense, that's when I start getting excited because you know what I do? I say, "Lord, this doesn't make a lick of sense to me. I need You to show me what You are saying, and then I start praying in tongues. Do you know what happens? All of a sudden the enlightenment comes bubbling up or it comes up later. That's where a lot of what I've preached and I've written has come from. Numerous times I have been writing a book and this has happened so many times. As I'm writing the thoughts are coming like a machine gun and all of a sudden I hit a brick wall. And I go, "I'm out, there's nothing else to say. I don't even know where I can go from here." Do you know what I do? I get up, I start pacing back and forth and praying in tongues. Guess what happens? Suddenly I feel like something opens up like a geyser and I sit back down and go for several more hours. When I thought I'm in a total complete dead end at this book and I don't have anywhere to go, one little revelation comes and just opens up everything and I know the direction to go.

Let me give you other examples. When I was a single man it was a mystery to me of who would be the right person for me to get married to. I always said to the Lord, "Lord knowing me, I'm going to marry some dizzy chick and she'll backslide in three years. I don't even trust myself to choose. I need your help because You know the girls I dated. Lord you're going to have to show me." I remember when I led Lisa to the Lord on our first date. I felt drawn to her because I hadn't been out with a girl for a year and a half and I told God I wouldn't date another girl until he brought my wife. I was three weeks away from graduating at Purdue and here's the wildest girl on Purdue's Campus and the Lord puts in my heart to take her to a Bible study picnic. Now I didn't realize it but she had another date that night and she thought I was just inviting her, but then I called and said, "What kind of meat do you want, hamburgers or hotdogs? She said, "Oh, my goodness this guy is asking me for a date." She ended up going which was a miracle in itself. The girl could drink anybody under the table because she was a party girl. One guy looked at me and said, "Do you know she's the wildest girl on this campus?" I said, "I know." So all the girls thought that I had backslid in the Bible study. Here I was the leader of the Bible study and one girl comes up to me at the Bible study picnic and says, "Do you know whom you're with?" I said, "Yeah." So that night she got saved at 1:30 in the morning and filled with the Holy Spirit at 2:15 and the Lord starts saying to me, "Keep going." I said keep going, I'm graduating in three weeks. I'm going to marry a pastor's daughter so I can't marry this girl. I've got a call on my life, what do you mean keep going? So I started and after a week I thought: this girl is my wife. So I started because I was praying about it. This is what I did. I said, "Lisa I feel that there is something here" and she said, "I do too." I said, "This is what we are going to do for thirty days– because I had graduated and went to Dallas and we were separated. For thirty days I want you pray in the spirit everyday for half an hour." I said, "I'm going to pray in the spirit everyday for half an hour. If you feel any check you tell me and if I feel any check I'll tell you." Well every time I prayed in the spirit I felt this velvet feeling when I was praying for her. I knew she was my wife.

We have to do this with business deals. Businessmen, if you just sit there and pray in tongues you wouldn't buy the wrong piece of property and then find out isn't fit to build anything on because the water table is wrong or something like that. Or you wouldn't make investments that

would end up sour. God would give you the ideas because that's what you're called to do. If you're called to be in the market place then guess what: if you pray in the spirit you will rise above the economy. The economy can be plummeting and you can be prospering. That's the wisdom that you need. There are a lot of things we need counsel on. There have been times when God has had me pray for family members. I didn't realize that they needed to be prayed for but I'd start praying in the spirit and all of a sudden, as I was praying for this person that the Lord would show me how to pray. Now the number one thing that people need help with is direction. A lot of times people go to counselors because they need help with direction. Well have I got good news for you– James says if any of you lack wisdom let him ask of God who gives liberally.

This is the way Lisa and I have functioned in the ministry. What we have done is we have prayed in the spirit and everything God has put in our heart we have done. Now after fifteen years of ministry we have never had one debt in the ministry and we have paid for a 1.4 million dollar building with cash. We've just recently acquired a plane to fly in and we didn't have to borrow for that. God has given us ways and ideas. Messages have come from praying in the spirit in the morning and this is what used to happen. I'd start praying in the spirit and after you get past the flesh– you know what I mean by past the flesh– you get by that and usually I'll just start singing for awhile or something else, but I get past that until I know I'm really in. What used to happen was things would start coming to my mind, such as titles for tapes, ideas for books or this person needs some money or needs to be visited. I would cast those things down and then one day I realized: wait a minute this is the Holy Spirit speaking to me. So what you do is to start writing down these ideas and then something else comes because what's happening is you're praying and He is giving you the wisdom. That is how the tape series, the books and everything else that we've done have come.

I will never forget when I was down in Monterey Mexico. I was asked to come down there and preach. The pastor had rented the gymnasium right in the middle of the city and I had prayed all afternoon. As I was praying in the spirit I had a vision. I saw a light coming down from the sky right down on top of the gymnasium. The Lord spoke to me and said: that's My unhindered power that shall flow in the meeting tonight. I thought this is great. The pastor and I were driving to the meeting that night and all the workers were getting everything ready. The pastor and I walk in and we notice a guy that was big and mean looking who had two armed soldiers with him. They were not policemen– soldiers. They came up to the pastor speaking in Spanish and the pastor had this concerned look on his face. I saw the pastor go over and talk to this guy. The guy was not talking very nice to him. So after five minutes the pastor came back to me and he said, "John you're not going to be able to preach tonight." I said, "What?" He said, " You're not going to be able to preach. I hate to tell you this but there is a law in Mexico. It's a fine print law and nobody ever enforces it but it says you can't preach the gospel without a permit unless you're a Mexican Citizen. Nobody enforces it but this guy is enforcing it and he wants to talk to you." I said, "Hold it, hold it, hold it. I didn't fly all the way down here to not preach tonight. Is this going to affect your church?" He said, "Yeah it will." I said, "Well, then I submit to you. Whatever you say. I want you to know if you're worried about me then don't worry about me. I'm preaching because I didn't come down here to not preach."

So we walked over to this guy and the guy looks at me and he is really gruff and he says, "" I have one question for you: do you speak Spanish?" I said, "No sir, I don't." He said, "Well I have one thing to say: you will say nothing to these people except church related activities." And then he started talking to the pastor about some grumpy stuff and so then the pastor looked at me and said, "I've got to go in there and I've got to do the service tonight." I'm really upset and so I go outside the building and I find the most remote place that I can. How many of you know in downtown Monterey Mexico

Lesson Ten

you're not going to find any place remote but I found this flag pole that was kind of tucked away and I just started walking around the flagpole praying in tongues. I thought if anybody sees me they'd just think I'm a crazy Frenchman. I just started praying in tongues, walking around the flagpole, and I am just stunned. I'm upset and all of a sudden this comes bubbling up from my spirit: put your Bible away and tell them about the greatest tourist that has ever visited Mexico.

I said, "That's it, that's it, Jesus, Jesus." So I went running in and the pastor has already started the service. We're in the back and the pastor's wife who spoke English looks at me and she said, "John he's calling for you, the Pastor is calling for you." So I went up, the pastor put his hand over the microphone and said, "God told me to tell you to obey Him." I said, "You got it." I said folks I'm here to tell you about the greatest tourist that's ever visited Mexico and His name is Jesus. I started preaching to them about the greatest tourist that ever visited Mexico for one hour. When I was done I gave an altar call; a bunch of people came up for the altar call and I see a policeman walking into the back of the building and I'm thinking I'm going to be arrested so I have to get them saved before I get arrested. I remember Peter and John got arrested before they could even pray the prayer, so I said, "All right we're going to pray" and here comes the guy. I bow my head, and I lead them in the sinner's prayer and say "Amen." I open my eyes thinking the guy is going to be standing right in front of me but when I open my eyes the policeman walks right in the curtain behind me. I thought that's good.

So the people start walking off and there's a guy with a crutch. He's walking and limping off and the Lord says, "That's the first one I want to heal. Pray for him right now." I laid hands on him. God heals this guy and I said, "Drop your crutch." He looked at me like I was crazy. He started limping, then he started walking, then he started running, and then he let go and ran back and forth. How many of you know the way Hispanic people are? They came running down just like that. There were hundreds of people all down in the front. My voice is gone, my interpreter is gone and I'm going to pray for people? There was a woman who was born deaf, God opens up here ears and she cried profusely. She had a light blue blouse on and that light blue blouse went dark blue from all the tears coming. There was a lady that got her eyes healed, there was another lady that was healed of cancer, there was a little five-year-old boy I prayed for, the power of God hit him and he got healed.

The pastor flies back up the next week and he says, "John I had to come and tell you about this." I said, "What?" He says, "First of all the newspaper was there and they reported that you were a fraud taking money." What is interesting is that I didn't take a penny out of the country because it was a total mission thing. He said, "The papers there said they genuinely saw people getting healed but you know the guy that said you couldn't preach?" I said, "Yeah." He sent two undercover agents or guards there that night to arrest you if you preached. He said they got there right when you were praying for the crippled guy and he said, "When the guy started running, the one looked at the other and said, "Do you think this is real?" The other guy said, "Well, I don't know let's go closer and look because the people are all down there." The usher followed them because the usher was listening to these guys and he said when he saw the deaf woman get healed, he cried. He said, "I think there might be something to this," to the other. Then they saw the little boy go under the power of God and get healed and the one looked at the other and said, "This is real." The two guys that came to arrest you came right up to you and you prayed for them to get saved. Now if I didn't have the ability to pray in tongues and draw the counsel of God I would have left that place a very frustrated preacher. Do you understand? So this is the beauty of being able to pray in the spirit.

Now I want to talk about the fact that when we pray in the spirit it builds our inner man. 1 Corinthians 14:4 says this, *"He who speaks in a tongue edifies himself."* The Greek word for edifies is: to build a house. Now this is interesting because our bodies are the temple of the Holy Spirit, we are the

The Language of Intimacy

building of God. Therefore when we pray in tongues we are enlarging our dwelling place for the Holy Spirit. We are giving Him more room to occupy. Of course this is not a physical sense, this is figuratively. W.E. Vine says that this word signifies to build whether literally or figuratively. So when we pray in tongues we enlarge our ability to contain His presence and power in our lives. W.E. Vines also tells us that this word is used metaphorically in a sense of promoting spiritual growth and developing character in unbelievers. Jude 20 confirms this, *"But you, beloved, building yourselves up on your most holy faith, praying in the Holy Spirit."* It's the same thing.

Hebrews 5:11 says, *"Of whom we have much to say, and hard to explain, since you have become dull of hearing."* Notice they became dull which means they were once maybe sharp hearing but then they became dull in hearing. Look at verse 14, *"But solid food belongs to those who are of full age* (or mature), *that is, those who by reason of use* (practice), *have their senses exercised to discern both good and evil."* I went to the gym today with Pastor Doug. Why did we exercise? To build up the body. When you pray in an unknown tongue you build yourself up, you exercise your spirit man. Now notice he says those who by reason of use have their senses exercised. Now how many of you know you have five physical senses? That is not what he is talking about; he is talking about your five spiritual senses. How many of you know that our spirit has five senses? Nobody? Let's go through it real quick. Psalms 34:8, *"Oh, taste and see that the Lord is good."* How are you going to taste God? He's not talking about taste here; He's talking about the spirit man. Psalms 119:103, *"How sweet are your words to my taste, sweeter than honey to my mouth."* Taste. We read about touch in 2 Corinthians 6:17, *"Therefore, come out from among them and be separate, says the Lord. Do not touch what is unclean."* Is he saying don't touch a sinner because you might get what they've got? No. He's saying don't touch what they touch in the realm of the spirit. Smell can be seen in 2 Corinthians 2:14-16, *"Now thanks be to God who always leads us in triumph in Christ, and through us diffuses the fragrance of His knowledge in every place. For we are to God the fragrance of Christ among those who are being saved and among those who are perishing. To the one who we are the aroma of death leading to death, and to the other the aroma of life leading to life."* For sight Paul says in Ephesians 1:18, *"The eyes of your understanding being enlightened; that you may know what is the hope of His calling, and what are the riches of the glory of His inheritance in the saints."* He is not talking about the eyes of your physical head he is talking about the eyes of your heart. In 1 Kings 18:41 Elijah talks about hearing saying, *"Then Elijah said to Ahab, go up, eat and drink; for there is the sound of the abundance of rain."* There wasn't even a cloud in the sky but he heard it in his spirit. Jesus said constantly he who has ears to hear let him hear. So we have five spiritual senses and when we pray in the spirit we develop and strengthen those spiritual senses.

There are people in the natural that have developed their physical senses. We have people that have trained their eyes to recognize false and true gemstones. They can tell you the cut, the color and the quality of a diamond. You can think you have the greatest diamond in the world and they will tell you no because it has this color, this many flaws and all this stuff. You can think you have a genuine diamond and they can look at it and say it's a fake. There are people that have trained their hearing in the natural. There are conductors that have trained themselves so they can hear if one musical instrument is off in the whole orchestra. I couldn't tell the difference but they know tones and pitches. Why? They trained they're hearing. There are people that have learned to train they're sense of smell. They know the top note in the undertones of a fragrance in the bouquet of spices and all the other stuff that are in there. I met a wine taster one time that told me all the years he spent practicing tasting wines. They can tell you if it was an early crop, a late crop, if it was a good rain that year, or a bad rain. These people have learned how to train their physical senses. God says the mature in the spirit are those who have learned how to train their spiritual senses.

Let me tell you why that is so important in regard to our intimacy with God. Let's talk about the natural. If you can't see, hear, taste, touch, or smell– I

Lesson Ten

can't communicate to you. I come to you and go, "Doug, Doug, Doug." He doesn't feel a thing because he can't feel. I go "Doug, Doug." but he can't see. I go "Doug" and yell but he can't hear. I can even put something ugly smelling under his nose but he can't smell. I have no way of communicating to him. God is saying I want to have intimacy with you. Many people come up to me and say, "I don't to hear God speak to me." Could it be your inward spiritual senses are dull? But when you pray in the spirit you're building. What you are actually doing is you're fasting your outward man and your outward senses and you're building your inner man. The reason God gave us the ability to speak in tongues is to enhance our intimacy with Him. When we pray in the spirit we build up our inner man and our inner man is sensitive to what He wants, what He loves and what He needs. We hear his voice easily.

FULL ASSURANCE OF FAITH

FULL ASSURANCE OF FAITH

Key Statement:
You will find intimacy with God when you draw near in full assurance of faith.

"Therefore, brethren, having boldness to enter the Holiest by the blood of Jesus, by a new and living way which He consecrated for us, through the veil, that is, His flesh, and having a High Priest over the house of God, let us draw near with a true heart in full assurance of faith, having our hearts sprinkled from an evil conscience and our bodies washed with pure water. Let us hold fast the confession of our hope without wavering, for He who promised is faithful."
Hebrews 10:19–23

Drawing Near with a True Heart...

1. In verse 19 another word for boldness is *confidence*. Paul is talking about coming into the:
[ ] Outer court
[ ] Inner court
[x] Holy of holies, the holiest place

2. This place is where _____*God speaks*_____ to you.

3. Remember in an earlier session we learned that God is looking for people to worship Him at the base level. In the verses above, what does "true heart" mean? It is the same root word used when Jesus said, "God is looking for those who *will worship Him in spirit and truth.*"

It means to come in from the base level of your heart. It means to come in with the fear of the Lord with true sincerity.

LEADER'S NOTES

(3–5 minutes)

Remind the group of a few key lessons by referring to these statements:

1. Tongues are how we receive God's counsel.

2. Praying in tongues gives us strength by building our inner man.

Set this session up with the Key Statement. Then go through the questions, asking for and providing the answers.

LESSON ELEVEN

LEADER'S NOTES

"But without faith it is impossible to please Him, for he who comes to God must believe that He is, and that He is a rewarder of those who diligently seek Him."
Hebrews 11:6

4. What grieved Jesus more than anything else?

When people didn't believe He would do what He said He would do.

5. What statement did Jesus make four separate times in Matthew? _____*What little faith you have*_____.

Jesus goes from disappointment to downright disgust in Matthew 17:17 (TEV):

"How unbelieving and wrong you people are! How long must I stay with you? How long do I have to put up with you?"
"Then Jesus answered and said, 'O faithless and perverse generation, how long shall I be with you? How long shall I bear with you? Bring him here to Me.'"
Matthew 17:17

6. In verse 20, Jesus again says, "You do not have enough faith." Why does it grieve Jesus when people do not have faith? Because it insults ___*His character*___. When you doubt God, you doubt ___*His integrity*___.

"God is not a man, that He should lie, nor a son of man, that He should repent. Has He said, and will He not do? Or has He spoken, and will He not make it good?"
Numbers 23:19

Key Statement:
God responds to your faith.

FULL ASSURANCE OF FAITH

Healing of a Paralyzed Man...

Everything we receive from the Lord is through faith. In Luke 5, Jesus was teaching in a house, and the power of God was present to heal. Yet it was a group of men from outside who brought a paralyzed person to Him.

"Now it happened on a certain day, as He was teaching, that there were Pharisees and teachers of the law sitting by, who had come out of every town of Galilee, Judea, and Jerusalem. And the power of the Lord was present to heal them. Then behold, men brought on a bed a man who was paralyzed, whom they sought to bring in and lay before Him. And when they could not find how they might bring him in, because of the crowd, they went up on the housetop and let him down with his bed through the tiling into the midst before Jesus.

When He saw their faith, He said to him, "Man, your sins are forgiven you." And the scribes and the Pharisees began to reason, saying, "Who is this who speaks blasphemies? Who can forgive sins but God alone?"

But when Jesus perceived their thoughts, He answered and said to them," Why are you reasoning in your hearts? Which is easier, to say, 'Your sins are forgiven you,' or to say, 'Rise up and walk'? But that you may know that the Son of Man has power on earth to forgive sins' —He said to the man who was paralyzed, 'I say to you, arise, take up your bed, and go to your house.'

Immediately he rose up before them, took up what he had been lying on, and departed to his own house, glorifying God. And they were all amazed, and they glorified God and were filled with fear, saying, 'We have seen strange things today!'"

Luke 5:17–26

LEADER'S NOTES

LESSON ELEVEN

LEADER'S NOTES

7. What are some indications that the men who brought the sick man had faith?

The men tried to bring the man to Jesus, but they couldn't get in because of the crowds. They persisted anyway, so they climbed to the top of the house and let him down through a hole in the ceiling.

8. Even though there were many religious leaders there and the power of God was present to heal them, why were none of them healed? *They had no faith.*

9. What were some indications that these religious leaders had no faith?

They accused Jesus of blasphemy and were amazed when the person was actually healed.

(5-10 minutes)

Ask the group question 10, opening it for discussion. The answer refers to earlier lessons and gives you a chance to refer to this journey.

10. How could it be that the most religious people there were the ones who grieved Jesus the most?

This journey to the heart of God is not about rules, regulations, or religion; it is about relationship. Just because the scribes and Pharisees appeared to look and act like they had a relationship, they did not possess a pure attitude in their heart. Outwardly they appeared to have wealth and knowledge, but inwardly they didn't worship Him in spirit and truth. They had a form of godliness but denied the power thereof. Just because someone goes to church regularly, prays lots of prayers, and seems religious doesn't make that individual a person who has faith.

FULL ASSURANCE OF FAITH

Casting Out Devils...

"But Jesus said to her, 'Let the children be filled first, for it is not good to take the children's bread and throw it to the little dogs.' And she answered and said to Him, 'Yes, Lord, yet even the little dogs under the table eat from the children's crumbs.' Then He said to her, 'For this saying go your way; the demon has gone out of your daughter.'"
Mark 7:27–29

11. What are some indications that this woman had faith?

Even though Jesus put her off because she was a Greek (the NLT renders this verse, "First I should help my own family, the Jews"), she responded boldly in confident expectation. She was persistent in her faith.

LEADER'S NOTES

12. What are some other examples you can think of like the paralytic and the woman's daughter that illustrate Jesus responding to faith?

Sample answers:
- *Healing of the leper in Matthew 8:1-3*
- *Healing of the centurion's servant in Matthew 8:5-13*
- *The woman with the issue of blood in Luke 8:43-48*

(3-5 minutes)

Ask volunteers to shout out their answers in orderly fashion.

13. Has Jesus ever responded to your faith in a miraculous way? How?

_____
_____
_____

(3-5 minutes)

Ask for one or two volunteers to share their answers to question 13. Use this as an opportunity to build your group's faith.

LESSON ELEVEN

LEADER'S NOTES

Key Statement:
Jesus responds to faith, not need. Faith is the key to receiving everything.

Below, we've left out the most significant words in James 1:6-7. This is a definitive statement with no gray areas. Fill the words in from your bible.

14. "But let him ask in _faith_, with no _doubting_ for he who doubts is like a wave of the sea driven and tossed by the wind. For let _not_ that man suppose that he will _receive anything_ from the Lord."

In Galatians, we see the reason so many have not received the Holy Spirit:

"This only I want to learn from you: Did you receive the Spirit by the works of the law, or by the hearing of faith?"
Galatians 3:2

Many hungry believers have sought more of God and perhaps have prayed once to receive the Holy Spirit's infilling, but nothing seemed to happen. Others have asked to receive but with a "maybe so" attitude. We must have determination like what we saw in our biblical examples above. We must be wise and know what the will of the Lord is, coming to Him in full assurance (Eph. 5:17).

15. Why do so many people have trouble getting into the presence of God? _They come with a "hope so" attitude._

FULL ASSURANCE OF FAITH

16. Drawing near to God is not a ___hit___ or ___miss___ scenario. Notice the second part of our flagship scripture and also James 1: 7-8

> "...purify your hearts, you double-minded."
> **James 4:8**

> "For let not that man suppose that he will receive anything from the Lord; he is a double-minded man, unstable in all his ways."
> **James 1: 7-8**

And Hebrews:

> "But without faith it is impossible to please Him, for he who comes to God must believe that He is, and that He is a rewarder of those who diligently seek Him."
> **Hebrews 11:6**

17. When God tells us to draw near to Him and He will draw near to us, He means it. You have a part to play, and God will always honor His Word. When you ___confidently___ draw near to God in the full assurance of faith instead of doubt, your life changes. He is a ___rewarder___ of those who ___diligently___ seek Him.

Notice that the writer to the Hebrews says "diligently." There will be times when you draw near to God and it seems dry or God seems distant. Pressing in is exactly what God is expecting you to do during those times. Remember, God is seeking those who will worship Him in spirit and truth. One of the truths of the spirit is that God will test you in the wilderness to see if you will persist in faith in drawing near.

LEADER'S NOTES

Lesson Eleven

Leader's Notes

Drawing near when it's "dry"

"I'm telling you that morning the Lord really spoke to me. I woke up to the fact that I was coming in with a 'hope so' attitude. See, that's something even I still have to fight sometimes, because that's the way we've been taught. But we've been taught wrong. God doesn't say it's a hit–or–miss scenario. He said, 'You come, and I will manifest Myself.' Now don't get me wrong. When He backs off, He is saying, 'Come on harder, come on harder, come on harder because I want to fill you more, because if you're hungry I'll fill you more.' Do you understand? But that's a very rare thing that happens, and I have to say tonight sometimes it does happen, OK? But listen, that is not the way it always is. It is not that you have to scream loud enough and cry hard enough and pray long enough, and finally God will say, 'OK, you've done it for five hours. Bam! There you go.' Are you kidding? You know what happens most of the time? I'm out there, and within a minute He's there. If I cleanse my heart and I've done everything we've talked about in these last several lessons, He's there. So this is the number one thing: we must have that full assurance of faith."

—John Bevere

Key Statement:
Faith is not a formula; it is a seed.

18. What can we learn from the examples of the servant plowing, the centurion soldier, and Abraham? God gives us faith in _seed form_, but the way we make the seed _grow_ is by _obedience to completion_.

FULL ASSURANCE OF FAITH

19. Who is an example of someone who was not obedient to completion? _Saul_.

20. Why? _He had been told to kill all of the Amalekites but he only killed most of them._

"If you really, really, really search the Scriptures, you will find something interesting. The people who had the greatest intimacy with the Lord are the people who understood kingdom authority, who were submitted to God with authority, and who submitted to the authority that He placed over their lives. They were obedient, and everything God told them to do, they did it to completion. If you really want to know the secret of having great faith that's going to give you the confidence to come into the very holy of holies, the place where the presence of God is, you need to be a person who obeys."

—John Bevere

---

21. Why is obedience so important?
Because it shows that we will follow through to completion, and as we do, our faith will grow.

22. Why is it important that our faith grows?
Here are some sample answers:
- _Without faith it is impossible to please God._
- _It is how we receive the Holy Spirit._
- _It is how we come to God in assurance of faith._
- _Like the earlier examples, it is how we are healed._

LEADER'S NOTES

Ask for answers for question 22 from your group.

Remind your group:

1. They should preview the next session and complete the personal discussion portions in their workbooks. If they would like, they may complete the entire section.

2. Pray for the group before they leave. Remind those who spoke in tongues for the first time to keep praying daily, and they will grow in their faith.

LESSON ELEVEN

Video Script for Lesson 11
FULL ASSURANCE OF FAITH

We are going to talk about the full assurance of faith in this lesson. Over the years I have met numerous believers that are filled with the Holy Spirit who love and fear God. They abstain from sin yet they say "why is it I just don't hear from God" and "why do I have so much trouble getting into His presence?" I sense the frustration of those people but after talking with them a few minutes, I always discover it comes down to this very point which we're gong to talk about in this lesson. We read in Hebrews 10:19, *"Therefore, brethren, having boldness to enter the Holiest by the blood of Jesus."* We talked about the priest who was in the outer court. There was also the holy. The most holy place or the holiest is where the very presence of God dwelt between the Cherubim. So Paul knows exactly what he is talking about here in Hebrews. He was not talking about coming into the Holy place where there is illumination with the lamp stand, revelation with the table of showbread, or where there is prayer and praise at the table of incense. He is not talking about that place. He's talking about coming into the Holy of Holies where the presence of God is. He's talking about coming right in where God speaks to us personally.

There is illumination and revelation in the Holy place but where God speaks to you personally and where there is intimacy is in the most Holy place because that's when God said to Moses, "It is right there that I will speak to you." Exodus 25:22 God says, *"And there I well meet with you, and I will speak with you from above the mercy seat."* That was the most holy place. Paul continues in Hebrews 10:19, *"Therefore, brethren, having the boldness (or confidence) to enter the Holiest by the blood of Jesus, by a new and living way which He consecrated for us, through the veil, that is, His flesh, and having a High Priest over the house of God, let us draw near with a true heart."* True heart is the same root word that Jesus uses when He says God is looking for those who worship Him in spirit and truth. It means to come in from the base level of your heart with the fear of the Lord and true sincerity. Verse 22 continued, *"Having our hearts sprinkled from an evil conscience and our bodies washed with pure water."* That pure water is the word of God. That is why it is so important to come and hear the Word of God especially from pastors who preach the word of God straight, pure, wonderful and lovely.

Let me detour a little bit and tell you something that I have learned. I used get up at 4:30 to 5:30 in the morning because that's when I like to go straight out to pray, because I love to pray. The Lord kept dealing with me about this and unfortunately I was being thick headed and I wasn't really listening but the Lord said, "Son I want you to read the scripture before you go out on the golf course and pray." I always prayed out on the golf course. It's the best place to pray. I'm telling you, it's wonderful. God just seems to speak to me at oceans, golf courses, and mountaintops. Now, I was wrestling with this because I love getting out there and praying really early before any of those workers come out there to cut the lawn and all that stuff but I started realizing that God is saying this to me over and over. Then I started realizing in the outer court of the Tabernacle was the brazen altar where they offered the lambs daily. The layer was also out there and the layer is where the priest had to wash himself in pure water before he could go in and get the revelation, the illumination, the prayer and the praise, he had to wash himself with the water. And I realized God was really trying to get me to see something. The Bible says in Ephesians 5 that Jesus sanctifies the church by the washing of the water of the word. Now you know what I noticed in the practical sense? I go out after reading the scripture and my mind would be in tune that much quicker to His voice. In the prayer closet I noticed that I was hearing revelation and illumination much quicker and easier if I read the scriptures first.

Verse 22 and 23, *"Let us draw near with a true heart in full assurance of faith, having our hearts sprinkled from an evil conscience and our bodies washed with pure water. Let us hold fast the confession of our hope without wavering, for He who promised is faithful."* It says to let us draw near with a true heart in full assurance of faith. Hebrews 11:6 says, *"But without faith it is impossible to please Him, for he who comes to God must believe that He*

FULL ASSURANCE OF FAITH

is, and that He is a rewarder of those who diligently (not casually) seek Him."

Did you get that? Without faith it's impossible. Now there are people who are upset with people who preach on faith. Stop and think about this: if you were the devil what would you do? Try to pervert everything that is important to God so people will run from it. So what do you do? You get a bunch of legalistic preachers that preach holiness as wearing your hair up in a bun and your dress down to your ankles, and you beat people up with this legalism. So what do people do? They run from holiness. But what my Bible says is without holiness no man is going to see the Lord. Holiness has nothing to do with the way you dress but it has everything to do about being His. When I walked down the aisle and I said that girl is mine– good-bye Jennifer, good-bye Helga, good-bye all you other girlfriends-Lisa you're mine and I'm yours. Holiness is that I'm completely His.

Then you get people and all they do is talk about is His money and they do perverted things with money. They love it and so these people say we're not even going to talk about offerings. Do you realize how you're holding people back by not talking about offerings? You are robbing from God's people by not enlightening them and telling them about offerings. We ought to look at the way Jesus took offerings. He sat next to the bucket and called his staff and said let's talk about how much everybody is putting in. Look at this on. This guy gave ten thousand, that one over there gave fifteen. Now look at this woman here, she gave two pennies but she gave more than that guy who gave ten thousand. She gave more than the one that gave fifteen. Jesus was talking to his staff about it. They came and put it at Peter's feet. He opened it and everyone knew what he or she was doing. You can keep the body of Christ from keeping her destiny in the last days.

Another bunch of people get a little bit too extreme with faith and they get way out there and become unbalanced. Then what people do is start running from faith. Any Christian that says they are not a faith man or woman is stupid because I don't know about you but I want to please God and my Bible just told me it is impossible for me to please God without faith. Let me give you an example. I had just been saved about a year and I was still a single man and I was living in Raleigh, North Carolina. I was working for IBM as a co-op engineer. I was an engineer from Purdue University and then every semester I'd go down to IBM and work for them then go back to the apartment I was living in. I'd only been saved for about a year and I was attending to a very denominational spirit filled church so I really didn't hear much about faith teaching at that point. I was sound asleep one night in one of those deep sleeps where you wake up and you wonder where you are. I'm in this deep sleep and all of a sudden I woke myself up by jumping up out of the bed screaming, "I'm just looking for someone to believe." I turn on the light, turn around and there's an outline of my body in sweat. My body is drenched in sweat. God just spoke to me and I thought, "well couldn't it have been a little more profound": "I'm just looking for someone to believe." I know that, so I went back to sleep. The next morning I got up and I kept hearing this in my head: "I'm just looking for someone to believe, I'm just looking for someone to believe, I'm just looking for someone to believe." Then all of a sudden I just stopped right in my tracks in the parking lot of the apartments and I said, "That's it." And I started thinking about what grieved Jesus more than anything else. It's not anger because the Pharisees angered him. What grieved Him was simply when people didn't believe that He would do what He said He would do. That was a profound revelation.

Let me show you how grieved Jesus was. I'm going to read you just a few scriptures out of the book of Matthew. I'm going to read it out of today's English version because it gives you a little better understanding of Jesus' tone. Listen to what Jesus says in Matthew 6:30, *"What little faith you have!"* Matthew 8:25, the disciples went to him and woke him up saying, *"Save us Lord we are about to die. Why are you so frightened Jesus answered, what little faith you have."* Matthew 14:31, *"At once Jesus reached out and grabbed a hold of him and said, What little faith you have, why did you doubt?!!!!"* Matthew 16:8, *"Why are you discussing among yourselves about not having any bread, what little faith you have."* Do you hear the tone of his voice? Now what is amazing is He's about to go from disappointed to disgusted in this next one. He is up on the mountain and He comes down with three of his disciples and His other disciples couldn't cast out a devil. Listen to what He says to his staff: *"How unbelieving and wrong you people are!!*

197

LESSON ELEVEN

How long must I stay with you? How long do I have to put up with you? Bring the boy here to me." Jesus gave the command to the demon and it went out of the boy and at that very moment he was healed. Afterwards the disciples came up and said "why couldn't we cast out the demon?" Jesus simply said it was because you did not have enough faith. In the New King James Version He said, *"Oh, faithless and perverted generation, how long do I have put up with you?"* Do you see how it really grieved Him when people just didn't have faith? It grieves him because it insults His character. Can you imagine my youngest boy who is nine-years-old and I say, "Arden, I am going to bring you home a brand new set of three golf balls which are your favorite ones." He's not going to school all day thinking my dad probably won't do it. He doesn't come in here looking depressed at me and saying, "Okay dad I know you didn't do it." He doesn't do that because that would insult my integrity. He comes in and says do you have my prize because he has faith in his daddy's integrity. When you doubt God you say I doubt Your integrity.

But God is not a man that He should lie. He watches over His Word to perform it. If you look in the gospels you will find there are places that Jesus was so excited. In Luke's gospel the fifth chapter you will find that He was in a house one time and there were so many teachers sitting there and the Bible says, *"The power of the Lord was there to heal them."* And you know what that means? It means some of those teachers and some of those Pharisees were sick and they needed to be healed because if the power of the Lord is there to heal it means somebody needs to be healed. God does not put the power of the Lord to heal and waste it but you know what–not one of them got healed. But there was a group of men that came and let down a paralyzed man through the roof because they couldn't get in and when Jesus saw their faith, He said to the man your sins are forgiven. The guys who were there that needed the healing said, "Who does He think He is? It's easy to forgive sins." Jesus said, *"What's easier for you to say: your sins are forgiven or to say to the man get up and walk?* So that you might know that I have power on earth to forgive sins He looked at me and said 'get up and walk'." The Bible says they were all amazed and they said we have seen strange things today. It is really sad because they could have been the one's being healed but they were the ones saying we were amazed because they simply didn't believe.

There was a Greek woman from Canaan who comes up to Jesus because she has a demon-possessed daughter. She looks at Him and says, " My daughter; she needs healing, she needs deliverance." Jesus says, *"You know it's not right for me to give the little dog's the children's bread of healing."* He called her a little dog. She looked back and said, "Even the little dog's need the crumbs that fall from the Master's table." Do you see the confidence and boldness that comes from faith? She didn't take no for an answer because she knew He was good for His word. I can just see Jesus smiling and saying, "Go on your way– you just got it– great is your faith woman." So faith is the key to receiving everything in the kingdom. James 1:6 and 7 is bold enough to state that when we come to God in prayer we must, *"Let him ask in faith, with no doubting, for he who doubts is like a wave of the sea driven and tossed by the wind. For let not that man suppose that he will receive anything from the Lord."* That's a pretty definitive statement. There is no room for question on that one. You come in faith or you don't get anything. God is trying to make sure we get this.

Do you know why so many people have not received the Holy Spirit? Galatians 3:2 says, *"This only I want to learn from you: did you receive the Spirit by the works of the law, or by the hearing of faith?"* Do you know how many times people have looked at me and said I prayed to the Holy Spirit once and it didn't work so it's not for everybody and tongues have ceased? What is really sad is there are a lot of people today in the church that have allowed their experience to dictate to them what they believe instead of allowing the Word of God to dictate their experiences. So they come with a "maybe so" attitude in regards to drawing near to God with intimacy and this is why so many people have trouble getting into the presence where He speaks. They come with a "hope so" attitude because preachers have made it hard sometimes by the way we preach. They say, "YOU GOTTA PRAY and really cry out and maybe God will meet you." I've noticed what we preached and we've made it hard for people to get in the presence of God. Last year the Lord said to me, "It is not a hit and miss scenario. When I said draw near to Me, then I will draw near to you; it is not a hit and miss." He said, "Am I a liar?" I said, "No." He said, "If I told you to draw near and then if you do that I will draw near to you,

FULL ASSURANCE OF FAITH

why are you coming in with this 'hope so' attitude?" I said, "whoa". I noticed everything changed because I started going in with a confidence. I had the full assurance of faith.

Let me give you some examples. I'm in the prayer closet recently and this happened. I was praying in the spirit and praying in English and I was in there for about twenty-five minutes, and it was just dry. Now don't get me wrong, there are times when God wants to know of you will still pursue Him even if He is not manifesting Himself yet. He'll test you to see just how hungry you are. But I know that most of the time I'm sitting there because of my lack of really believing. So I'm sitting there praying for twenty to twenty-five minutes and all of a sudden I realize: what am I doing? I said, "Lord, you said if I asked I would receive, if I seek I would find, if I knock, it would be open. You said if I draw near You would draw near to me. And all of a sudden, wham there was His presence. That morning the Lord really spoke to me because I woke up to the fact that I was coming in with a "hope so" attitude. I still have to fight that "hope so" attitude sometimes because that's the way we've been taught and we've been taught wrong. God doesn't say it's a hit and miss scenario– He said you come and I will manifest Myself. When He backs off He is saying, "Come on harder and harder because I want to fill you more because if you're hungry I'll fill you more." Sometimes He desires this but that 's a very rare thing that happens but that is not the way it always is. You do not have to scream loud enough and cry hard enough and pray long enough and then finally God will say okay you've done it for five hours so bam there you go. What happens most of the time is I'm out there and within a minute He's there. If I cleanse my heart and I've done everything we've talked about in these last several lessons He's there. The number one thing is we must have that full assurance of faith.

The thing I want to talk about real quickly is, how do we develop that faith because let me tell you something, faith is not a formula: it's something that produces a confidence in us, a knowing even before you ever say you know. How do you develop that? Luke 17:5, *"And the apostles said to the Lord, Increase our faith. So the Lord said, If you have faith as a mustard seed, you can say to this mulberry tree, be pulled up by the roots and be planted in the sea, and it would obey you."*

The first thing He talks about is His faith being a seed. If you plant it and it grows up it will obey you. In growing the Mulberry tree, the mountain, or whatever it is, it is going to ultimately obey you but He said faith starts in seed form. How do we get the seed of faith? Roman says this, *"So then faith comes by hearing, and hearing by the word of God."* He says hearing and hearing and hearing and then hearing.

Remember I talked about the inward senses in the last session? When I come into a meeting, I don't write everything the preacher says. I write what explodes in here; I hear the voice in the voice and that's what I write down. Every word that proceeds out of the mouth of God is what the Bible says we live by. Not proceeded past tense. Not the written Word, it's the spoken word. It's when a person may read the written Word and all of a sudden is spoken in here. I heard and heard–that's the seed. Now, how many of you know I can put a seed on this podium right here– I can dance, I can praise, I can do this for ten thousand years, I can pray for ten thousand years– and that seed is not going to grow. We have to make that seed grow because inside that seed is everything needed to produce the wonderful tree with all the fruit– which in this case would be moving the Mulberry tree, moving the mountain or whatever the need is because everything in the kingdom is received by faith. He's going to tell you how to get it to grow in Luke 17:7, *"And which of you, having a servant plowing or tending sheep, will say to him when he has come in from the field, 'Come at once and sit down to eat'? But will he not rather say to him, 'Prepare something for my supper, and gird yourself and serve me till I have eaten and drunk, and afterward you will eat and drink'? Does he thank that servant because he did the things that were commanded him? I think not. So likewise you, when you have done all those things which you are commanded."*

First he talks about faith as a seed and then He starts talking about a servant in the field. You are thinking what does this have to do with anything, yet it has everything to do with anything. He talks about faith being a seed and we know it comes by hearing, but how do you get it to grow? He goes on in the parable to tell you how to get it to grow. Let me ask you this: why would you as a master hire a servant to tend your flocks, your fields? The ultimate goal is to put food on your table. Jesus is saying why are you going to let this guy tend your flocks and your fields and then he's going to come right up to the

199

Lesson Eleven

place of putting food on your table and you are going to say, "It's okay you just eat and drink and I'll starve." He's talking about obedience to completion. That's why He goes on to say, *"So likewise you, when you have done all those things which you are commanded."* So He immediately talks about it all coming back to obedience again.

The man who had the greatest faith in Israel that Jesus had ever met was not a person who was an Israelite, he was a Roman soldier, an officer. He probably had very few seeds but what he had was good because he understood authority and he understood obedience. Jesus marveled when He saw how great his faith was. The Roman soldier said, "Jesus I am a soldier and I am under authority; I'm an officer and I'm under authority and I have men under me. And because I'm under authority all I have to do is say one word and those men move. And you are under your Father's authority and therefore all you have to say is one word and that demon, that mountain has to leave my servant." He understood that Jesus was very obedient and obeyed to completion therefore he had great faith.

Look at Abraham. God tells Abraham to offer up Isaac. I'll show you something very interesting. In Genesis 22, God tells Abraham to go and sacrifice Isaac. How many of you know that is a tough thing to obey? But early the next morning Abraham's on his way, and not only does he go on his way; he goes all the way to the top. The reason God gave him three days was in case he wanted to think it over and turn back but Abraham obeys all the way to completion. He builds the altar, puts Isaac on the altar, lifts up the knife and is ready to put the most important person to death in his life and the angel said "stop". In verse 15 an the angel of the Lord called out to Abraham a second time out of heaven and said, *"By Myself I have sworn, says the Lord, because you have done this thing, and have not withheld your son, your only son– blessing I will bless you, and multiplying I will multiply your descendants as the stars of the heaven and as the sand which is on the seashore; and your descendants shall possess the gate of their enemies. In your seed all the nations of the earth shall be blessed because you have obeyed My voice."* God said you just secured everything I promised you because you obeyed My voice. What is Abraham called? The father of faith. In other words his example is the example to us of how we cause our faith to mature and grow to its full completion.

God gives it to us in seed form but the way we make the seed grow is by obedience to completion. Saul did not obey to completion-- he only did 99% of what he was told to do by killing most of the Amalekites. If you look at Saul he had zero intimacy with God. You look at Abraham and he is the friend of God. If you really search the scriptures you will find something interesting out: the people who have the greatest intimacy with the Lord are the people that understood kingdom authority, who were submitted to God's authority, and submitted to the authorities that He had placed over their lives. They were obedient and everything God told them to do they did it to completion. If you really want to know the secret of having great faith that's going to give you the confidence to come into the very Holy of Holies where the presence of God is near, then you need to be a person who obeys.

Remember what God said to Moses and the children of Israel. He brought them out there to have intimacy with Him. He was revealing Himself to them and He said, " I brought you out of Egypt and brought you to myself, so they could have intimacy with God. In Deuteronomy chapter 5 God said,"Moses the reason they can't come near Me is they do not have a heart that fears Me and they do not keep all My commandments. If they wanted, they could hear Me so you tell them to go back to their tents, they can't have intimacy with Me but you stand by Me and I'll talk to you. That is why obedience is so important.

Video Session 12

DRAWING NEAR

Key Statement: ~~START~~

A journey is not something that can be taught; it is something that is lived.

"To You I will cry, O LORD my Rock: Do not be silent to me, lest, if You are silent to me, I become like those who go down to the pit."
Psalm 28:1

1. You must be the one who draws near and makes the effort to be intimate with the Lord. If we cry out to God, He will not be silent to us. God through the Holy Spirit confirms His Word. This is how we know our life is _____*different*_____ from the life of unbelievers.

2. To teach about drawing near could be compared to giving detailed instructions to one who is about to be _____*married*_____. You can only teach so much, and the rest flows from the heart. But there are some practical guidelines that can help.

The Practical Side of Drawing Near...

3. In approaching the Lord, what is the first thing you need to remember? _*We are created in the image of God.*_
_____

(3-5 minutes)

Remind the group of a few key lessons by referring to these statements:

1. You will find intimacy with God when you draw near in full assurance of faith.

2. Jesus responds to faith, not need. Faith is the key to receiving everything.

3. Faith is not a formula; it is a seed.

Set this session up with the Key Statement. Then go through the questions, asking for and providing the answers.

LEADER'S NOTES

4. What are some of the attributes we share with God?

Moods, emotions, laughter, weeping, peace, etc.

5. God draws near to people who have His *interests* at *heart*.

6. If we are to touch the Lord's heart, we must seek to know what He *desires* and *needs*.

> "…inasmuch as you did it to one of the least of these My brethren, you did it to Me."
> **Matthew 25:40**

7. Maybe you never thought of God as having needs. How does this verse show that?

We are the family of God, and God cares about all of us from the greatest to the least. God considers us one with Him, so when one of His family has a need, it is essentially the same as Him having a need.

8. What can you do to answer those needs?

As the Scriptures teach, we can minister to people, visit those in prison, care for widows, bring up our children properly, assist the poor, always be praying for people, etc.

DRAWING NEAR

9. God gave man a free ___will___ and by giving man a free will, He made Himself ___vulnerable___, because He brought man into His kingdom and made him His ___family___.

10. In Isaiah 58, God's people were coming to Him diligently, seeking Him daily, and delighting to know His ways. Why wasn't the Lord responding? ___Because they were living for themselves___.

11. What was it that God asked John when he was praying in New York that caused him to weep? "Son, ask My people, if they want Me to be ___as faithful to them___ as they ___have been to Me___. Do they want Me to be as ___committed to them___ as they've been ___committed to me___?"

"What causes fights and quarrels among you? Don't they come from your desires that battle within you? You want something but you don't get it. You kill and covet, but you cannot have what you want. You quarrel and fight. You do not have, because you do not ask God. When you ask, you do not receive, because you ask it with wrong motives, that you may spend it on your own pleasures. You adulteress people… submit yourselves, then, to God. Resist the devil, and he will flee from you. Come near to God and he will come near to you."
James 4:1–4, 7–8, NIV

Key Statement:
To know God is to be a servant.

LEADER'S NOTES

LESSON TWELVE

LEADER'S NOTES

12. What is practical step number one of drawing near to God? _____
We must lose our lives for His sake and the gospel.

13. [ ] True or [x] False: This means our lives will not have any times of pleasure and refreshment.

14. Can you back up your answer with Scripture?

First Timothy 6:17 says, "God...gives us richly all things to enjoy."

15. [x] True or [ ] False: There is a difference between enjoying something and living just to have a pleasure.

16. What is it we need to know and teach our children?
• *Life is serving, being a servant, and working*
• *The privileges you get for working hard are the times of refreshment*

17. [x] True or [ ] False: Everyone in the kingdom is a servant.

Finding and knowing what God has called YOU to do is critical if you are to please God. That is one of the things this journey is all about. Feeding the poor, preaching the Word, finances, music - these are all gifts God uses to meet the needs of people.

18. [x] True or [ ] False: There are people called to preach the Word who would be disobeying God if they left the Word of God and tried to serve God in another way.

19. [x] True or [ ] False: There are people who are disobedient to God because they want to try to preach when they are supposed to be feeding the widows' tables or ushering in the church or working out in the parking lot. We should all just do our part.

20. What are some of the things the church needs to be able to function properly?

You need to have people who will usher, count the money, help with the parking lot, drive the bus that brings the poor people, etc.

21. What happens if we don't find our part and serve in the local church?

The local church can't function and the gospel isn't preached.

> "'He made sure that justice and help were given to the poor and needy, and everything went well for him. Isn't that what it means to know me?' asks the LORD."
> **Jeremiah 22:15–17, NLT**

22. God said to know Him is to meet the needs of *hurting humanity.*

LEADER'S NOTES

Lesson Twelve

Leader's Notes

(10 minutes)

This is the opportunity you've been waiting for. Here is where people really get a chance to put substance to all the Drawing Near teaching and all the prayer time they've been having

• *Open a discussion about gifts, talents, and how God uses the seemingly "least" skill or talent or experience for meeting the needs of people.*

• *Encourage people to acknowledge their gifts and to see you about how God wants to "plug" them in, getting them to use their callings in the church.*

• *Have church materials ready to distribute, listing areas of ministry and areas of need. Remember, not all people are at the same level. Many have no idea what is involved or in what ways they can be of service to God in the local church.*

• *Give examples or real-life stories of people who have helped in church and been so blessed in their lives.*

Maybe you never put much thought into meeting God's needs. Your body is the temple of the Holy Spirit. God has given all of His children gifts, talents, skills, and callings to use for the kingdom. Part of your journey to God's heart must be service in your local church. It's simple. *If you aren't involved, who will be?* It's easy to look around and see other people taking care of the "business of the church." Other people will never be able to be intimate with God *for you*, nor will other people be able to serve God for you.

Ephesians 4 says God gave apostles, prophets, evangelists, pastors, and teachers, and the whole body of believers functions when every person does his or her part. Romans 12 says that we are mutually dependent on one another having gifts that differ according to the grace that's been given us.

You Have a Part to Play in your Church...

23. List here your talents, skills, and experience:

Don't be afraid to list the smallest or biggest things.

- Is your talent using a sewing machine? Maybe the children's church needs curtains, pillow covers, or stuffed animals.
- Do you own a janitorial company? Maybe the church floors need to be waxed.
- Do you teach gym? Maybe someone in the youth group needs help with baseball.
- Are you a student? Maybe you could help in the church office.

DRAWING NEAR

LEADER'S NOTES

24. The list of human needs is endless. The great news is that the list of God's provisions through His people's gifts is also endless. List here ways your gifts might serve the church, meeting the needs of humanity:

___

25. When you minister to God's people, it equates to ministering to God. Generally people are only using a small proportion of their gifts and talents for the Lord. Put in some time of prayer in the Spirit and meditating on these things. Then write how you can use more of your gifts and talents and when and how you plan to do it:

___

Leader's Notes

Don't be rash; don't make promises you are not going to keep. It is the Holy Spirit who will lead you and empower you, so be prepared to take more than one time of prayer. Also, don't be timid. The world is never short on needs, and the gift God has given you will find its place. You are valuable to God!

Lastly, find out from your church what they need right now. Inquire as to what ministries (such as food pantry, Sunday school, greeting, etc.) exist and how you can "plug in." Don't underestimate what God can do through you.

Key Statement:
When you draw near to God, be quick to listen and slow to speak.

"Guard your steps when you go to the house of God. Go near to listen rather than to offer the sacrifice of fools, who do not know that they do wrong. Do not be quick with your mouth, do not be hasty in your heart to utter anything before God. God is in heaven and you are on earth, so let your words be few. As a dream comes when there are many cares, so the speech of a fool when there are many words."
Ecclesiastes 5:1-3, NIV

26. What are some practical things you can do to approach God this way?

- *When reading your Bible, sit there and close your eyes and meditate on what you read.*
- *Instead of just singing songs during worship, make sure your heart is focused on God. It is coming and being sensitive to Him.*

27. When you come to God, remember He has _feelings_. Be _sensitive_ to those _feelings_.

28. Instead of always going into your prayer time telling God what _you_ need, go in and ask God what _He_ needs.

29. When you pray in the Spirit, it makes you _sensitive_ to God's needs.

30. How do you reconcile the fact that some scriptures tell you to come before God with joyful noise and others speak of silence?

Because it is relationship we have with God and not law .

31. What is the correlation we keep seeing on this journey between intimacy with God and the intimacy between a husband and wife?

We are the bride of Christ. God calls us into the holiest of holies for a passionate relationship. In the same way a formula would never work for the love affair between a husband and wife, neither would a formula work in our relationship with God.

32. This journey as we learned from our first day provides a _road map_ and the Word gives _guidelines_, but it is up to _you_ to go do it.

LEADER'S NOTES

LESSON TWELVE

LEADER'S NOTES

Key Statement:
We must learn to develop a listening ear at all times and practice His presence.

33. What are some of the many ways God speaks to us?
- *Strong voice*
- *Still, small voice*
- *Other people*
- *Books*
- *Visions or dreams*

34. What is the way God usually speaks?
The still, small voice

35. How do you know it's God?
- *Absolute alignment with Scripture*
- *An inward peace*

36. If we are to draw near to God, we must learn to develop a listening ear at all times and practice His presence. Remember David said, "I will always set the Lord before me." God is with you at all times. If you __*acknowledge*__ His presence at all times, you will start having interaction and continuous __*communication*__.

John closes this session with a scripture that gives you everything you need to continue in your journey:

"'I will bring him near and he will come close to me, for who is he who will devote himself to being close to me?' declares the LORD."
Jeremiah 30:21, NIV

37. What progress have you made along this journey?

Leader's Notes

(5-10 minutes)

Go over questions 37-39 with your group.

38. How has it affected your prayer life?

39. How has it changed your view of God himself?

Enthusiastically congratulate your group, then pray the prayer with them, boldly and aloud.

Remind your group:

1. Pray daily in the Spirit.

2. Follow through on their "Feet to your faith" and "Samaritan's Road" sections.

3. That they should get involved with the local church.

Congratulations on your choice to participate and be obedient to completion in the journey to a life-long intimacy with God!

Pray this prayer as you complete your last session:

Lord, I devote myself to You. My journey certainly has not ended. I commit to You in the power of the Holy Spirit and by all that is within me to give myself to drawing near for my entire lifetime. I know You will continue in me the work You have begun. I will press in, I will pray in the Holy Ghost, I will study Your Word, and I will go into all the earth. I will not draw back; I will draw near.

I will resist Satan in the name of Jesus and by the Word of God. Father, Your Word in these sessions has been sown in the good ground of my heart. I will not neglect it. I will fight the good fight of faith and be who You've called me to be. I will run this race to its finish, for I long to hear You say, "Well done, thou good and faithful servant." Amen

When you devote yourself to being close to Him, draw near to Him, and He will draw near to you.

Video Script for Lesson 12
DRAWING NEAR

Tonight we are going to talk about the practical aspects of drawing near but before we do I just want to remind you about some of the scriptures we studied about in this series. First of all one of the words that I love so much is found in Exodus 34:14. Moses made the statement *"for He is a God who is passionate about His relationship with you."* That is the New Living translation. He's passionate about His relationship with you. Now I want to tell you something that happened when God started dealing with me about Drawing Near. I was out in the prayer closet early one morning and this time I was at the school, not the golf course because we have a school by us too. I was really pouring out my heart to God that morning and I just screamed– you know how you just get so deep in prayer that you say something before you realize what you say? In other words your ears hear it for the first time after your mouth says it. I was in that place of deep prayer and out of my spirit comes this: "Father, if I can't have intimacy with you on this earth then just take me home to heaven now." And all of a sudden my knees started shaking and I thought that might not have been a smart prayer to pray. Immediately my mind starts thinking, is that scriptural, but I knew it was a deep cry.

That afternoon I got on an airplane to fly down to Pastor Tommy Barnett's church in Phoenix, Arizona because I was scheduled to preach there on Sunday morning and it was on a Saturday that I got on the plane. I plop my briefcase down, pulled out my Bible and you know how you do one of those things where you just open up your Bible and your eye looks down and it's the first scripture you read. I opened up my Bible, looked down, saw this and I just started reading what David said, *"To you I will cry oh, Lord my rock. Do not be silent to me, lest if you are silent to me I become like those that go down to the pit."* Do you know what David just said? He said Lord if you don't talk to me I'm no different than those that go to hell. I reached and grabbed my new Living Translation because I carry the new King James and the New Living with me all the time in my briefcase and I opened it up and David said, *"If you are silent I might as well give up and die."* I thought, I did pray a scriptural prayer!

One of my favorite scriptures in the whole Bible found in the New Living Translation is this one: Psalms 27:8. Write it down and get yourself a New Living Translation and read it. *"My heart has heard you say, "Come and talk with me and my heart responds, "Lord I'm coming."* That is an amazing scripture! Can I read it again? "My heart has heard you say, *"Come and talk with me and my heart responds, "Lord I'm coming."*

In this final lesson I want to get real practical but to get practical could be almost like trying to tell a guy how he is going to make love to his new bride on his wedding night. You can only say so much but then it really happens when they get in the bed chamber. You've got to be the one that goes in there and has the intimacy but there are some guidelines that we can give you to help.

In approaching the Lord, the first thing you have to remember is that we are created in His image. We all have moods, don't we? Now there is nothing wrong with moods as long as moods don't control you. God has moods too. There are mornings when I have gone into prayer and I'm telling you He's serious; there's mornings I've gone into prayer and He wants me immediately praying in tongues; there's mornings that I've gone into prayer and He's in a joyful singing mood. I've caught Him at times when He's in a joking mood. He said something to me just a couple months ago about me and I laughed so hard you cannot even believe it. If my wife had said it she would have been in trouble but He nailed me about me with a joke– a funny thing– and I laughed so hard and hysterically. You don't want to know where I was but I just sat there and laughed and laughed. So there are times that I come in singing, there are times that I come in broken, there are times I come in boldly and there are times I come in trembling.

In times of prayer with God we will experience laughter, we will experience weeping, we will experience worrying and we will experience times of peace and tranquility. When you just sit there in His presence and there is nothing to be said, there is communication

Lesson Twelve

going on by saying nothing. Somebody said, "you mean there's times you will go in and it's time to war?" Oh yeah. Let me give you an example of the different times. Imagine there's a criminal trying to break into a family's house. While this criminal is trying to break in and bring harm to the family imagine the son comes into the father's office and says, "Oh dad, I just want to tell you that you are a great dad. You are wonderful and I just think you're the best." The father is looking at the son thinking what is wrong with you. Will you get a baseball bat, get to the front of the house and protect your mother and sisters with me. The father is almost upset because he's not sensitive to what the need is. Then imagine everything being peaceful on the home front and the son comes running into the dad's office with a baseball bat and says, "I'm ready, let's get them. The father says, "Son, would you please chill."

My sons really please me (I've got to be careful because my oldest son, Addison is sitting over there) when they are sensitive to the atmosphere of the house. There are times when maybe Lisa is going through a struggle or something is going on, and my sons will come in and they are totally insensitive to the atmosphere and that disappoints me because that's a lack of maturity. So when you come into the presence of God, first of all find out what is going on. You'll know and you'll be sensitive to Him. It's the most amazing thing. Today is different; I need to really come in a sober moment: He wants me to intercede because there are people in trouble. Can you imagine having a friend and all they ever do is talk to you about their interest. They always talk about themselves and what they want. You who are parent's understand what it's like to have a child in school and all he ever does is call you and say, "I need money, I need clothes, I need this", and that is the extent of your conversation with that child. Do you understand how disappointing that is as a parent? You don't maintain really close intimate friends when all they ever do is come to you and say, "I'm feeling really bad; I'm really good, you should see how good I am." You don't want friends like that and God doesn't draw near to people like that. God draws people near to people that have His interests at heart.

If we're going to touch the Lord's heart we must seek to know what He desires and what He needs. God has needs too. Remember Jesus said, *"I was hungry and you gave me food, I was thirsty and you gave me drink, I was a stranger and you took me in, I was naked and you clothed me, I was sick and you visited me, I was in prison and you came to me."* He said inasmuch as you did to the least of these my brethren you've done it to Me. God gave man a free will and by giving man a free will He made Himself vulnerable because He brought man into His kingdom and made him, His family and made him one with Him. He made Himself vulnerable and that's why He said when I was hungry you fed me. That is why He said to Saul you are persecuting Me. Saul wasn't persecuting Jesus in heaven, physically, he was persecuting the people he was one with. There was a time when God's people at one point were coming to Him diligently and He even said to them in Isaiah 58:2, *"They seek me daily, and delight to know My ways."* These people were coming everyday to seek Him and they wanted to know His ways but the Lord wasn't responding and they finally said, "God why aren't you responding? We're seeking You daily and we delight to know Your ways." In the New living Translation Isaiah 58:3 and 4 He said, *"I will tell you why it's because you are living for yourselves."*

I will never forget when I was in New York and I'd been praying for about two hours out in the woods. There was a trail in the woods right by the hotel where we were staying. I had been praying for about two hours and a cry came into my heart and the Lord said, "Son ask My people if they want Me to be as faithful to them as they have been to Me. Do they want Me to be as committed to them as they've been committed to Me?" My heart broke and I wept and I wept and I wept. I thought He ever lives to make intercession for me, if He let me go for just five seconds I'd be annihilated. He says, "You're seeking Me daily and delight to know My ways but the reason I 'm not responding is because you're living for yourselves even while you are fasting. You keep right on oppressing your workers so what good is fasting when you keep on fighting and quarreling.

Remember the flagship scripture in James? It says, *"What causes fights and quarrels among you? Don't they come from your desires that battle within you? You want something but you don't get it. You quarrel and fight and you do not have because you do not ask. When you ask you do not receive because you ask it with the wrong motives that you may spend it on your own pleasures. You are an adulteress people. Submit yourselves to God, resist*

DRAWING NEAR

the devil, he will flee from you, draw near to God and he will draw near to you" So there you have it folks.

Here is the practical step number one of drawing near to God: we must lose our lives for His sake and the gospel. There are no shortcuts on this one. Does this mean our lives will not have any times of pleasure or refreshment? Absolutely not, because 1 Timothy 6:17, says this, *"God gives us richly all things to enjoy."* There is a difference between enjoying something and living just to have pleasure. This is something we have to teach all of our children. How many of you know if you left a child to his self all he'd ever do is party and have fun, play golf, play tennis, play basketball and never work? We've got to teach children that life is really serving. Life is being a servant, life is working, and the privilege you get for working hard is the times of refreshment and playing. Everyone in the kingdom is a servant.

Now there are those that believe that they are not fulfilling God's wishes, unless they are physically helping the poor. I have got to address this. I almost felt at times there were people that were saying, "You know our ministry is we feed the poor." Let me make a statement: Peter had a bunch of poor widows that needed food one time and he said it is not desirable that we leave the Word of God to wait on tables. Choose seven men that will wait on those tables. You have to understand that God is into us meeting needs whether it is spiritually, socially, financially, physically– He just wants us to meet the needs of people. There are people that are really called to preach the word because Peter said I would be disobeying God if I left the Word of God and waited on those tables. There are people that are disobedient to God because they want to try to preach when they are supposed to be feeding the widows tables, ushering in the church or working out in the parking lot. We all just need to do our part.

I can walk on my hands. People can walk on their hands. Have you ever seen gymnasts that can walk on their hands? But that's not the efficient way to walk. Your feet were made to walk. Yes, there is going to be times when God says, "John, reach out to this person that needs something to eat or this or that. That is going to happen, but if I were going to give my life doing that, then I would be disobeying God because I'm called to preach. Peter was called to preach. He said I'm going to give people food if they need it and I'm going to clothe them if they need it but I'm called to preach. So always remember it's just meeting the needs of people. Find out what you are called to do in the body in the church. In order for a church to be able to be successful you have to have people in there that will usher, you've got to have people to count the money, you have to have people out in the parking lot and you have to have people that drive the bus that brings the poor people in. You've got to have all these different facets and if you don't do them we're not reaching out to the needs of people. That's why it is heartbreaking when I see young people that are thirteen, fourteen, fifteen, sixteen, seventeen, eighteen years old and they are not doing anything in the church. They are part of the church too. For those who have the Lords interests at heart are those that come more easily to Him.

If you look at Moses, David, Daniel and all those people, one of those people that really had God's heart was a guy named king Josuah. Look what God said about him in Jeremiah 22:15-17, God said he made sure that justice and help were given to the poor and to the needy and everything went well for him. That's what it means to know Me. He made sure justice and help was given to the poor. Poor doesn't just mean physically poor, it means poor in any realm. God said to know Me is to meet the needs of hurting humanity.

We are going to find the next practical step in Ecclesiastics chapter 5. I am reading out of the New International version. We read in Ecclesiastics 5:1-3, *"Guard your steps when you go to the house of God. Go near or draw near to listen rather to offer the sacrifice of fools, who do not know that they do wrong, do not be quick with your mouth and do not be hasty in your heart to utter anything before God. God is in heaven and you are on earth so let your words be few as a dream comes when there are many cares so the speech of a fool, when there are many words."* I have found such success in the last couple of years in being quiet when I approach the Lord. I have found now that a lot of my prayer time is spent being quiet because I'm listening. There is a pastor of a very large church in the Northeast part of the United States. I was with him last year doing a conference with him and he said, "You know John, I got to the point where I was tired of hearing myself talk in the prayer closest. I told the Lord I'm not saying anything until you talk to me. The Holy Spirit really tested me because

Lesson Twelve

there were several mornings that I went in and there was nothing and I just sat. But I was determined and I knew God would speak and after several mornings God spoke to me and what he spoke to me revolutionized my life and my ministry. I preached on it for weeks from my pulpit and it is one of the most profound revelations God has ever given me for my church." God says draw near to hear.

I've learned a very powerful way of coming into the presence of the Lord is by taking my Bible and just reading scripture, especially out of the New Testament or the book of Psalms. What I'll do is just read a scripture, maybe one sentence of the scripture or maybe the whole scripture or half of the scripture and I'll just sit there and close my eyes and meditate on what I just read. And many times I have sensed the Lord's presence come near. When I sense that it's not so strong, I'll read the other half of the scripture and there is His presence. Many times when I've walked into praise services I do not start singing immediately because I want to make sure my heart is drawn near and then I begin to sing to Him. It is a much quicker and efficient way of getting into His presence. Many times people just sing the songs to sing the songs. Many times when I have altar calls I will tell the people not to play anything on the keyboard or I will tell them to play something nobody knows because if you play a song on the keyboard that they know, their mind starts singing it and they don't focus and draw near because they're off singing a song. I have had the Lord tell me to turn off the stereo in my car and I'm playing Christian praise music because He said, "I would like to speak to you." It's coming and being sensitive to Him. Imagine a friend who never comes into your presence and he is never sensitive to you-- he's only sensitive to what he wants. He is not going to be that close of a friend. When you come to the Lord remember that He's got feelings so be sensitive to His feelings.

I had a dear friend and we were both on the staff of a very large church back in the 1980's. We prayed three mornings a week: Monday, Wednesday and Friday. We would pray an hour and a half before the staff opened and I am telling you there was such flow when we prayed together. I remember one of the first mornings that we were in there and God gave him a word. He started speaking that prophetic word and the Lord said this to him, "He said why is it so many of My children when they come into the throne room all they do is bring Me requests? He said I will answer those requests, but when will My children start coming and saying Father what do you need? And so we determined in our own personal time we would not pray requests, but whenever we came together three times a week, we went in and said Lord what do you need. We were quiet and listened while we prayed in the Spirit. How many of you know that praying in the Spirit will quiet your mind? See a lot of my prayer time is listening in silence, praying in tongues or speaking the Word because when I'm praying in tongues I know I'm praying the perfect will of God. When I'm speaking the word, I'm speaking His word and I'm a little more reluctant to do that unless I really sense that's what to do. Speaking in the word will edify myself; it will build my personal faith but to get me sensitive to what God's needs are, I'll pray in the Spirit. So we came into that room three mornings a week and we'd just start praying in the Spirit and I'm telling you, you wouldn't believe some of the things that happened in that prayer closet. There were times when we knew we were in Oriental Nations, there were times when we knew we were in Middle Eastern Nations and we knew it because our whole tongues would change and we would sense things and even see things in our spirit. Those were amazing times of prayer.

So there are times I walk into a praise and worship service and I sensed its "go". Have you ever just sensed Jesus walked in and God's going "Let's go" and that would be perfectly scriptural because listen to Psalms 95:2, *"Let us come before His presence with thanksgiving; let us shout joyfully to Him with psalms."* Psalms 100:2, *"Serve the Lord with gladness; come before His presence with singing."* So there is one verse that says draw near to listen and not to speak. There is another verse that says come into his presence with singing. It's a relationship; it is not a law. What is really sad is that we try to make a formula out of it. Can you imagine a guy walking in to make love to his wife and he's got his seven-step card. Step 1: tell her that her eyes are beautiful. "Honey your eyes are beautiful." Step 2: tell her you love her. "Honey I love you." Step 3: turn down the lights. Step 4: oops I can't read, I need a flashlight. See how spiritless and mechanical that is and yet that is what people have done with prayer. How can I teach you to have intimacy with God? I can give you the road map, I

216

can give you the word that gives you the guidelines, but you're the one that has to go. The other thing that it says in Ecclesiastes is to not be hasty with your words. Even in natural relationships we learn from this. When somebody rambles too much we tend not listen to him or her too closely. I've met people that were very careful with their words and they got my ear. One of my board members who was an attorney for thirty-five years and he is like a dad to me. When he speaks I listen because he doesn't speak a lot but when he speaks he's got something to say. Now there are other people that are very careful with their words and they may do a lot of talking. I have friends that I'll sit there and we'll talk on the phone for an hour and a half and all of a sudden I've have to go, yet everything has been rich. I'm not saying you won't say a lot of words but I'm saying be careful with your words, don't be hasty because there are a lot of people who make very vain promises to the Lord. You better know that you mean what you are promising Him. There have been times when I had to go to the Lord and say I was rash with my mouth, I was a fool, would you please release me from my commitment. And you know what, I find I get far with the Lord because I was honest. I was rash with my mouth so please forgive me. I made a commitment that I just couldn't keep.

Back in 1985 I had been praying every day for three years and I missed very few days. I remember when the Lord put in my heart that I was supposed to pray every morning. I love praying in the mornings because there is something about the mornings. Now don't get upset with me because I'm saying this. You can pray in the middle of the night, you can pray in the afternoon, you can pray anytime but there is something about the mornings when your mind is quiet and you don't have to repent for everything you did wrong that day. It's a new day; you just wake up and go, His mercies are new, thank you so much Father. Because you did all the repenting before you went to bed and, but you know what I'm talking about. You are just fresh. So I made a commitment. I said the Lord really dealt with me about getting up and praying so I said I was going to pray an hour every day. I remember the first day I got up in 1982, I went out to the couch to pray and within five minutes I was sound asleep. An hour later my wife walks out and she goes, "Honey why are you sleeping on the couch?" I was so frustrated. So then what I started doing was I would get an entire lemon and squeeze the entire lemon into a glass, fill it up with a little bit of water, put it in the microwave for thirty seconds and then guzzle as fast as I can. That will wake you up faster than any Starbucks on the planet. Then I go outside and pray outside. Now I got to the point where I started praying from five to seven every morning and I was almost getting proud of it. How many of you know God knows how to nail that pride? And so one morning I'm walking back to my apartment and the Holy Spirit screams this, "I would like the other twenty-two hours of the day." And all of a sudden I realized what kind of relationship would I have with Lisa if Lisa said to me, "Your time is every day between four and six" and I had to say something to her at 10:00 in the morning and went, "Babe I have to talk to you," and she said, "John wait a minute, your time is not for another six hours. So you go home at lunch and you say, "Babe I have to talk to you about this, it is urgent, and she says, "John its noon, your time is not for another four hours." So finally you wait until 4:00 and you come in at 4:00 O'clock and you have something so urgent to say and she starts talking non-stop for two hours." "You're trying to go, " ah, ah, ah" and she talks non-stop for two hours and at 6:00, she says, "Well it's been great talking to you, see you tomorrow at 4:00." You didn't get a word in edge wise. The Lord says, "Son that's what you do every morning. You come out here and you talk non-stop for two hours and then you say "Amen" and you shut me off for the next twenty-two hours.

Now there are many different ways that He speaks to us. Sometimes we will hear Him speak in a strong voice that is so strong, and this is very rare, you almost think you hear it with your physical ear. Other times it's the still small voice and I find that's the way He usually speaks. Now let me tell you how to recognize it. With His still small voice will be two things: absolute alignment with the scripture and secondly there will be an inward velvet peace. That's why the Bible says let the peace of Christ rule your heart. Sometimes He'll communicate through another believer or leader as they speak or you are reading their writing. You hear His voice within the voice. That's how you know an anointed book. You sit down and read an anointed book and within thirty minutes if you're not getting something out of it, chances are it's not anointed, unless your heart is not right. If your heart is right God's going

Lesson Twelve

to be there and you are going to hear God's voice in that book. He'll speak to you through a vision or a dream. Many times if you have dreams, ask God if this means anything? Is this because I had pizza last night at 11:00 or is this because You are saying something to me? Usually when God is saying something to you it is very vivid and it sticks with you. One time God was trying to get something through to me and I had the same dream four times in two weeks and I finally said, "Lord what are you trying to say? And He blurted to me what he was trying to say and it was a correction for me. Another way He will speak is that we will just know things that we didn't previously know. That is a frequent way He'll speak. Another way He will speak to you is He will deposit His word in you and it's not unveiled until you speak. As you open your mouth and speak, the illumination comes. This happens a lot when I'm praying with friends. We start talking after we pray and fresh revelation and illumination starts coming because He has spoken to us. That's what happened with Peter on the day of Pentecost. Peter gets up and just preaches this marvelous message that he had no time to study because God deposited something in him when he was filled with the Holy Spirit and out it came.

I want to say this as we close: please read the book. There is so much more and there is no way I could have covered it in twelve sessions of thirty minutes each. Spend time with the Lord. Remember what I taught you are the guidelines to keep you from falling into pit falls and traps. Learn to develop a listening ear at all times and practice His presence. Remember what David said, *"I will always set the Lord before me."* He is with you at all times. If you acknowledge His presence at all times, you will start having interaction and continuous communication. I am going to end the whole session with Jeremiah 30:21 out of the New International Version, *"I will bring him near and he will come close to Me, for who is he who will devote himself to being close to Me, declares the Lord."* Will you devote yourself to being close to Him? Draw near to Him and He will draw near to you. Amen.

"Drawing Near" Leader's Guide

Additional Notes

"Drawing Near" Leader's Guide

Additional Notes

Your Journey never ends...

We hope this *Drawing Near* Series has helped guide you as you continue on the *life-long* adventure available to those who make the decision to live each day in intimacy with God.

Giving God glory...

If there is a personal story you would like to share about how this Drawing Near Curriculum has strengthened your relationship with God, we would love to hear from you.
mail@messengerinternational.org

Master Code Page

Please remember to watch for the icon to view the additional bonus content on these discs.

Disc 1

DVD Extra Feature

Introduction & Welcome

The first time you watch the DVD, please choose the "Leader's" path. You will be asked to enter the code below for a personal welcome from John. **Enter code: 963**, to watch this bonus feature as you begin your journey.

Enter code: **865**, to watch the 1st bonus feature in *Session 1* of your DVD.
Enter code: **855**, to watch the 2nd bonus feature in *Session 1* of your DVD.
Enter code: **782**, to watch this bonus feature in *Session 2* of your DVD.
Enter code: **596**, to watch this bonus feature in *Session 3* of your DVD.

Disc 2

DVD Extra Feature

Enter code: **985**, to watch this bonus feature in *Session 4* of your DVD.
Enter code: **784**, to watch this bonus feature in *Session 5* of your DVD.
Enter code: **452**, to watch this bonus feature in *Session 6* of your DVD.

Disc 3

DVD Extra Feature

Enter code: **738**, to watch this bonus feature in *Session 7* of your DVD.
Enter code: **357**, to watch this bonus feature in *Session 8* of your DVD.
Enter code: **545**, to watch this bonus feature in *Session 9* of your DVD.

Disc 4

DVD Extra Feature

Enter code: **969**, to watch this bonus feature in *Session 10* of your DVD.
Enter code: **472**, to watch this bonus feature in *Session 11* of your DVD.
Enter code: **468**, to watch this bonus feature in *Session 12* of your DVD.

To reach us please call:
U.S. - 1-800-648-1477
Europe - 44 (0) 870-745-5790
Australia - 1-300-650-577 (outside AUS. +61 2 8850 1725)

Appendix A

OUR NEED FOR A SAVIOR

There are two standards for living; one set by society and one set by God. Our culture may deem you "good" according to its parameters, but what does God think? Scripture tells us every person has fallen short of God's standard of right: "As the Scriptures say: 'There is no one who always does what is right, not even one.'" (Rom. 3:10 NCV) and again, "For all have sinned; all fall short of God's glorious standard." (Rom. 3:23 NLT)

To sin means to miss the mark of God's standard. Man was not created to be a sinner; rather Adam chose this course of his own free will. God placed the first man, Adam, in a beautiful world without sickness, disease, poverty, or natural disasters. There was no fear, hatred, strife, jealousy, and so forth. God called this place Eden, the very garden of God.

Adam chose to disobey God's command and experienced an immediate spiritual death, even though he did not die physically until hundreds of years later. Darkness entered his heart, and this spiritual death differs from physical death because in physical death the body ceases to exist; however, spiritual death is best described as separation from God, the very giver and source of all life.

Sin had entered Adam's makeup, and he fathered children after this nature: "And Adam lived one hundred and thirty years, and begot a son in his own likeness, after his image" (Gen. 5:3).

As a father his offspring were born after his nature and from this point forward each and every human is born into the image of his sin through their parents. Adam gave himself and his descendants over to a new lord, Satan, and with this captivity the natural world followed suit. A cruel lord now had legal claim to God's beloved creation. This is made clear in the following verses: "Then the devil, taking Him [Jesus] up on a high mountain, showed Him all the kingdoms of the world in a moment of time. And the devil said to Him, 'All this authority I will give to you, and their glory; for this *has been delivered to me,* and I give it to whomever I wish'" (Luke 4:5-6, *author's emphasis*).

Notice it was delivered to him. When? The answer is in the garden, for God originally gave the dominion of earth to man (see Gen. 1:26-28). Adam lost it all…this included himself and his seed for all generations. Again we read, "The whole world lies under the sway of the wicked one" (1 John 5:19).

Before God sent Adam from the garden, He made a promise. A deliverer would arise and destroy the bondage and captivity mankind had been subjected to.

This deliverer was born four thousand years later to a virgin named Mary. She had to be a virgin, as the father of Jesus was the Holy Spirit who impregnated her. If Jesus had been born to natural parents, He would have been born into the captivity of Adam.

He was Fathered by God and His mother was human. This made Him completely God and completely man. It had to be a son of man, who would purchase our freedom. For this reason Jesus constantly referred to Himself as the "Son of man." Though He was with the Father from the beginning, He stripped Himself of His divine privileges and became a man in order to give Himself as an offering for sin.

When He went to the cross, He took the judgment of our sin on Himself to free us from our bondage. Scripture declares, "He personally carried away our sins in his own body on the cross so we can be dead to sin and live for what is right." (1 Peter 2:24, NLT)

It's amazing: man sinned against God, and yet God (manifest in the flesh) paid the price for man's grave err. We read again, "For God made Christ, who never sinned, to be the offering for our sin, so that we could be made right with God through Christ." (2 Cor. 5:20-21, NLT)

Notice it says we could be made right. We do not receive the freedom which He paid so great a price for until we believe in our hearts that He died for us and was raised from the dead, and receive Him as our Lord; that is when He becomes our personal Savior. As Scripture states, "But to all who believed him and accepted him, he gave the right to become children of God. They are reborn! This is not a physical birth resulting from human passion or plan – this rebirth comes from God." (John 1:12-13, NLT)

When we receive Jesus Christ as our personal Lord and Savior, we die and are spiritually reborn. We die as slaves in the kingdom of Satan and are born as brand new children of God in His kingdom. How does this happen? Simple, when we believe this in our heart all we have to do is confess with our mouth Jesus as our Lord, and we are born again. Scripture affirms this: "For if you confess with your mouth that Jesus is Lord and believe in your heart that God raised him from the dead, you will be saved. For it is by believing in your heart that you are made right with God, and it is by confessing with your mouth that you are saved." (Rom. 10:9-10, NLT)

It's that simple! We are not saved by our good deeds. Our good deeds could never earn us a place in His Kingdom. For if that was true, Christ died in vain. We are saved by His grace. It is a free gift that we cannot earn. All we have to do to receive is to renounce living for ourselves and commit our life to Him as Lord, which means Supreme Master. "He died for all, that those who live should live no longer for themselves, but for Him who died for them and rose again." (2 Cor. 5:15)

So if you believe Christ died for you, and you are willing to give Him your life and longer live for yourself; then we can pray this prayer together and you will become a child of God:

> *God in Heaven, I acknowledge that I am a sinner and have fallen short of Your righteous standard. I deserve to be judged for eternity for my sin. Thank You for not leaving me in this state, for I believe you sent Jesus Christ, Your only begotten Son, who was born of the Virgin Mary, to die for me and carry my judgment on the Cross. I believe He was raised again on the third day and is now seated at Your right hand as my Lord and Savior. So on this day of _____, 20__, I give my life entirely to the Lordship of Jesus.*
>
> *Jesus, I confess you as my Lord and Savior. Come into my life through Your Spirit and change me into a child of God. I renounce the things of darkness which I once held on to, and from this day forward I will no longer live for myself, but for You who gave Yourself for me that I may live forever.*
>
> *Thank You Lord; my life is now completely in Your hands and heart, and according to Your Word I shall never be ashamed.*

Now, you are saved; you are a child of God. All heaven is rejoicing with you at this very moment! Welcome to the family!

Appendix B

How To Be Filled With The Holy Spirit

Receiving the fullness of the Holy Spirit is as easy as receiving Jesus as your Lord and Savior. Some struggle, become discouraged, and can't receive most often due to the neglect of receiving basic scriptural instructions before asking. I've learned it is always best to show seekers what God says before praying, as this develops their faith to receive. So before I lead you in a prayer to receive, allow me first to instruct. (Note: It is important that you have read Chapter 11 in the *Drawing Near* book before proceeding any further.)

First and foremost, you must have already received Jesus Christ as your personal Lord and Savior (see John 14:17).

There can be no pattern of disobedience in your life. We are told that God gives His Spirit "to those who obey Him" (Acts 5:32). I've learned from experience this especially includes the area of unforgiveness. In our meetings I've seen many times hundreds receive the Holy Spirit and immediately speak in other tongues, yet a dozen or two of the hundreds stand and look bewildered. In almost every case in going to those few dozen I would find the Lord leading me to deal with harbored offense. Once the seekers forgave they immediately received and spoke in tongues. So before we go any further let's pray together.

> *Father, I ask that you would search me and show me if there is any disobedience in my heart. Please show me if there is any person I have withheld forgiveness from. I purpose to obey and forgive no matter what You reveal to me. I ask this in the name of Jesus and thank You so very much.*

To receive the Holy Spirit all you have to do is ask! Jesus simply says, "If a son asks for bread from any father among you, will he give him a stone? Or if he asks for a fish, will he give him a serpent instead of a fish? Or if he asks for an egg, will he offer him a scorpion? If you then, being evil, know how to give good gifts to your children, how much more will your heavenly Father give the Holy Spirit to those who ask Him!" (Luke 11:11-13). He is simply saying that if our children ask us for something which is our will to give them, we won't give them something evil or different. In the same way, if you ask the Father for His Spirit, He won't give you an evil spirit. All you have to do is ask the Father in Jesus' name, and you will receive His Holy Spirit.

You must ask in faith. The New Testament tell us it is impossible to receive from God without faith. James 1:6-7 states: "But let him ask in faith, with no doubting, for he who doubts is like a wave of the sea driven and tossed by the wind. For let not that man suppose that he will receive anything from the Lord. So ask yourself at this moment, "When will I receive? Will it be when I speak in other tongues, or will it be the moment I ask?" Your answer should be – the moment you ask! For in the Kingdom, we believe then receive. Those who do not have faith say, "Show me and I will believe" but Jesus says, "I say to you, whatever things you ask when you pray, believe that you receive them, and you will have them" (Mark 11:24). Notice you believe first, and then you will have what you've asked for.

Acts 2:4 says, "And they were all filled with the Holy Spirit and began to speak with other tongues, as the Spirit gave them utterance." Notice they spoke with tongues; it was not the Holy Spirit who spoke in tongues. They had to do it, as the Spirit gave them the words. So there is a yielding! I can be in a swift moving river, but if I don't pick up my feet and yield to the river, I won't flow with it. So there are three areas we must yield: First, our lips. If I don't move my lips, words, whether in English or in a Foreign language, a heavenly tongue cannot come forth. Second, our tongue. If I don't move my tongue, I cannot speak. Third, our vocal chords. If I don't yield my vocal cords to my lungs, then I cannot speak.

You may at this point think I'm being sarcastic, but I'm not. After years of seeing people struggle, I've learned many subconsciously think the Holy Spirit is going to grab ahold of their lips, tongues, and vocal cords and make them speak. No, we speak, or yield, as He gives the utterance.

Jesus says, "'He who believes in Me, as the Scripture has said, out of his heart will flow rivers of living water.' But this He spoke concerning the Spirit, whom those believing in Him would receive; for the Holy Spirit was not yet given, because Jesus was not yet glorified" (John 7:38-39). When you ask for the Holy Spirit, you may have a syllable bubbling up, or rolling around in your head. If you will speak it in faith, it will be as if you open a dam, and the language will come forth. I like to see it as a spool of thread in your gut and the tip, or beginning of the thread, is glimpsed at your tongue, but as you begin to pull (speak), out comes the rest of the thread. Some think they are going to have the entire language in their mind then they will speak. No, we are to speak in faith.

I remember when my wife prayed to receive the Holy Spirit she didn't speak in tongues for a time, then she and a few friends were praying a few weeks later and she began to speak in tongues. She then said, "I had that syllable running through my head the past few weeks while praying, but didn't yield to it till tonight." I believe this is the case for so many – they ask, receive, but don't yield.

Scripture states, "The spirits of the prophets [spokespersons] are subject to the prophets" (1 Cor 14:32). This simply tells us that we are the ones who speak, and that the Holy Spirit will not force Himself on us. I recall the day after I was filled with the Holy Spirit I didn't know how to speak again. I went to another brother at the gym and asked, "How can I do it again?" He said, "John, you just do it!" I went out for a run and began to speak in tongues again while running. I was overcome with joy. We must remember the Holy Spirit is always ready to go; we are the ones who must yield. It is like a water fountain. The water is always there; all you have to do is turn the knob and out comes the water. So pray in tongues frequently!

Now that you have received basic instructions from the Scripture, if you believe you will receive we can pray together. One last thing: you cannot speak English and Spanish at the same time. Even so you can't speak in English and tongues at the same time. So remember, just believe and yield! Let's pray:

> *Father, in the name of Jesus, I come to you as Your child. You said if I asked You for the Holy Spirit You would give Him to me. With joy I now ask in faith; please baptize and fill me at this very moment with Your Holy Spirit. I receive all You have for me including the ability to speak in tongues. So now in faith I will speak in new tongues! Amen!*

John Bevere Presents: THE DRAWING NEAR
INDIVIDUAL CURRICULUM KIT

THE NEXT STEP of your JOURNEY WITH GOD

You have finished the group kit, don't stop there! Continue your growth with John's first ever INDIVIDUAL kit that you can now take home. Designed for a one-on-one personal encounter with your Creator, and featuring a beautifully bound personal 84-day devotional journal with instructions and a place to record your daily communion with God. Specifically written and prepared to lead you into times of deep, private intimacy with the Holy Spirit.

"A 'must-have' for every serious believer"

This Beautiful Kit contains:

- John's newest hardcover book, *Drawing Near*
- 4 interactive DVD's with bonus content
- Devotional Journal
- Engraved Pen

Begin Your Journey

Please contact us today to receive your free copy of Messenger International's newsletter and our 24 page color catalog of ministry resources!

The vision of MI is to strengthen believers, awaken the lost and captive in the church and proclaim the knowledge of His glory to the nations. John and Lisa are reaching millions of people each year through television and by ministering at churches, Bible schools and conferences around the world. We long to see God's Word in the hands of leaders and hungry believers in every part of the earth.

Messenger International
www.messengerinternational.org
with John and Lisa Bevere

UNITED STATES
PO Box 888
Palmer Lake, CO 80133-0888
800-648-1477 (US & Canada)
Tel: 719-487-3000
Fax: 719-487-3300
E-mail: jbm@messengerinternational.org

EUROPE
PO Box 622
Newport, NP19 8ZJ
UNITED KINGDOM
Tel: 44 (0) 870-745-5790
Fax: 44 (0) 870-745-5791
E-mail: jbmeurope@messengerinternational.org

AUSTRALIA
PO Box 6200
Dural, D.C. NSW 2158
Australia
In AUS 1-300-650-577
Tel: +61 2 8850 1725
Fax +61 2 8850 1735
Email: jbmaustralia@messengerinternational.org

The *Messenger* television program broadcasts in 214 countries. Some of the major networks include The God Digital Network in Europe, the Australian Christian Channel and on the New Life Channel in Russia. Please check your local listings for day and time.

LIFE TRANSFORMING MESSAGES

Under Cover Curriculum - This kit contains the Best Selling Book, *Under Cover*

The Promise of Protection Under His Authority

Are you living under the shadow of the Almighty where there is liberty, provision, and protection? *Under Cover* is a life-transforming message that will revolutionize the way you see authority. Most people try to use kingdom principles with a democratic mindset and the kingdom of God is not a democracy, it is a kingdom with rank, order and authority. The majority of people in America do not like the subject of authority but I believe as we go through these twelve lessons and you listen carefully, you will find that you not only like authority, you will develop a passion to seek it and live it in your own life.

LEADERS GUIDE • STUDENT WORKBOOK
5 VHS TAPES • 2 DVDS • 6 AUDIO CDS

The Bait of Satan Curriculum - This kit contains the Best Selling Book, *The Bait of Satan*, A Leaders Guide, A Student Workbook, 5 VHS Tapes, 2 DVDs, and 6 Audio CDs.

"It is impossible that no offenses will come" - Luke 17:1

LEADERS GUIDE • STUDENT WORKBOOK
5 VHS TAPES • 2 DVDS • 6 AUDIO CDS

This powerful Multimedia Curriculum Kit is written for individuals or small groups who desire to break free from the snare of the devil. This program exposes one of Satan's most deceptive traps to get you out of God's will--offense. *The Bait of Satan* Multimedia Curriculum Kit includes daily or weekly discussion questions, scriptures, prayers, action steps, and other interactive study tools for group or individual study. Don't be fooled! You *will* encounter offense, and it's up to you how you're going to let it affect your relationship with God. Your response will determine your future.

OTHER RELATED RESOURCES
to Drawing Near

Intimacy with the Holy Spirit
2 Videos or 2 DVDs

Paul writes, "The communion (intimate fellowship) of the Holy Spirit be with you" (2 Cor. 13:14). Yet so many do not enjoy this…why? As with all things in the Kingdom, we enter into this communion by faith. This faith is quickened by hearing His Word on how He communicates with us. In this important two-part series John addresses: Is the infilling of the Holy Spirit for all? Is the gift of tongues only for a select few? Why even speak in tongues? The benefits of praying in the Spirit. How God reveals His secrets. How to communicate with God on His level and much more!

These messages will ignite a passion and bring understanding of how to have intimacy with the Holy Spirit. It is a must for you and those you love.

> Our Special Edition "Intimacy with the Holy Spirit" DVD packaging comes with an attractive custom shaped die cut package and holographic gold foil image on the case.

The Hidden Power of Humility - 2 Cassettes, 2 Cd's, 2 DVD's or 2 Videos
The Key to your High Calling

Humility strengthens and protects you from the enemy. It keeps you sensitive to the heart of God so He can reveal His ways... and it empowers us to complete the race. In Psalms 25:9 we learn God leads the humble in what is right, teaching them His way. Humility is a characteristic of His nature we are to excel in. Yet too many do not know what true humility is. They mistake it for a weakness or lack of courage. Without it we lead a fruitless Christian life. Now more than ever before we need to acquire a good understanding of humility and the skills to walk in it.